ANTHROPOLOGICAL PAPERS OF
THE UNIVERSITY OF ARIZONA
NUMBER 40

T0289302

MULTIDISCIPLINARY RESEARCH AT GRASSHOPPER PUEBLO ARIZONA

Edited by
WILLIAM A. LONGACRE
SALLY J. HOLBROOK
MICHAEL W. GRAVES

Contributors:

Larry D. Agenbroad

Eric J. Arnould

Walter H. Birkby

Vorsila L. Bohrer

Jeffrey S. Dean

Gerald K. Kelso

Charmion R. McKusick

J. Jefferson Reid

John W. Olsen

Stanley J. Olsen

William Reynolds

William J. Robinson

Izumi Shimada

Stephanie M. Whittlesey

David R. Wilcox

THE UNIVERSITY OF ARIZONA PRESS
TUCSON, ARIZONA
1982

About the editors...

WILLIAM A. LONGACRE has conducted archaeological research in the southwestern United States since 1958. He was Associate Director of the University of Arizona Archaeological Field School at Grasshopper for the 1965 season and Director from 1966 through 1978; since 1979 he has been Institutional Director. Several of his published articles and monographs investigate the application of anthropological concepts to archaeological research methods. Recently he has pursued ethnoarchaeological studies in the Philippines. He received his doctoral degree in anthropology from the University of Chicago in 1963, and is Professor of Anthropology at the University of Arizona, Tucson.

SALLY J. HOLBROOK, Associate Professor of Biological Sciences at the University of California, Santa Barbara, received her doctoral degree in zoology from the University of California at Berkeley in 1975. She spent several summers at the Archaeological Field School conducting microfaunal studies in the Grasshopper region, and she has authored numerous publications on microfaunal ecology.

MICHAEL W. GRAVES served on the staff of the Archaeological Field School at Grasshopper from 1975 through 1979. He assisted Sally Holbrook with microfaunal studies and supervised various excavation projects. After receiving his doctoral degree in anthropology from the University of Arizona in 1981, he accepted a position as Assistant Professor of Anthropology at the University of Guam.

THE UNIVERSITY OF ARIZONA PRESS

Copyright © 1982
The Arizona Board of Regents
All Rights Reserved

This book was set in Alphatype CRS (English series) Times Roman.
Manufactured in the U.S.A.

Library of Congress Cataloging in Publication Data

Main entry under title:

Multidisciplinary Research at Grasshopper Pueblo,
    Arizona

    (Anthropological papers of the University of
Arizona; no. 40)
        Includes bibliographical references and index.
        1. Grasshopper Pueblo (Ariz.)—Addresses, essays,
lectures.   2. Mogollon culture—Addresses, essays,
lectures.   I. Longacre, William A., 1937-
II. Holbrook, Sally J.   III. Graves, Michael W.
IV. Series.
E99.M76M84   1982   979.1'3   82-13715

ISBN 0-8165-0425-3

CONTENTS

FIGURES

TABLES

ABOUT THE AUTHORS

LARRY D. AGENBROAD received a doctoral degree in geology from the University of Arizona, Tucson, in 1967, and he earned a master's degree in anthropology from the University in 1970. He served on the staff of the University of Arizona Archaeological Field School at Grasshopper in 1965, and has contributed to the teaching program there in subsequent seasons. He is Associate Professor of Geology at Northern Arizona University in Flagstaff.

ERIC ARNOULD was a student at the Archaeological Field School at Grasshopper in 1975. He has been employed by Arid Lands Studies at the University of Arizona, Tucson, and he received his doctoral degree in anthropology from the University in 1982.

WALTER H. BIRKBY has been a consultant in physical anthropology for the Archaeological Field School at Grasshopper since 1963, and in 1968 he was appointed Physical Anthropologist on the staff of the Arizona State Museum, Tucson. He received his doctoral degree in anthropology from the University of Arizona in 1973.

VORSILA L. BOHRER, Research Professor of Anthropology at Eastern New Mexico University in Portales, was granted a doctoral degree in botany by the University of Arizona in 1968. She has published numerous articles on pollen and plant remains from southwestern archaeological sites.

JEFFREY S. DEAN, Professor in the Laboratory of Tree-Ring Research at the University of Arizona, Tucson, received his doctoral degree in anthropology from that institution in 1967. His extensive tree-ring studies have helped to establish archaeological chronologies, especially in the northern regions of Arizona, and he has applied broader anthropological concepts to chronological research.

GERALD K. KELSO pursued pollen studies while he was a student at the Archaeological Field School at Grasshopper, and he received a doctoral degree in anthropology from the University of Arizona, Tucson, in 1976. He is Assistant Professor of Archaeology and Anthropology and Coordinator of Laboratories at the Center for Archaeological Studies at Boston University.

CHARMION R. McKUSICK, a Research Associate with the Amerind Foundation, Inc., Dragoon, Arizona, resides in Globe where she continues her research on mammalian bones and avifaunal remains from archaeological sites in the southwestern United States. For several years she conducted studies on faunal specimens from Grasshopper Pueblo.

J. JEFFERSON REID is Associate Professor of Anthropology at the University of Arizona, Tucson, and is the Director of the Archaeological Field School where he has played an active role in the Grasshopper research program since 1970. He is interested in establishing reliable reconstructions of Mogollon prehistory and in using the unique Grasshopper record to focus on some of the general problems apparent in archaeological method and theory. He received his doctoral degree in anthropology from the University of Arizona in 1973.

JOHN W. OLSEN received his doctoral degree in anthropology from the University of California, Berkeley, in 1980. His dissertation research focused on the analysis of faunal remains from Grasshopper Pueblo. He has conducted field work in Belize, Egypt, the Philippines, and the People's Republic of China, and he is particularly interested in the relationships between humans and their environment in prehistory.

STANLEY J. OLSEN, Zooarchaeologist with the Arizona State Museum and a Professor in the Department of Anthropology, University of Arizona, Tucson, has specialized in the analysis of faunal material from archaeological sites in the southwestern United States, including Grasshopper Pueblo. He served as Vertebrate Paleontologist at Harvard University and with the Florida Geological Survey, and he is investigating the origins of domestic animals in the People's Republic of China.

WILLIAM REYNOLDS received his doctoral degree in anthropology from Arizona State University, Tempe, in 1981 and he has been employed by Esca-Tech in New Mexico. He served on the staff of the Archaeological Field School at Grasshopper in 1975 and 1976, and was a student there in 1972.

WILLIAM J. ROBINSON lectured and demonstrated tree-ring field techniques at the Archaeological Field School at Grasshopper for many years, and he has coauthored a series of publications compiling all tree-ring dates obtained from archaeological sites in various sections of Arizona. He is a Professor in the Laboratory of Tree-Ring Research at the University of Arizona, Tucson, and he received his doctoral degree in anthropology from that institution in1967.

IZUMI SHIMADA, Assistant Professor of Anthropology at Princeton University, New Jersey, received his doctoral degree in anthropology from the University of Arizona, Tucson, in 1976. He attended the Archaeological Field School at Grasshopper as a student and was a staff member during the 1972 and 1973 seasons.

STEPHANIE M. WHITTLESEY served on the staff of the Archaeological Field School at Grasshopper in various capacities from 1972 through 1975, and she was Assistant Director for the 1976 season. From 1979 through 1981 she conducted studies at Grasshopper as a Research Associate. She is employed by the Arizona State Museum, Tucson, and she received her doctoral degree in anthropology from the University of Arizona in 1978.

DAVID R. WILCOX is an Assistant Archaeologist with the Arizona State Museum, Tucson. Since receiving his doctoral degree in anthropology from the University of Arizona in 1977, he has continued to investigate architecture and the use of space in archaeological sites of the southwestern United States. He was on the staff of the Archaeological Field School at Grasshopper in 1969 and 1970.

PREFACE

The Hemenway Expedition of 1887 to 1888 in the Salt River Valley of southern Arizona was one of the first examples in the Southwest of a multidisciplinary approach to archaeological research. On that project a physical anthropologist worked jointly with archaeologists to present a fuller understanding of the prehistoric culture and its people. During the intervening years specialists from disciplines other than anthropology were often consulted by archaeologists, but usually on a post hoc basis. They were asked to identify and interpret, if possible, various kinds of data recovered from the archaeological record, and the resulting appendixes were of relatively little use to either the archaeologist or the consulting specialist. The multidisciplinary trend has intensified in American archaeology during the 1960s and 1970s, and by actively participating in the development of research designs, sampling strategies, and data collection procedures, specialists in various fields are now producing significant additions to archaeological interpretations. This book presents an overview of a project at Grasshopper Pueblo in east-central Arizona that engaged scientists from a variety of disciplines in the original research design and its subsequent revisions.

After A.D. 1250 Mogollon populations in east-central Arizona aggregated into large pueblo communities, and our research in the Grasshopper region has been designed to investigate the nature of this cultural development in the Mogollon area. To identify the selective pressures leading to this readaptation, relevant aspects of the environment before, during, and after occupation at Grasshopper have been studied. Changes through time in such systemic variables as residence-unit size, status and activity differentiation, residence patterns, inheritance, and other aspects of social organization have also been examined (Longacre 1966, 1970a, 1970b).

The specific goals of this research have included (1) delimiting the economic basis of the prehistoric society, (2) testing the hypothesis that a slight climatic shift occurred about A.D. 1300 (Schoenwetter and Dittert 1968), (3) determining the causes for abandonment of Grasshopper Pueblo and the surrounding region about A.D. 1400, and (4) defining and investigating the nature of interaction among the prehistoric societies in the Grasshopper region (Tuggle 1970) and interaction between the Grasshopper region and areas farther to the north and south. Valuable comparative information has been provided from the north by work in the Upper Little Colorado region directed by the late Paul S. Martin of the Field Museum of Natural History, Chicago, and from the south by 15 years of excavations in the Point of Pines region directed by Emil W. Haury of the University of Arizona.

Most of the chapters in this volume are revised, expanded, and, in some cases, updated versions of presentations prepared for a symposium entitled "Multidisciplinary Research at the Grasshopper Ruin, East-Central Arizona," held at the 37th annual meeting of the Society for American Archaeology in Bal Harbour, Florida, in 1972. Because work at the site has continued each summer since 1972, and will continue for some years to come, quantitative data are constantly increasing, more sophisticated statistical manipulations are used, and research designs are evaluated and often revised. Despite the obvious changes that may emerge when the final history of Grasshopper Pueblo is written, we feel it is worthwhile and useful to others contemplating multidisciplinary studies to present in this volume some of the interim results and to document the various thought processes, the direction and redirections, applied to our research program.

Preliminary remarks by William Longacre and Michael Graves concerning the nature of multidisciplinary studies at Grasshopper are presented in Chapter 1 (submitted 1981). The modern environment of the region is discussed in Chapter 2 (submitted 1981) by Sally Holbrook and Michael Graves, based on work conducted in the field earlier by Thomas W. Mathews and B. Dean Treadwell; original papers by the latter are on file in the Archives of the Arizona State Museum Library, Tucson. In Chapter 3 (revised 1980), J. Jefferson Reid and Izumi Shimada identify different patterns of growth in the development of the Pueblo that raise interesting questions about the mechanisms and rates of growth in various portions of the prehistoric community. The dates and building sequence for the three major room blocks indicate that most of the construction at Grasshopper was completed within 50 to 60 years, by A.D. 1360. David Wilcox (Chapter 4, revised 1981) reviews the history of the cornering project at the site, and discusses room-set additions to the Pueblo and some of the problems encountered in identifying building sequences.

Interpreting the stratification in Plazas I and II, excavated under the direction of Stephanie M. Whittlesey, involved a study of formation processes of archaeological sediments. In Chapter 5 (revised 1981), Whittlesey,

Eric Arnould, and William Reynolds show how sediment typology was used to interpret the depositional history of Plaza I and they suggest inferences about past activities carried out in the three plazas at Grasshopper Pueblo.

Walter Birkby, an osteologist at the University of Arizona, served as a consultant for the collection and analysis of the human skeletal material. Along lines described by Lane and Sublett (1972), Birkby (1973) analyzed nonmetric, discontinuous traits that may delineate biological differences among the Grasshopper population related to patterns of cultural behavior (Chapter 6, submitted 1972).

Larry D. Agenbroad focused on the geological history of the site and the valley, and the use of geological resources by the prehistoric population (Chapter 7, submitted 1972). Dendrochronological and dendroclimatological research was undertaken by personnel at the Laboratory of Tree-Ring Research at the University of Arizona, at that time directed by Bryant Bannister. More than 2000 tree-ring samples were analyzed, providing 164 dates as well as environmental and behavioral information (Jeffrey Dean and William Robinson, Chapter 8, revised 1977).

Stanley J. Olsen of the University of Arizona analyzed reptilian, amphibian, and fish remains from the site (Olsen and Olsen 1970), and the macaw and canid remains (S. J. Olsen 1967, 1968; Olsen and Olsen 1974). His work on fish and amphibian material, along with McKusick's identification of waterfowl, led to the discovery of the prehistoric reservoir underlying the historic pond just north of the ruin (Chapter 9, submitted 1972).

In 1969 Thomas W. Mathews and Jerry Greene of the Southwest Archeological Center, National Park Service, Globe, Arizona, began analyzing all the worked and unworked mammalian bones recovered at Grasshopper, attempting to identify each piece to the species level. Charmion McKusick took over the project in 1972 and has since studied all the avifaunal remains. Her identification and interpretation of various species of waterfowl and of both domesticated and wild turkey have been especially important (Chapter 12, revised 1979). More recently, John and Sandra Olsen completely organized and analyzed approximately 40,000 skeletal and egg shell fragments and artifacts. This material and the previous analyses form the basis of their studies of the prehistoric environment (Chapter 10, submitted 1981), animal exploitative activities, and bone tool manufacture and use (Sandra Olsen 1979).

Through her analyses of microfaunal material and modern rodent relationships in the area, Sally J. Holbrook (1979a, 1979b) has provided important evidence for subtle climatic shifts since the period of occupation at Grasshopper Pueblo (Chapter 11, submitted 1981).

Research on fossil pollen, seeds, and plant parts recovered through flotation, and on modern botanical and pollen collections has been conducted by Vorsila Bohrer. Her conclusions add to the information on climate and the nature of the prehistoric environment as well as the cultural use of plants and the exploitation of wild plant resources (Chapter 13, submitted 1972). The pollen analyses by Gerald Kelso (Chapter 14, submitted 1972) augment the work of Bohrer.

To conclude the book, Michael Graves, Sally Holbrook, and William Longacre (Chapter 15, revised 1981) discuss aggregation and abandonment at Grasshopper Pueblo, incorporating research results presented in the preceding chapters, and they review evolutionary trends in the late prehistory of the region.

ACKNOWLEDGMENTS

The Grasshopper archaeological field station is located on land leased from the White Mountain Apache Tribe and the excavations proceed under an agreement with the White Mountain Apache Tribal Council. The University of Arizona is grateful to the White Mountain Apache people for their continued interest in and encouragement of this program of scientific investigations, and we deeply appreciate their hospitality. Apache crews have been especially helpful in both the excavations at the site and the various archaeological survey projects undertaken in the Grasshopper region.

Support for the Archaeological Field School from the Advanced Science Seminar Program, Division of Graduate Education, National Science Foundation, began in 1964 and continued for eight years (GE-4601, GE-7781, GZ-22, GZ-397, GZ-745, GZ-1113, GZ-1493, GZ-1924). In addition, research grants for the study of prehistory at Grasshopper were awarded to the University of Arizona by the National Science Foundation (GS-2566, GS-33436, SOC-72-05334, SOC-74-23724), the Wenner-Gren Foundation, and the National Geographic Society. Other support was provided by a Historic Preservation Survey and Planning Grant-in-aid from the Arizona State Parks Board through the State Historic Preservation Officer. The basic research that underlies the dendroclimatic analyses was generously supported by the National Science Foundation, the National Park Service, and the Advanced Research Projects Agency.

Nearly two decades of research at Grasshopper Pueblo have been completed, and during those years, several hundred students and staff members participated in the Field School. Their careful studies and meticulous record keeping form much of the basis for this volume, but their contributions are far greater than those revealed in the tangible results of their work at the site. Their creative thought and insightful suggestions have led to important scientific advances, and have helped to solve major problems posed in the research design. Several of their significant comments are noted in the text and authors not cited have written research papers that are on file in the Grasshopper Collection, Department of Anthropology, University of Arizona, Tucson. In addition, numerous colleagues have read, commented on, and assisted with individual papers in this volume, and their aid is gratefully acknowledged: Michael Collins, Patricia Crown, Donald Graybill, C. Vance Haynes, Candace Johnston, Meade and Sandra Kemrer, Michael B. Schiffer, Linda

Stacy, Richard Thompson, H. David Tuggle, Carol Weed, and Susan Wilcox. Patricia Crown and Betsey Brandt helped conduct plaza excavations for the sediment experiments (Chapter 5).

John W. Hannah and Richard L. Warren patiently recorded the ring characteristics of a vast amount of charcoal, and Linda G. Drew, then on the staff of the Laboratory of Tree-Ring Research, University of Arizona, competently assisted in computer analyses of the dendroclimatic material. A substantial part of the archaeological analysis in Chapter 8 was abstracted from a research paper by Alan P. Sullivan, then a graduate student at the University of Arizona; we are grateful to him for making his results available to us.

In addition to the funding sources mentioned above, the microfaunal studies (Chapter 11) were supported by the Academic Senate of the University of California. The Arizona Game and Fish Department issued permits for that field work.

Most of the prehistoric plant remains were identified by Vorsila Bohrer (Chapter 13). Paul Fryxell, Crops Research Geneticist with the U.S. Department of Agriculture at College Station, Texas, identified the prehistoric cotton seeds. Caryl Sagar, University of Arizona Herbarium Technician, kindly identified the modern plants collected in the Grasshopper area; they now are filed as vouchers at the Herbarium. Separate envelopes of flowers and seeds were collected with the Herbarium specimens to furnish modern comparisons. Both Carl Eric Granfelt (Whiteriver, Arizona) and Caryl Sagar provided valuable information on seasonality.

These papers were first compiled and edited by William A. Longacre during a fellowship year at the Center for Advanced Study in the Behavioral Sciences at Stanford University, California. Many members of the Center's staff were helpful in this project, and special thanks are extended to Dr. Perry Gluckman, Susan Custer, and Mrs. H. A. Page. The volume was assembled in final form by Michael Graves in 1981 and edited by Carol A. Gifford in 1982. Typing services were provided by Doris Sample, Ida Edwards, and Natalie Harding. Illustrations were provided by each author, and Charles Sternberg produced final drafting of Figures 1.2, 4.1, 4.2, 5.1, 5.3, 5.4, 5.5, 13.1, 15.1, 15.3, and 15.4. The base map used in Figures 1.1, 7.1, 8.3, 8.4, and 8.5 was furnished by the Laboratory of Tree-Ring Research at the University of Arizona.

The continuing interest expressed, the helpful suggestions, and the unending support of our productivity by Raymond H. Thompson, Director of the Arizona State Museum and formerly also Head of the Department of Anthropology at the University of Arizona, have been of inestimable value throughout the Grasshopper research program.

All the authors join us in extending special appreciation to the highly competent staff members of the University of Arizona Press, directed by Marshall Townsend, for their fine efforts in the production of this book.

William A. Longacre
University of Arizona

Sally J. Holbrook
University of California, Santa Barbara

Michael W. Graves
University of Guam

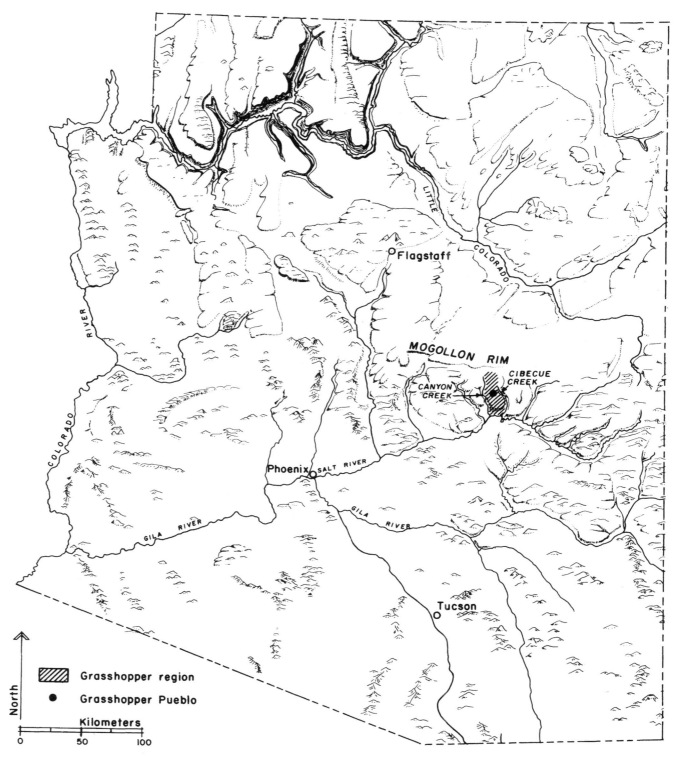

Figure 1.1. Location of the Grasshopper region, Arizona.

1. MULTIDISCIPLINARY STUDIES AT GRASSHOPPER PUEBLO

William A. Longacre and Michael W. Graves

Grasshopper Pueblo, a fourteenth century community located in the western half of the Fort Apache Reservation, has long been recognized as an important late pueblo site in eastern Arizona. Walter Hough of the U.S. National Museum visited the ruin in 1918 and returned the following year to conduct limited excavations. He published two brief notes on this work and later wrote a longer and more inclusive paper on the Grasshopper site and several others in the area (Hough 1919, 1920, 1930). Leslie Spier also visited the site briefly during the same period (Spier 1919: 384). Their early archaeological work was the only formal investigation at the site until Raymond H. Thompson began assessing the potential of the site in 1963 and the University of Arizona embarked on a long-term research program in the area. These investigations are being made in conjunction with the Archaeological Field School program as a joint endeavor of the Department of Anthropology and the Arizona State Museum. In addition to excavations at Grasshopper Pueblo (Arizona P:14:1 in the Arizona State Museum Site Survey), archaeological survey in the region (Tuggle 1970) and investigations of historic Apache sites have also been conducted (Longacre and Ayres 1968; Griffin, Leone, and Basso 1971).

The surrounding area, the Mogollon Rim, is a geological transition zone between the Colorado Plateau to the north and the Basin-and-Range province to the south. The vegetation is also transitional, with components from both the Upper Sonoran Desert and the Evergreen Woodlands (Lowe 1964). Topographic diversity in this region enhances its biotic diversity.

The current vegetation in the vicinity of Grasshopper consists of upland stands of pinyon pine (*Pinus edulis*), juniper (*Juniperus*), and ponderosa pine (*Pinus ponderosa*), with a mixture of grasses (*Bouteloua, Euphorbia, Erigeron, Agropyron,* and *Plantago*) in the valley bottoms. Extensive areas support open shrub associations of oak (*Quercus*), manzanita (*Arctostaphylos*), sumac (*Rhus*), juniper (*Juniperus*), and mountain mahogany (*Cercocarpus*). The mean annual precipitation is 475 mm and comes as late summer thunderstorms and winter rain and snow (U.S. Department of Commerce, Climatological Data).

DESCRIPTION OF GRASSHOPPER PUEBLO

The ruin is in east-central Arizona (110°40'E, 34°5'N) on the Salt River drainage, 17.4 km northwest of Cibecue on the Fort Apache Indian Reservation (Fig. 1.1). Eleva-

tion is about 1829 m. The masonry pueblo contains approximately 500 rooms, distributed among 13 room blocks of varying sizes and 15 smaller groups of room spaces and construction units. The three largest room blocks are situated on either side of the old channel of Salt River Draw and are collectively referred to as the main ruin (Fig. 1.2). To the east of the old channel is Room Block 1, consisting of 95 room spaces; Room Blocks 2 and 3 are on the west side. Room Block 2 is adjacent to the west bank of the old channel and contains 92 room spaces and Plaza III, which was converted into the Great Kiva. Room Block 3 has 101 room spaces. Together these two room blocks bound Plaza I and Plaza II. Access to the exterior was obtained through a long roofed corridor to the south of Plaza I and a short corridor to the east of Plaza II (Fig. 1.3). The presence of rooms with a second story has been demonstrated for all three room blocks of the main ruin, although the frequency of their distribution is unknown. No three-story structures have been identified.

Outlying room blocks are located adjacent to the main ruin and on the surrounding low hills. The outliers are different from the main ruin in several ways. Outlier rooms have appreciably lower walls than those in the main ruin and their fill lacks comparable quantities of charcoal and other related roofing material. Along with other evidence this suggests rooms of low stone walls supporting a superstructure, perhaps like a ramada, with sides open or walls constructed of jacal. Another form is a partially enclosed or three-wall ramada delimiting an unusually large area. The walls are low with only a few courses of stone in place.

About 50 years ago, a local stockman built an earthen dam across the wash just north of the ruin creating a reservoir on top of the location of a prehistoric one. As a result of subsequent silting, the historic pond backed up, and just east of the site Salt River Draw cut a new course through a large trash deposit on the eastern flank of the ruin.

EXCAVATION ACTIVITIES

In 1963 students investigated the stratigraphic history of selected areas, and the old stream bed between the two major units was trenched. Extensive areas of trash were excavated uncovering various features and burials, and revealing a set of contiguous masonry ovens. The first rooms were excavated in Room Block 1. In 1964, further hand trenching was undertaken, more rooms

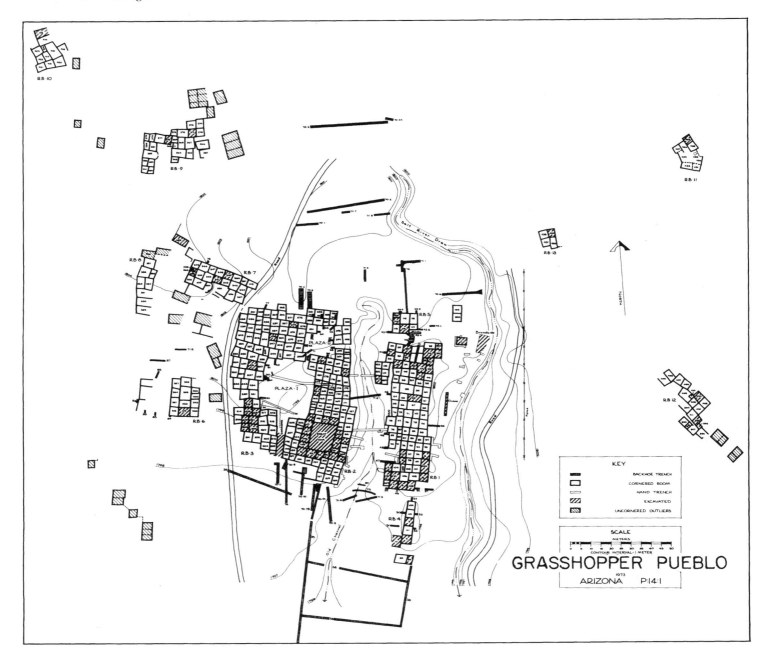

Figure 1.2. Plan of Grasshopper Pueblo showing the location of major room blocks and plaza areas.

were completed, and the Great Kiva was excavated to floor level with the aid of a backhoe provided by the Museum of Northern Arizona. The investigation of the Great Kiva-Plaza complex continued in 1964 with an examination of the deposits below the Great Kiva floor and of selected two-story rooms surrounding that structure. Backhoe trenching began in open, alluviated areas to the north and south of the main pueblo units. The investigation of the plaza floors and burials underlying the Great Kiva was completed in 1966. A distinctive cemetery was revealed (Griffin 1967) and a preliminary examination of burial patterning was completed (Clark 1967, 1969).

Probability sampling techniques were initiated in 1967. Student researchers exposed at least two corners of each of the 95 rooms in Room Block 1, and a backhoe located outside walls around the unit. From these data architectural units and room sizes were categorized, and a stratified sample of rooms was selected for excavation. Work began on these rooms in 1967 and continued in 1968. In addition, approximately 70 rooms in Room Block 2 were cornered and the entire site, including outliers, was mapped. Backhoe trenching provided material for environmental and stratigraphic analyses. Intensive pollen sampling was completed and extensive burial areas were revealed. Stratigraphic information for microtemporal

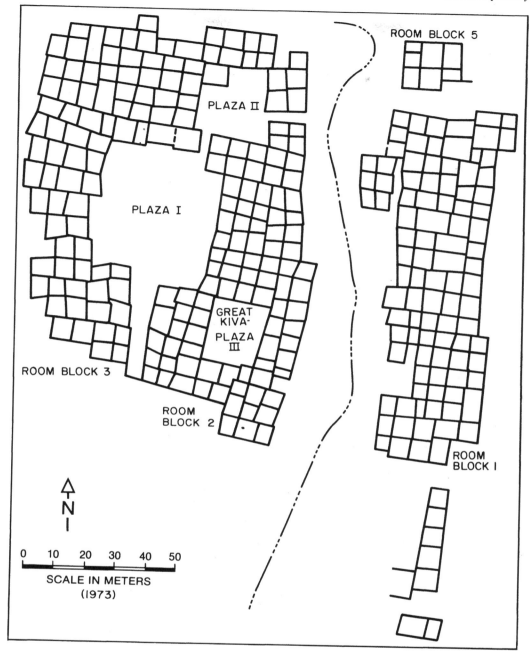

Figure 1.3. Major room blocks at Grasshopper Pueblo.

control was collected. A report detailing the results of the first three years of research at Grasshopper Pueblo has been published by Thompson and Longacre (1966), and Longacre and Reid (1974) have presented a summary of the subsequent years of research.

The investigation of sequences of room construction leading to the isolation of groups of rooms, designated as construction units and as aggregation units built as a single construction event, has illuminated the nature of the growth of the pueblo. These units appear to represent important social and behavioral segments of the community (Reid, Schiffer, and Neff 1975: 219). From this work and a growing list of tree-ring dated material

establishing approximate dates of room construction, the direction and processes of pueblo growth can be estimated. The three major room blocks, for example, were established at approximately the same time, between A.D. 1295 and 1305, although the number of core rooms initially constructed varied among the units. Multiroom sets of between 4 and 20 structures were added to core construction units during the early period of growth. By about A.D. 1320 the two room blocks located west of Salt River Draw were joined at their southern extension by a roofed corridor. The relatively early construction for the corridor indicates rapid expansion for these room blocks.

During these years of excavation, nearly 700 skeletons

were found distributed among at least seven cemeteries (Birkby 1973). Whittlesey (1978) attributes variability in mortuary practices (for example, style of interment, size of grave pit, associated grave structures, and mortuary offerings) to the age and sex of the individual and the relative date of interment. Men and women received different sets of grave offerings and the quantity and quality of offerings and energy expended on interment increased with the age of the individual. Burials during the early period of occupation received relatively more elaborate mortuary treatment than later interments. Other analyses of the human skeletal remains recovered from Grasshopper indicate that over half of those interred died before reaching reproductive age, and most of these died before the age of five (Longacre 1976). Simulation studies by Longacre (1975, 1976) suggest that a rate of population increase in excess of four percent annually would be necessary to account for the final size of the community (measured in terms of number of rooms). The most economical explanation for the rapid population increase associated with aggregation at Grasshopper is migration into the area from the local region.

MULTIDISCIPLINARY RESEARCH

In order to better understand the cultural processes of aggregation, growth, and abandonment at the Grasshopper Pueblo community, the multidisciplinary approach has been designed to investigate three broad areas of causality. One is the nature of the environment and the potential of environmental change in the Grasshopper region as a selective pressure responsible for the aggregation of population at the site. Both environmental deterioration and the possibility of climatic change leading to a more beneficial environment for subsistence agriculture have been investigated. Another causality is the possibility of major systemic change in the economic sector of cultural systems in this area of the Southwest during the thirteenth and fourteenth centuries. Intra- and interregional economic relationships involving food stuffs, resources, and locally produced goods may be responsible for changes in community size and organization. Major involvement in large-scale trading enterprises, perhaps originating and orchestrated in Mesoamerica during this period, has also been considered. Thus, the pressures for aggregation and relocation of populations may involve social and economic interaction with other communities in a network of trading relationships. A third causality is the possibility of a major adaptive change in subsistence strategies that resulted in more efficient utilization of available energy, a change not triggered, necessarily, by direct environmental pressures,

but perhaps by population pressure. Clearly, these hypotheses are interrelated, and environmental change may have resulted in greater agricultural opportunities for families in the Grasshopper locality that in turn affected population growth at the community.

The location and structure of activities, households, and suprahousehold levels of organization across the prehistoric community were affected in a complex manner by the expansion of the Pueblo. Early constructed rooms were probably single story units (Haury 1934), with an expanse of land between construction units. Although secure evidence is unavailable throughout the Pueblo, household activities at this time may have been carried out within several contiguous rooms connected by doorways and nearby extramural areas.

As the pueblo community grew, second story rooms were added to many of the early constructed core units and extramural areas decreased in extent, replaced by three plazas enclosed by room construction. During the latest period of occupation the community was apparently functionally zoned into central and peripheral areas (Ciolek-Torrello 1978: 170; Morenon 1972). Central areas are marked by early constructed rooms or second story additions around the two major plazas and the Great Kiva (formerly Plaza 3). The peripheral zone was utilized as the primary habitation area of the community, organized in a manner similar to early habitation units and characterized by the same range of activities. Many of the households within the central zone were organized vertically with domestic habitation activities performed on second story floors or rooftops and specialized manufacturing or refuse disposal conducted in ground floor room spaces. Outdoor areas, especially the two plazas, were no longer associated with individual household use. They were utilized for communally-based activities incorporating larger segments of the community.

The growth of functional zoning and specialized manufacturing at Grasshopper suggests that as the population expanded many members of the community may have engaged in occupations (on at least a part time basis) that were not directly involved with agricultural production. Analyses of White Mountain Red Ware vessels from Grasshopper indicate that they may have been imported to the community (Whittlesey 1974) in large quantities and possibly redistributed or traded to smaller villages in the region (Graves 1978). These lines of evidence attest to the growth of functional differentiation among members of the prehistoric community as the local population grew, in which individuals increasingly participated in activities unrelated to agricultural production. This form of organization marks a significant and novel development in this region of the Southwest.

2. MODERN ENVIRONMENT OF THE GRASSHOPPER REGION

Sally J. Holbrook and Michael W. Graves

Grasshopper Pueblo is situated within a geological transition zone between the Colorado Plateau to the north, and the Basin-and-Range province to the south. The up-tilted southern portion of the plateau, the Mogollon Rim, forms an abrupt geological boundary. There is no general agreement on regional geochronology or actual formative processes, but intensive faulting and erosion since the mid-Tertiary have produced a diverse physical environment of canyons, valleys, and mountains that vary considerably in dimensions. Some of the intermontane valleys form closed basins or playas, but most of them are dissected by drainage systems ultimately tributary to the Colorado River. The portion of the Rim that includes Grasshopper drains into the Salt River, a part of the Gila River Basin. These watersheds range in width from one to more than thirty miles (48.3 km), and many exhibit local changes in altitude of over a thousand feet (305 m; Wilson and Moore 1959). Moore (1968) places the Grasshopper locality within a physiographic subprovince designated as the Carrizo Slope, and describes the region as a badland incised by south-flowing streams on an incline extending south-southwest from the northern border of the Rim. Differential erosion caused by the varying hardness of the rock strata results in several major exceptions to the general direction of stream flow.

The actual site lies within the narrow drainage valley of Salt River Draw, once a perennial tributary of the Salt River, but only intermittent in recent years. The elevation is slightly over 5900 feet (1829 m) and the topography is not particularly rugged in the immediate area.

The Mogollon Rim and all of the Southwest has a biseasonal climate regime characterized by winter and summer rainstorms separated by periods of drought. Lowe (1964) provides an excellent summary of this precipitation pattern. Specifics for the Grasshopper locality, taken from Cibecue, ten miles east and almost 900 feet (275 m) lower, include a mean annual rainfall of 18.61 inches (47.27 cm), often with substantial snowfall, and mean temperatures ranging from 37° to 74° F (2.3° to 23.3° C) with normal extremes approaching 20° and 95° F (-6.7° and 35° C; Greene and Sellers 1964). Based on records for the last twenty years, the average length of the growing season (frost free days) is 140 days.

GENERAL VEGETATION OF THE MOGOLLON RIM

Vegetation of the Rim country represents a continuum between the Upper Sonoran Desert of the Basin-and-Range province and the Evergreen Woodlands of the Plateau (Table 2.1). In addition, the extreme topographic diversity, with its considerable influence on local climate and microhabitats, accounts for innumerable variations of these biotic communities. There are two reasons to consider these biotic communities, even though not all of them are directly associated with Grasshopper. The first is that in the narrow geographical area occupied by the Rim, all communities were within easy access to the prehistoric inhabitants of the Pueblo. Second, it is likely that these communities may have altered to some extent in composition, location, or size within the last thousand years. These small changes in the environs and its corresponding biota may be significant to archaeological interpretations.

VEGETATION COMMUNITIES AT GRASSHOPPER PUEBLO

Both the geographic location and the climate place Grasshopper at the lower border of the Transition Life Zone, an ecotonal situation accounting for the mixtures of vegetation types. The area includes certain species common to the next higher or lower life zone, but at the same time, it lacks some typical constituents of those other zones. The result is intermediate associations that characteristically support a greater diversity of species than might normally be expected.

The major communities represented in the Grasshopper vicinity include grassland and woodland associations, and a ponderosa forest consociation (a community dominated by a single species). Two other minor vegetation types are also present. A poorly developed riparian community occurs along drainages and around localized seepages. It occupies little area compared to the other associations, but it does include several species possibly of economic importance. In areas where the original vegetation has been removed either by natural fires or range modification practices, there is chaparral vegetation. In some instances delineations between adjacent communities are abrupt, and they seem to be related to variations in the substrate (Figs. 2.1, 2.2). The soil types present are discussed with each vegetation type. Complete soil profile descriptions for each community are on file in the archives of the Arizona State Museum, Tucson.

Both random samples and plant materials along transects were collected during the late spring, summer, and early fall months. Those species not encountered are probably infrequent or rare forms of ground cover, and

Figure 2.1. Aerial view of vegetation in the Grasshopper region. Solid lines delineate major vegetational communities; dashed lines indicate variations within a community. Vegetation transect locations: A, ponderosa pine; B, woodland; all transects oriented east-west. S indicates soil pits. Only areas worked are outlined. (Approximate scale, 10 cm equals 1.6 km.)

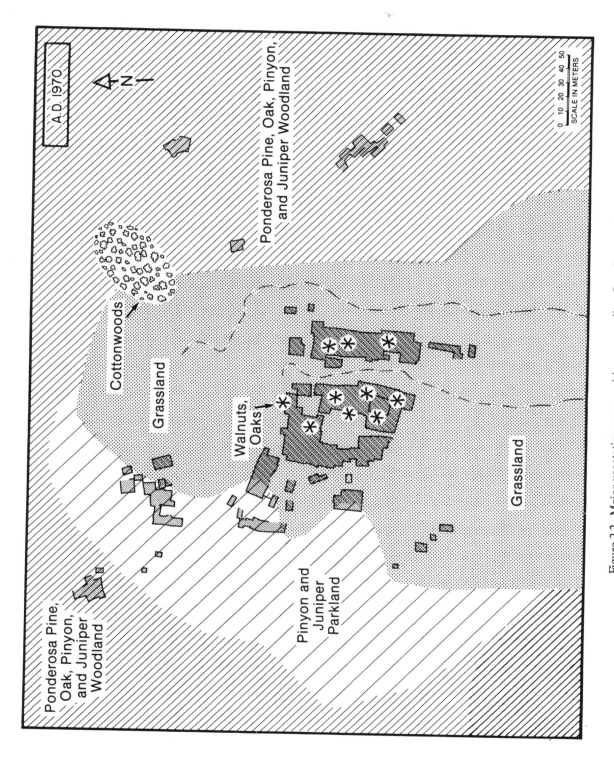

Figure 2.2. Major vegetation communities surrounding Grasshopper Pueblo.

TABLE 2.1

Vegetation Communities of the Mogollon Rim[1]

Vegetation Communities	Life Zones
Desert Formation-Class[2]	
Southwest Desert Scrub Formation[3]	
Palo Verde-Saguaro Association	
Grassland Formation-Class	Lower Sonoran
Desert Grassland Formation	
Plains Grassland Formation	
Mountain Grassland Formation[4]	————
Chaparral Formation-Class	
Woodland Formation-Class	Upper Sonoran
Evergreen Woodland Formation	
Juniper-Pinyon-Oak Formation	
Deciduous Woodland Formation	
Riparian Woodland Association	————
Forest Formation-Class	
Coniferous Forest Formation	
Ponderosa Pine Forest Association/Consociation	Transition
Douglas Fir Forest Association	Canadian ⎫ — Boreal
Spruce-Alpine Fir Association	Hudsonian ⎭

1. Adapted from Lowe (1964). Some additional communities occur in Mogollon–Sub-Mogollon regions; those listed above are related to the Grasshopper locality.
2. Formation-Classes are from the World Ecological Classification system.
3. Formations are from the Subcontinental Classification System.
4. Not properly included in the Upper Sonoran Life Zone.

early spring (February to May) annuals and perennials in all communities. The inventory has been estimated by Eric Granfelt of the Bureau of Indian Affairs in Whiteriver to be two-thirds complete.

The grassland complex was not sampled because it proved to be an altered association resulting primarily from grazing activities, and, therefore, was not particularly applicable to archaeological interpretation. Grazing does affect all the communities, but it is not so pronounced in those dominated by tree and nonbrowse shrub species. Results of a survey of grassland areas made by V. E. Scott during a study on the wild turkey are included in the grassland discussion.

The woodland and pine forest communities were extensively sampled. The line-intercept technique (Cox 1967) used consisted of a series of parallel lines at either 50 or 100 m intervals. In the analysis these lines were added consecutively and considered as one, a method that assumes the composite vegetation for each community was homogeneous. At Grasshopper, where these communities are well delineated, such an assumption is probably valid, but it would be violated in areas where intergrading and gradual transitions prevail. The problem of evaluating stratified vegetation (woodland with an upper canopy of tall trees, a subcanopy of older seedlings, a woody shrub layer, and finally a ground cover) was partially solved by recording the species, abundance, and pattern of the subdominants. Analysis revealed that the subdominants were not of the same species and density composition as the canopy, and therefore we inferred that a successional stage was represented.

Grassland Association

Grassland in the Grasshopper area most closely resembles the Plains Grassland Formation (Table 2.1). Both elevation and mean annual rainfall are within the range of the Plains type, which extends into the lower Transition Zone and is frequently associated with woodlands. The grassland association at Grasshopper, however, does have some characteristics of the Desert Grassland Formation as well. Certain floral constituents, specifically *Sporobolus cryptandrus*, and species of *Aristida* and *Eragrostis* are indicative of the more xeric formation. Locally, the community occurs on deep, well-drained alluvial soils with little surface rock. Topographic variations are negligible and afford minimal potential for erosion. Table 2.2 shows the density composition by percent, based on Parker Three-Step Survey data collected by Scott.

The fairly continuous ground cover (bare soil is less than 10 percent) instead of clumped open bunch grass is a characteristic of the Plains grassland. A soil pit located 100 m south of the site revealed deep alluvial soils (2 m) underlain by sandstones and limestones of the Naco or Supai formations. Cultural outwash material occurred to a depth of 60 cm. This pit best represents the soil type of the area immediately adjacent to the site, and the detailed horizon description is available in the Arizona State Museum archives. Further sampling of this association might yield information useful in archaeological interpretation of the prehistoric grassland complex, especially if made in conjunction with a palynological

TABLE 2.2
Grassland Density Composition
Near Grasshopper Pueblo

Species	%	Species	%
Bouteloua gracilis	34.7	*Astragalus* sp.	3.6
Euphorbia sp.	12.4	*Aplopappus gracilis*	3.5
Erigeron divergens	6.2	*Agropyron smithii*	2.9
Plantago sp.	5.6	*Erodium cicutarium*	2.9
Eragrostis lutescens	4.7	*Achillea lanulosa*	2.4

Note: Eight other species were 1.0 to 2.0 percent; 51 species were less than 1.0 percent and 26 of them were less than 0.1 percent. Litter and bare ground equaled 6.9 percent.

TABLE 2.3
Proposed Species of an Unaltered
Grassland in the Grasshopper Locality

Scientific Name		Common Name
Bouteloua curtipendula	(dominant)	side oats grama
B. gracilis	(common)	blue grama
B. hirsuta	(possible)	hairy grama
B. eriopoda	(possible)	black grama
Eurotia lanata		winter fat
Hilaria jamesii		galleta
Koeleria cristata		June grass
Lycurus phleoides		Texas-timothy (wolftail)
Muhlenbergia repens	(infrequent)	red muhly
M. wrightii	(infrequent)	spike muhly
Andropogon sp.		blue stem
Poa sp.		blue grass
Agropyron smithii	(mesic locations)	western wheatgrass
Panicum obtusum	(mesic locations)	vine mesquite
Carex spp.	(mesic locations)	sedges

study. Granfelt identified the probable constituents of an unaltered grassland association in the Grasshopper locality and they are listed in Table 2.3.

Juniper-Pine-Oak Woodland Association

The juniper-pine-oak association occurs on ridges with residual soils underlain by limestones and sandstones. The soils may be virtually absent on rock outcrops or be more than two m deep. The vegetation is generally open, with coverage by dominant taxa less than 40 percent. A substantial area estimated at 30 to 40 percent of grassland clearings is characteristic of this community type. The woodland proper ranges from moderately open to a dense, stratified community, with the more open parts exhibiting a limited nursemaid type understudy (Fig.

Figure 2.3. Profile of a densely stratified view of the woodland association. Foreground clearing results from shallow soil over a limestone outcropping, as shown by the cobbles. Yuccas were common in these areas.

2.3). Distribution of subordinate species seems to be influenced by variations of exposure resulting from topographic effects.

The species composition of the upper strata (canopy, seedling subcanopy, and shrub) is moderately diverse and includes six genera, four with two or more species that constitute 87.3 percent of the relative density and 32.9 percent of a total 38.5 percent coverage. *Juniperus* is both the most frequent and abundant genus, but *Pinus* has the highest coverage value; it occupies 125 percent of the ground cover value for junipers, reflecting the greater proportion of juniper seedlings and the larger average size of ponderosa pines. Species of the herbaceous strata are numerous. Important values for the nonherbaceous species of both woodland and forest communities are presented in Table 2.4.

The low importance value of the pinyon pine (*Pinus edulis*) in the woodland association is significant. Mixed woodlands are often referred to as Pinyon-Juniper, but pinyon is more common at higher elevations or more northern localities. For archaeological considerations, pinyon may be an important food and fuel plant, while the other pines contribute wood for construction.

Pine Forest Consociation

In the pine forest near Grasshopper, *Pinus ponderosa* dominates in all quantitative values, and its importance value is more than three times that of *Juniperus* (Fig. 2.4). The stand varies from moderately open to dense, with an average cover value of 46.9 percent. Open clearings are fairly common and initial analysis of surface soil samples indicates this pattern might be the result of substrate variation. The majority of subordinate tree species is composed of seedling individuals under 5 m, and the shrub understory, which is exclusively *Rhus trilobata*, is largely restricted to the margins. Several observations suggest that this particular stand may have developed within the last 300 years or so. Although most

TABLE 2.4

Importance Values of Woodland and Forest Flora

	Taxon					
	P. ponderosa	*Juniperus*	*Quercus*	*P. edulis*	**Shrubs**	**Yucca**
Woodland	90.9	100.9	67.6	10.9	13.7	6.4
Forest	180.3	56.8	33.4	5.4	14.4	9.7

Note: Value is derived as the sum of relative frequency, density, and coverage.

Figure 2.4. Ponderosa pine consociation with foreground moderately open and background dense (trees within 2 m of each other). Differences in height are not attributable to age. Note the near absence of any understory. Subdominant woody species are almost entirely restricted to juniper seedlings and squaw bush.

Figure 2.5. Old alligator-bark juniper with limb debris within a dense ponderosa pine stand.

nonpine species are seedlings, it is not uncommon to see occasional large solitary junipers or oaks, and tree-ring cores from these individuals indicate minimal ages of 250 years (Fig. 2.5). In contrast, the oldest pine located within the consociation is 117 years or more. While the pines divide into three distinct height categories, height difference must be attributed to either genetic origin or microhabitat variation because all ages are within 50 to 75 years of each other, whether the tree is 10 or 20 m

tall. Two pines, one marginal to the forest and the other within the woodland, date respectively as 295 and 332 years. This age discrepancy between woodland pines and forest pines suggests recent development. Removal of the older forest pines by fire has been considered but that explanation is unsatisfactory because fire would not select pines only and leave behind junipers and oaks of the same stand. Logging activities also cannot account for the absence because there are still older pines within the woodland that are much more accessible for lumbering. Although the longevity of pines may be less than that for oaks and junipers along the Mogollon Rim, the discrepancy remains unanswered because one would expect the pines in the forest to be at least of comparable age to those in the adjacent woodland.

Additional supportive evidence is derived from analysis of soil profile pits. The woodland, as noted previously, occupies ridges with residual soils, while both the grassland and pine communities occur on deep alluvial soils that may be of Pleistocene origin. The pines are situated uphill on a gentle slope from the grassland. The well-developed profiles and buried horizons of these soils required long periods to form and these subsurface horizons are similiar throughout the alluvial deposits, indicating a common developmental history. Of the five basic soil-forming factors—parent material, climate, time, topography, and vegetation—the first three are constant for the immediate locality, and the slight topographic variations are probably of negligible influence. It is possible to conclude, therefore, that the fifth factor, vegetation, must have been of a uniform type because similar soils result only from the same composite of soil-forming factors. While the surface horizons exhibit certain expected characteristics of the respective current vegetation types (such as granular structure in the grassland resulting from the dense root network, and accumulation of coniferous litter producing a platy structured, acidic soil in the pine forest), these surface features can develop within a shorter time period of hundreds of years and thus do not negate the view of recent development.

Even though the evidence on the temporal origin of the pine stand near Grasshopper is inconclusive, the future direction of the stand seems clear. Using a functional definition of climax communities, which requires that the understory consist of the same species in the same proportions as the canopy, it is apparent that this particular stand is not maintaining itself through reproduction. Further, the prevalence of juniper in the understory indicates that the woodland is encroaching. These observations suggest that the pine stand is, then, a stage in a seral progression.

Enough data are available to surmise the probable distributional pattern of these communities. The woodland appears indigenous along the stable ridge habitats; it may well be the original post-Pleistocene vegetation type. The alluvial sediments undoubtedly supported a grassland vegetation type once depositional activities subsided enough to allow growth. Where the two communities merged in ecotonal situations, the landscape must have been a juniper-oak savanna, a pattern probably extending down the gentle alluvial slopes from the woodland as far as moisture conditions allowed.

Such a situation is the locus of the pine stand today. There are substantial indications that water availability in the Grasshopper locality has decreased considerably since prehistoric times (see Chapter 9). At some time during this transition, the higher slopes dried out sufficiently to allow ponderosa pine from the woodland to occupy this habitat, but, as current observations indicate, the opportunistic pines could not retain their position against the woodland association.

3. PUEBLO GROWTH AT GRASSHOPPER: METHODS AND MODELS

J. Jefferson Reid and Izumi Shimada

In that region bound by the ruins at Kinishba, Fourmile, Chavez Pass, and Lake Roosevelt, an area of approximately 3400 square miles (8772 square kilometers), Grasshopper was the most prominent fourteenth century pueblo community. In less than 125 years, it was established, grew to 500 rooms, and was abandoned forever. The relatively short duration of such a prominent community prompts questions concerning major events and processes operating in the late prehistory of the Southwest. But as often happens in archaeology, to answer questions concerning these larger issues requires first that problems on a much smaller scale be solved. This chapter chronicles the development of such solutions to the ongoing research problem of reconstructing pueblo growth.

One of the most interesting questions confronting the research team at the Field School has been how environmental factors influenced the development of Grasshopper Pueblo and how the inhabitants solved the inevitable problems of making a living in this rugged portion of the Arizona mountains. Within this broader range of problems specific research by Reid (1973, 1978) focused on responses to environmental stress, itself a problem of some concern in southwestern archaeology (Dean 1969; J. N. Hill 1970b; Longacre 1970b). Was environmental stress late in the history of the Pueblo responsible for abandonment? Could shifts in subsistence routines be identified and further interpreted as responses to such stress? Answers to these questions required a temporal framework for investigating pueblo establishment, expansion, and abandonment and the rate at which these processes proceeded. The Growth Project that began in 1971 was designed to provide this necessary framework (Longacre and Reid 1974).

THE GROWTH PROJECT

Growth is defined as an increase in units resulting in an increase in size. The units are architectural and in basic form are labeled rooms (see Chapter 4). Concern, then, is with pueblo growth through the addition of rooms rather than with establishing population estimates. The necessity for building a temporal frame for pueblo growth with which to study possible increases in environmental stress and the behavioral responses to it dictated this research direction.

The complexities involved in establishing a complete and accurate architectural history of a large pueblo ruin are staggering because that architectural structure is the product of numerous processes. Activities of construction and occupation are made more complex by remodeling, reoccupation, abandonment, and recycling of materials. David's (1971) analysis of a small African settlement in the ethnographic context is a lucid illustration of this complexity. Further modifications result from the natural processes that produce deterioration and collapse of pueblo rooms. In this fashion the original forms that pueblo construction took are often obscured by subsequent processes, both natural and cultural (Schiffer 1976, Ascher 1968). There can be no simple architectural history of a pueblo or a room, for the processes that alter both lack their obvious visibility in the archaeological record. Unraveling this contextual tangle is neither a simple matter nor one resolvable by any single technique. The expansion of the technical repertoire developed in attempting to reconstruct the growth of Grasshopper Pueblo is briefly chronicled.

The goal of Growth Project research was to formulate sets of artifacts that could be assumed to possess classificatory contemporaneity (Dean 1969) and thus be suitable for comparison. To accomplish this goal a construction sequence was required in which sets of contemporaneously constructed rooms and their artifact arrays could be identified. The field strategy of the Growth Project thus began with the excavation of room corners to identify bond-abutment patterns of room walls, a procedural outgrowth of the antecedent cornering project (see Chapter 4; Wilcox and Collins 1971). These patterns were to be used to reconstruct the sequence of building events that produced the final configuration of the ruin. Information from excavated rooms such as datable tree-ring specimens and stratigraphic relationships were expected to link the construction sequence to other events, and especially to absolute time. The idea was rather naively entertained that early constructed rooms would possess early floors covered with early artifacts, and that late floors and associated artifacts would be found in late constructed rooms, a situation that would have provided the necessary sets of artifacts possessing classificatory contemporaneity.

Unfortunately, this simplistic notion did not correspond to the realities of the archaeological record. A construction sequence based solely on bond-abutment analysis proved incapable of providing an unambiguous temporal ordering of critical behavioral events or artifact sets. Both past behaviors and natural processes had conspired to distort the information obtained from wall corner relationships and to obscure the temporal associations between room construction and use. The methodological innovations that corrected these difficulties and finally provided the elusive temporal information are discussed below.

The discovery of these difficulties in the original field strategy and the solutions proposed for them led to a reevaluation of concepts and objectives initially proposed for the cornering project in 1967 and formalized in 1969 (Wilcox and Collins 1971). The outcome of this reevaluation has been the creation of some new concepts and the redefinition of some old terms that have been useful in thinking about and observing pueblo architectural phenomena. The resulting lexicon forms a working vocabulary with which to describe and discuss pueblo growth.

Concepts and Definitions

Recovery space labels the class of spatial units such as squares, trenches, and levels that are the locus of *present* archaeological activity. On the other hand, the class of analytically defined areas of *past* human behavior is labeled *behavioral space* (Reid 1973; Reid, Schiffer, and Neff 1975). Recovery space refers to archaeological context phenomena, or to material remains as they are found today, while behavioral space refers to systemic context phenomena or material remains as they participated in a past behavioral system (Schiffer 1976). As such, the two classes of space are not necessarily isomorphic. Thus, specific labels are required to differentiate spatial context.

In the context of past behavior, the minimal unit of growth should specify a discrete activity or activity set. These activity areas are more than the space defined by the easily recognized pueblo room. Conventional labels include storage, habitation, or ceremonial rooms, rooftops, courtyards, ramadas, plazas, corridors, and exterior activity areas not associated with any architectural form (Dean 1969, 1970; J. N. Hill 1970a; Ciolek-Torrello 1978).

The possibilities and complexities increase when one considers variability in architectural form. Architectural forms delimit behavioral space. They also impede or channel the flow of matter and energy—light, wind, rain, heat, sound, dogs, or people. For example, masonry walls with doors and those without restrict the movement of people and the loss of heat in different ways. The movement of individuals and access to households may be directed, restricted, and redirected according to organizational constraints such as kinship relations, and these constraints will be manifest in architectural remodeling that may obscure previous relationships (see Rohn 1965, 1971; Schiffer 1973b; Wilcox 1975). Additionally, space bounded by four walls but lacking a roof may delimit activities different from those of a typical pueblo room or an open courtyard, even though each may contain superficially similar artifact arrays. These processes clearly impinge on the problem of reconstructing an accurate architectural history of a large pueblo ruin. The solution to the problem was to concentrate on the pueblo room.

A typical pueblo *room* at Grasshopper is bounded by stone masonry walls on all sides, the earth below, and a roof above. The walls extend to support a roof constructed of timbers, dirt, and a variety of other materials.

In most cases four walls can be recognized prior to excavation while the roof is assumed to have been present until demonstrated otherwise. In practice, the term room has at times been used to label phenomena in both the archaeological and systemic contexts. But as Wilcox points out in Chapter 4, some distinction should be made between what is labeled a room before excavation and what functioned as several rooms with various superimposed floors that are revealed through excavation. Room space is a reasonable label for such archaeological context phenomena, although it also seems consistent with traditional usage to view a room in the archaeological context as a recovery space that is revealed by excavation to possess a series of activity surfaces referred to as a roof, a second-story floor, a series of first-story floors, and possibly preroom surfaces such as portions of a plaza. Room and room space are used here to label these distinctions in context.

Rooms signify architectural forms that bound different activity areas. The associated activities define particular classes of room function. Identification of activities and their associated architectural forms is not a simple task. Whereas architectural forms may be unaltered during a room's occupation, activities performed within rooms often change through time as indicated by floor superposition and the rearrangement or removal of facilities such as hearths and mealing bins. Therefore, activities conducted on the latest floor may not be the same as the activities intended at construction and related to architectural form (see David 1971; Sullivan 1974). For example, a small storage room may be converted into a habitation room. In such a case, association between the latest activities and architectural form may be spurious, or, the reverse may happen and architectural features may be altered along with changes in room function. The dismantling of typical special features such as masonry bench and ventilator, when a kiva was converted to habitation functions, is perhaps the most obvious example. It is possible that room configuration may change while activities remain constant, but this has not been demonstrated.

This lack of simple equivalence caused difficulties in earlier attempts at Grasshopper to correlate room size with function. The problem of identifying original room function when floors are superimposed has been successfully resolved by several approaches (see Chapter 13; Sullivan 1974; Ciolek-Torrello and Reid 1974; Ciolek-Torrello 1978; Hill and Hevly 1968).

The remainder of this rather spare metalanguage comprises three labels for architectural phenomena—construction unit, core construction unit, and room block —and a method for ordering construction events, the construction phase.

A *construction unit* (CU) is a continuously bonded wall and the set of spaces directly associated with it. A construction unit may include one wall or any combination of walls and associated spaces. The activities delimited by these spaces and the temporal relations among these activities can only be identified through excavation. Although it is possible to posit courtyards and other architectural forms prior to excavation, it has not been possible to tie these units temporally to other walls and spaces in order to identify construction units of mixed forms. Therefore, room spaces have been employed as the elemental units combined together to form construction units of continuously bonded walls.

The *room block* (RB) is the next higher level architectural unit representing a set of contiguous construction units separated spatially from other architectural units. Isolated rooms are not given both a room space number and a room block number. Large room blocks expanded from one or more *core construction units,* which are the original or earliest construction units in the block.

Construction phase is a label for construction units ordered sequentially within a room block in terms of their relation to the original or core construction units (Reid 1973). The core construction units are designated Construction Phase 1 and succeeding construction unit additions are consecutively numbered until the peripheral and last construction units in that room block are included. Prior to excavation we infer that these construction phases approximate a relative measure of the construction events among *contiguous* construction units. Therefore, a construction unit was built after *contiguous* units of the preceding phase and before *contiguous* construction units of the succeeding phase. Noncontiguous construction units of the same numbered construction phase were not necessarily built at the same time, although in practice it has proved convenient at times to assume that they were.

Methods and Measures

Anchoring construction events in absolute time and estimating the temporal range of growth phases has relied exclusively on dates provided by the Laboratory of Tree-Ring Research at the University of Arizona. Dean and Robinson discuss their analysis of this material in Chapter 8.

With tree-ring dates it is possible to estimate the time of construction for crucial architectural features in the development of the pueblo. This is not to suggest that tree-ring dates resolved the problems of this research. Because there are no architecturally-associated cutting dates, few architectural proveniences with a sufficient number of dates to form clusters, and a number of dates from specimens of ambiguous provenience association, tree-ring dates could not be used to define an unambiguous construction sequence. Several other techniques of data collection and analysis augmented the information provided by tree-ring dates.

Bond-abutment Analysis

It became clear during early stages of field work that bond-abutment patterns observed in a large pueblo ruin do not provide unambiguous information on the construction sequence. Corner relationships as they are observed today are made ambiguous by the natural deterioration processes that operate to collapse pueblo walls. Correspondingly, determination of original relationships

is made less secure. Furthermore, bond-abutment patterns alone cannot be used to determine if remodeling of rooms took place, although any architectural remodeling would certainly obscure original corner relationships. A partial solution to this problem was to substitute wall-face analysis for observations of bond-abutment patterns.

Wall-face Analysis

For some time there had been a working hypothesis at Grasshopper that walls with a smooth face were once exterior (see Rinaldo 1964a: 49). Smooth-faced walls were equated to walls composed of dressed slabs with horizontal chinking between courses. This wall type and three additional types have been defined by Scarborough and Shimada (1974). Further investigation demonstrated that the relationship is true for the majority of cases in both the main ruin and the outliers. However, it is clear that masonry in the main ruin possesses a higher degree of uniformity than that of the outliers.

This analysis recorded wall-face types throughout the main ruin, distinguishing smooth-faced walls from rough-faced walls, as well as the degree of lithological homogeneity of stones used. These distinctions formed a more consistent basis for identifying construction sequences and eventually they replaced bond-abutment patterns in the designation of construction phases. Wall-face distinctions finally fulfilled one of the original goals of the Growth Project, the generation of a model of the construction sequence.

Room Abandonment Measure

Despite the greater confidence given to the construction sequence by wall-face analysis, still unsolved was the problem of establishing temporally equivalent sets of artifacts—information crucial to the study. The construction sequence could not disclose the subsequent occupation and abandonment of rooms. As observed earlier, there is no necessary relationship between initial room construction and its subsequent use-history because abandonment, remodeling, reoccupation, and simple decay create that use-history. In fact, geological analysis of exposed wall faces in some cases revealed considerable lithological diversity, suggesting intrasite recycling in remodeling and rebuilding. The room abandonment measure (Reid 1973) was developed to resolve this difficulty and provide the necessary, comparable sets of artifacts.

The measure was formulated within the framework of formation processes involved in the deposition of refuse (Schiffer 1976). It was proposed that the behavior believed to be associated with the abandonment of artifacts could be used to identify a relative abandonment period for excavated rooms and thus to order artifact sets temporally. The measure is predicated on the plausibility of two related assumptions. Rooms abandoned while Grasshopper was still occupied contain little or no de facto refuse, defined as tools, facilities, and materials that, although still usable, were abandoned at an activity area on the last utilized floor. These rooms do contain in the room fill, however, a high density of secondary refuse, defined as trash discarded away from its location of use (Schiffer 1976: 30, 33). Second, rooms abandoned at or near the time of Grasshopper's abandonment should have a high density of de facto refuse on the last utilized floor and a low density of secondary refuse in the room fill. This assumption obtains at Grasshopper because of particular conditions of abandonment seemingly uncommon at many other large pueblo ruins.

These views lean heavily on the belief that rooms abandoned while the pueblo was still occupied have a higher probability of being scavenged for usable items. Furthermore, it is assumed that people do not live in the same room into which they, or others, are dumping trash. If sufficient quantities of secondary refuse are identified, then the abandonment of that room during the occupation of the pueblo can be inferred. The inverse relationship posited between secondary and de facto refuse provides an index by which periods of room abandonment can be estimated.

Secondary refuse in room fill is measured by counting all sherds in the fill above the last ground floor and dividing that total by the area of the room in square meters. Sherds alone are used because they are consistent indicators of refuse and because sherd counts are more accessible. The result is a density measure normalized for room area.

De facto refuse is measured by the number of ceramic vessels on the last ground floor. These two variables, when plotted as a scattergram, permit rooms to be grouped by inspection into Room Abandonment Classes (RAC):

Room Abandonment Class 1—Late abandonment
Room Abandonment Class 2—Probable late abandonment
Room Abandonment Class 3— Early abandonment
A cluster and discriminant function analysis support this grouping (Reid 1973). Subsequent work by Richard Ciolek-Torrello (1978) demonstrates that the measure does function using only sherds as secondary refuse in room fill. Furthermore, his analysis of room function permits the provisional merging of Classes 1 and 2.

The distribution of these classes conforms to the assumption that rooms with a high sherd density have no ceramic vessels on the floor and that rooms with high de facto refuse have a low sherd density in the fill. It is inferred from these measures that rooms of the former configuration had been abandoned early enough for secondary refuse to accumulate and before rooms of the latter class were abandoned. This measure of differential abandonment temporarily satisfied the research objective of identifying early artifacts and associated behaviors that could be compared to late artifacts and behaviors (Reid 1973). However, the room abandonment measure alone does not explicate pueblo growth at Grasshopper.

Stratigraphic Analysis

Other techniques were used to correlate room construction and abandonment data. Traditional stratigraphic analysis was employed during excavation of Plaza II, for example, to match activities occurring in plaza space with the construction of rooms in and around the plaza. A plaza activity surface occurring below a room can be identified as being in use prior to the construction phase associated with that room. Features occurring on this surface are also tagged with a relative temporal label. In this way activities and artifacts not qualifying for a construction phase tag by themselves are linked with architectural units that do qualify.

Because the architectural history of a large pueblo ruin is complex, it is not advisable to rely solely on one technique or set of data for the purpose of reconstruction. It is helpful to remember that the event identified by a technique may be unrelated to the event presupposed in the analysis. To identify construction events is to record precious little concerning occupation, abandonment, and reoccupation events.

The Developmental Cycle Model

Discussion of pueblo growth at Grasshopper has undergone expansion and refinement since the period of initial consideration (Griffin 1969; Longacre and Reid 1971) and has been enhanced by the notions of domestic groups and their developmental cycles (Buchler and Selby 1968: 47-68; Fortes 1971: 14; Goody 1971). The popularity of the developmental cycle of domestic groups is seen in studies by Reid (1973), Ciolek-Torrello and Reid (1974), Kemrer (1973), Rock (1974), Wilcox (1975), and D. P. Morris (1975).

The model of the developmental cycle was formulated by Fortes in order to conceptualize the time dimension of an enduring social unit, the domestic group. The domestic group is a "householding and housekeeping unit organized to provide the materials and cultural resources needed to maintain and bring up its members" (Fortes 1971: 8). It is not a static unit, but undergoes patterned, cyclical changes.

> The domestic group goes through a cycle of development analogous to the growth cycle of a living organism. The group as a unit retains the same form, but its members, and the activities which unite them, go through a regular sequence of changes during the cycle which culminates in the dissolution of the original unit and its replacement by one or more units of the same kind (Fortes 1971: 2).

Fortes divides the developmental cycle of domestic groups into an expansion phase, a dispersion or fission phase, and a replacement phase. The expansion phase "corresponds to the period during which all the offspring of the parents are economically and jurally dependent on them" (Fortes 1971: 4-5). The dispersion phase, often overlapping the first, "begins with the marriage of the oldest child and continues until all the children are married....The replacement phase ends with the death of the parents and replacement in the social structure of the family they founded by the families of their children" (Fortes 1971: 5). In the following application an establishment and an abandonment phase have been substituted for the replacement phase.

Here the utility of the Fortes model of the developmental cycle is not in its application to archaeological problems of identifying domestic groups but in the framework it provides for constructing models applicable to the understanding of pueblo growth. Thus, the developmental cycle model is not used to identify domestic groups, but to proceed on the assumption that the growth of Grasshopper Pueblo is a reflection of growth and change in its constituent domestic groups. The Fortes model provides a framework to structure discussion of processes of establishment, expansion, dispersion, and abandonment of Grasshopper on the community and regional level.

In this expanded application of the developmental cycle the referent is the pueblo community, the aggregate of domestic groups. An establishment phase refers to the initial construction and occupation of core rooms at the pueblo. During the expansion phase, new rooms are added to the original core rooms to form room blocks. Coeval with this expansion process is the establishment of new groups at the pueblo through immigration (Reid 1973; Longacre 1975, 1976). The dispersion phase refers to movement away from Grasshopper to form satellite villages. The abandonment phase encompasses the emigration or death of the last occupants of the pueblo and the cessation of ongoing domestic activity. The developmental cycle at Grasshopper is replaced by community growth at another location or locations.

The model distinguishes periods during which certain significant processes occur. These processes need not be mutually exclusive. Furthermore, it is understood that in spite of the superficial linearity of such a model, more complex cycles are not precluded. It is possible that communities may have been established, expanded, and dispersed, and then have experienced expansion again without ever being totally abandoned. Other permutations are possible (see Adams 1968). Developmental phases of pueblo communities are placed in regional perspective when seen as recurrent, cyclic responses to local social and natural environmental conditions by a mobile population composed of autonomous ceremonial-domestic groups. Such a notion is consistent with prehistoric reconstructions (Dean 1969, 1970; Schoenwetter and Dittert 1968; Thompson 1958; Vivian 1970; Schwartz 1970) and ethnographic information (Dozier 1966, 1970; Eggan 1950, 1964; Titiev 1944).

Data used in the application of the model to Grasshopper come from bond-abutment patterns, wall-face patterns, the room abandonment measure, stratigraphic relations, and tree-ring dates. No single analytic procedure guided the interpretation of data, because none alone proved capable of handling these different and often incomplete sets of observations. The outcome of the growth analysis is essentially the product of intuition operating with the development cycle model on the available data. However, this reconstruction of pueblo growth at Grasshopper has not been significantly altered by subsequent analysis since it was first proposed (Reid 1973). The methods, measures, and models described and the lexicon developed can be used to reconstruct how the pueblo reached its final configuration.

GROWTH AT GRASSHOPPER PUEBLO

Establishment Phase
(A.D. 1275–1300)

The factors affecting initial settlement at Grasshopper were first observed by Hough (1930: 3):

The location of the Grasshopper sites was determined by the strong and permanent spring, the basin-like area in which water could be impounded, the excellent land available for cultivation, and the supply of wood for fuel, together with the good conditions for an abundance of game. Beams and stone for building and flint for various implements were also factors of advantage.

Significant to the development of the pueblo was the stable water supply provided by the spring and a walk-in well or small pond (Chapters 7, 9; Olsen and Olsen 1970). Stratigraphic evidence indicates the "basin-like" area was immediately north of the main ruin beneath the sediments of the historic pond noted by Hough. The presence of these water resources in the north flat posed an initial and continuing constraint on construction and the direction of subsequent expansion (see Tuggle 1970: 36).

In general, the nearest sources of construction stone were exploited to minimize time and energy expended in building the masonry pueblo. At times, ease of quarrying and shaping rocks was also a prominent concern (Shimada 1978). Wall building techniques further reflect an efficient use of materials (Scarborough and Shimada 1974).

The main pueblo at Grasshopper, described in Chapter 1 (see Figs. 1.1–1.3), developed from seven separate core construction units ranging in size from 5 to 21 rooms. Although dated tree-ring material has been recovered from core construction units in the three room blocks, no cutting dates have been obtained. Michael Graves has suggested, however, that for certain species the exterior ring approximates the death of the specimen within seven years. Tree-ring dates from early constructed rooms in Room Block 3 date between A.D. 1290 and 1310, most of them clustering after 1300. Room 164, a core room in Room Block 2, dates to A.D. 1298+ on the basis of one specimen. Room 35 of Room Block 1, although not the earliest constructed room in the block, was built by A.D. 1310. Construction on all three major room blocks probably began around A.D. 1300.

Climatic conditions during this period were characterized by subnormal precipitation and above average temperatures, an interval known throughout the Southwest as the Great Drought. Dean and Robinson (Chapter 8) suggest that the drought may have decreased tree cover, an effect associated with degradation in the old channel of Salt River Draw with a subsequent lowering of the water table and draining of the once moist flats in low-lying areas around Grasshopper. This pattern of drainage may have opened up the area for intensive agriculture. They further note that during the drought this region was affected less than areas to the south and to the north on the plateau, and thus Grasshopper may have possessed more favorable environmental conditions for habitation than surrounding regions. These factors are thought to be responsible for the immigration that led to the establishment of the Grasshopper community.

Expansion Phase
(A.D. 1300–1330)

The interval of most rapid expansion extended from A.D. 1300 to around 1330. During this period of accelerated growth, the major architectural features of the main pueblo were formed and Grasshopper assumed its basic configuration.

The direction of expansion in all room blocks was toward the south and west away from the water resources in the north. Building to the north did not exceed the limits of Room Block 5, and construction to the west in Room Block 1 and to the east in Room Block 2 was constrained by the old channel of the draw. Eastward expansion in Room Block 1 was presumably limited by the low-lying area where the present channel now runs. The extensive secondary refuse found there may represent an attempt to fill in this low area.

The southern expansion of Room Blocks 2 and 3 formed the roofed southern corridor about A.D. 1320 (Chapter 8). Both Plaza I and Plaza III were in use by this time. Growth of Room Blocks 2 and 3 toward the north joined isolated construction units to form Plaza II after A.D. 1320. Later expansion focused inward on Plaza I and outward principally on the higher ground to the northwest of Room Block 3. In Room Block 1, expansion was oriented to the south, joining a separate construction unit to the west toward the bank of the old channel of the draw, and toward the north but not joining Room Block 5. Toward the end of this period Plaza III was roofed and converted into the Great Kiva.

The water resource in the north flat continued to constrain the location of new rooms. Other low-lying areas were similarly avoided, possibly because of occasional flooding as indicated by the environmental reconstruction of Dean and Robinson (Chapter 8) for the period around A.D. 1300 to 1330. The limits of the main ruin are located today within the area circumscribed by the 1798 meter contour. This elevation may parallel the prehistoric level below which flooding at times occurred, suggesting systematic avoidance of these areas. Lending additional support to this idea are the depositional events in Plazas I and II, which indicate that flooding did occur.

Building during the initial period of expansion of the main pueblo consisted of multiroom construction units, while later building was largely of double- or single-room units, especially in Room Blocks 1 and 3. The earlier multiroom units probably represent the establishment of large, individual domestic groups at Grasshopper. Later construction emphasis on double- and single-room units represents the expansion and dispersion of these original domestic groups (Reid 1973: 128; Ciolek-Torrello 1978).

These 30 years were marked by high precipitation. Dean and Robinson note that the possible effects of the increased rainfall on the local Grasshopper environment are difficult to assess. It is thought to have caused the forest to become more dense and it may have enhanced agriculture in the newly opened bottom lands, making farming possible in areas previously unsuitable during the drought. However, the lower average temperatures that accompanied the increased rainfall may have adversely affected agricultural productivity by shortening the growing season.

Dispersion Phase
(A.D. 1340–Abandonment Phase)

Both expansion and dispersion processes are characterized by a relatively larger population size that required a corresponding increase in energy expended for construction, subsistence, and other maintenance activities. If a local environment cannot supply the increased energy demands, yet is still productive on a temporary basis, then an adjustment less costly than total abandonment may be chosen. Seasonal occupation of a village is one such option; it would bring other villages into the developmental cycle and thereby complicate further the developmental cycle of a single pueblo. Such seasonal movement might play a transitional role, mitigating the impact of permanent abandonment by allowing ongoing utilization of the original village until a point of diminishing returns was reached, and by providing initial exploration of future village locations.

To understand this phase of the developmental cycle at Grasshopper, it is necessary to look at growth at the villages of Red Rock House and Canyon Creek (Haury 1934), cliff dwellings to the southwest of Grasshopper. Canyon Creek Pueblo reached its maximum expansion shortly after A.D. 1340, at the time construction began at Red Rock House. A second phase of building occurred at Red Rock House after A.D. 1360.

Red Rock House and similar small outlying cliff dwellings in the region may have been established by groups emigrating from Grasshopper who occupied them, at least initially, on a seasonal basis (Chapter 8; Longacre and Reid 1971).

According to Michael Graves, the evidence of stockpiling timbers at Canyon Creek suggests an initial seasonal occupation, perhaps during the late summer or fall. Haury (1934: 18) notes that most of the primary beam construction timbers were cut during the growing season, which extends through the summer.

The canyon region where these cliff sites are located supplies a greater diversity of floral resources within a given radius of a site than is available within a comparable distance around Grasshopper. The edge effect (Odum 1971: 157–159) is greater in this region, and the canyons provided a superior collecting environment. In addition, mule deer (the largest single source of meat at Grasshopper) leave the ponderosa pine forests to spend the fall and winter in the lower canyon elevations (Griffin 1969: 161; W. Swank 1958: 46). The procurement of deer, as defined by the room abandonment measure, increased during the dispersion phase (Reid 1978).

Also indicative of a fall-winter occupation in the canyons is the southern exposure of Canyon Creek and the other cliff ruins in the area. This position maximizes heat retention in contrast to valley floor and bluff top locations (Longacre and Reid 1971: 108–109).

Haury (1934: 52) observed that no true kivas were found at Canyon Creek and only Room 22-B, a second story room, offered any evidence of ceremonial use. Volkman (1972) suggested that the room was modified from a previous habitation room, indicating that this modification was made sometime after A.D. 1342, late in the construction sequence, which ended after 1348. She hypothesized that the appearance of this ceremonial room might indicate a shift from seasonal to permanent habitation. Alternatively, Canyon Creek might have changed from satellite dependence on another village for religious support to independence and religious autonomy.

Although a dispersion phase has not yet been demonstrated for Grasshopper Pueblo, present data are parsimoniously interpreted in terms of this reconstruction.

Abandonment Phase
(Dispersion Phase-A.D. 1400)

Only limited construction was undertaken after 1350, indicating reduced expansion requirements, and Grasshopper gradually became abandoned by A.D. 1400. Structures suitable for domestic expansion were acquired through reoccupation of previously abandoned rooms.

For example, Room 216 was constructed during the expansion phase but was abandoned late. The superpositioning of hearths in this room indicates a long occupation sequence with repeated modification of floors. Reuse of construction materials may also be partly responsible for tree-ring evidence of limited construction after 1350.

The evolution of a piece of research and the results this research produced have been described, underscoring the necessarily dynamic character of archaeological methodology. The model of pueblo growth outlined here serves a dual function. On the one hand, it provides a framework for orienting thoughts about various processes operating in the past, a structure for examining past behavior. On the other hand, and perhaps more importantly, the model suggests questions of human behavior to be explored in future research. As more is learned about Grasshopper Pueblo itself, it becomes obvious that there is a need to expand understanding to include neighboring communities and their relationships both to Grasshopper and to the environmental context in which these prehistoric communities played out one segment of developmental cycles that continued elsewhere into historic times.

4. A SET-THEORY APPROACH TO SAMPLING PUEBLOS: THE IMPLICATIONS OF ROOM-SET ADDITIONS AT GRASSHOPPER PUEBLO

David R. Wilcox

Like any other human behavior, archaeological research may be treated formally as a system of activities subject to behavioral analysis. When research is conceived in this way, it is appropriate to ask: "How do the actors make decisions, what are the regularities in their decision-making processes, what set of rules can be specified that models those regularities?" Once such rules are stated, it becomes possible to evaluate their efficacy as ways in which to solve the research problems that delimit the goals of the research. In the context of such an evaluation, it may be fruitful to consider alternative rules that if adopted might better accomplish the requisite solutions. When evaluation activities are built into a research activity system, they may function as important mechanisms to improve the quality of the final research outcome.

During excavations at the Grasshopper site from 1967 to 1970, two rules were followed to select quadrilateral spaces in room blocks for excavation. The first, used for three years, was derived from a stratified random sampling approach, and the second, from a set-theoretic approach (Wilcox 1975). Both rules depended on information derived from an excavation procedure called the cornering project. A historical review of the cornering project and of the process of formalization that grew out of it shows that a change in the rule for selecting room spaces for excavation emerged from a change in what was conceived to be the goal of the cornering project. This difference in goal was of fundamental proportions, involving both different concepts of archaeological systematics as well as the nature of archaeological field work. This paper discusses the conceptual results of the process of formalization, first as it affected the objectives and potentials of the cornering project, and second as it transformed our understanding of the nature of pueblo sites and the ways they may be used to study anthropological problems.

THE CORNERING PROJECT, 1967-1970

Grasshopper Pueblo is a single component Pueblo IV site that includes numerous room blocks and about 500 room spaces altogether (see Fig. 1.2); a few of these are only partially enclosed and may have been part of outdoor activity areas. There are an unknown number of collapsed second story room spaces, but there is no evidence so far for any third story. Two of the three largest room blocks are located on the west bank of Salt River Draw, a dry stream bed, the other is opposite on the east bank (see Fig. 1.3); they are called respectively the West Unit and the East Unit. Other room blocks are called "outliers." The presence of preroom occupation surfaces below rooms in each of the three largest room blocks has been demonstrated, as well as the common occurrence of multiple floors in a room space. Roofs often were used as activity areas, and vacated room spaces commonly have trash above the abandoned floor surface. Ground-surface indications of rooms consist of the upper ends of wall remnants, which in nearly all cases at Grasshopper form quadrilateral spaces.

The general sampling problem at Grasshopper may be stated thusly: what excavation units and what rules for their selection can lead to a maximum recovery of information pertinent to and adequate for solution of the major research problems (Thompson and Longacre 1966: 256-257, 270-272). One solution to the sampling problems was suggested by James Hill (1967: 147-148):

> If...the sampling procedures are essentially the same in all portions of a site, then one can begin to interpret differential densities of material in terms of differences in function (activity), differences in social units, or temporal changes in these things....
> It appears, then, that a truly representative sample is one that covers all areas of a site to an equivalent degree.

Based on his experience at Broken K Pueblo, Hill suggested that the "ideal" way to have sampled the room blocks at that site would have been to use architectural units and size-classes of room-space area as strata in a stratified random sample (Hill 1967: 148-151, 154, 157).

Field work to implement a stratified random-sampling approach for selection of room spaces was initiated at Grasshopper in 1967 by William Longacre. A site map was to be prepared showing all room blocks and the outlines of all room spaces within them so that room size-classes and architectural units could be determined. Room corners were excavated so that points on the map could be drawn accurately.

Not all room corners were excavated. Because most room spaces at Grasshopper are quadrilateral in floor plan, it was apparent that an efficient rule for deciding which corners to dig in order to map the room spaces in a room block was to select any two diagonal corners in one room and the same two in all others. Additional corners were exposed as needed to finish the map. Bond-abutment wall relations were interpreted and recorded for all exposed corners.

During the 1967 season this work was completed in the East Unit. Each quadrilateral space was numbered, its area was computed to the nearest tenth of a square meter, and this information was displayed in a histogram. Six modal clusters were defined by inspection as size classes. On the basis of two rows of wall abutments, the room block was also divided into three architectural sections. A sample of five spaces in the northern section was then selected for excavation using room size-and-shape classes and architectural units as strata in a "stratified random sample." It was felt at the time that these "strata" might well be a "sensitive key to the total archaeological structure of the site and thus one key to our sampling procedure" (Thompson and Longacre 1966: 271). Work done since then, however, does not appear to support this idea.

Stimulated by the identification of three "architectural units," staff members P. Bion Griffin and H. David Tuggle began to ask questions in 1968 about possible building sequences and about the location in the architectural grids of domains of different social groups. In effect, they switched the focus of attention from rooms to sets of rooms. Before their questioning had proceeded very far, however, the cornering project was completed that year in the east block of the West Unit.

The cornering project in the West Unit was continued in 1969. A sketch map was made of the room block and, for convenience, bond-abutment relations were recorded on it. When potential patterns of wall abutments showed up on the work map, we postulated that certain sets of room spaces may have been added to earlier room blocks. To test these hypotheses, corners were dug where two walls would have to be abutted if a hypothesis was true or bonded if it was false. Proceeding in this way it was soon possible to show sets of room spaces that formed an ordered sequence, one room set abutted to the next. These sets of room spaces were called *construction units* and a contiguously ordered series of them was called a *growth mode sequence.*

The preliminary results of this study led to a formal decision to change the rules for selecting room corners for excavation. In the future corners would be chosen to facilitate testing of an expanding set of hypotheses concerning wall relations and the boundaries of a set of room spaces. As before, additional areas needed to complete the room map were also exposed. The research goal of the cornering project was thus expanded to include the definition of "construction units" as well as the production of a map of each room block. Several growth mode series and a single core construction unit in the west block of the West Unit were located. By applying the same decision-making rules to the east block of the West Unit, it was possible to demonstrate that a series of "construction units" were present there as well.

When the map of room spaces was completed, room areas were computed from it, and a modal histogram similar to that in the other mapped room blocks was identified. Acting on the assumption that patterns in the data may be behaviorally meaningful (Thompson and Longacre 1966: 270), we began looking for patterns in the room-area data. At first none were found. The distribution of the modal classes in terms of the room block as a whole and in terms of construction units showed no obvious repetitive patterns. When rooms within each of the construction units with five to nine room spaces were ranked by size (without regard to the modal size classes) and the distribution of ranks was displayed, many clear patterns emerged. From one construction unit to the next the size of rooms in any given pattern category was often highly variable. This result brought into serious question an assumption in earlier work that absolute room-size classes were behaviorally significant at Grasshopper Pueblo. On the other hand, it did appear that *relative* size and position relations within room sets might form behaviorally-meaningful patterns.

The working hypothesis was then entertained that the construction units with five to nine room spaces in the west block of the West Unit were the domains of different social groups (Wilcox 1970; Wilcox and Collins 1971). One of these was arbitrarily selected for excavation in 1970 to provide a context for investigating that hypothesis. Like corners in the cornering project, room spaces also were selected for excavation in terms of hypotheses based on evidence already at hand. As the process of logically analyzing and formalizing the concept of a "construction unit" proceeded, however, such strong inferences based on it were soon shown to be premature, and excavation later confirmed this (Rock 1974). Nevertheless, the process of formalization eventually produced a set of concepts that are adequate to solve the problems of identifying the domains of domestic groups in pueblo sites (Wilcox 1975). The same concepts have also been applied to the analysis of domestic groups in Hohokam sites (Wilcox, McGuire, and Sternberg 1981).

THE PROCESS OF FORMALIZATION

Initially, a "construction unit" was little more than an intuitive interpretation of a pattern in the distribution of bond and abutment wall relations that was visible on the work map. Any archaeological interpretation based on that pattern could be made more objective if it were treated as a logical argument and judged accordingly. Concepts were given a rigorous, logical definition; concepts that were the result of interpretation were specified as the outcome of postulates that asserted relations within the first set of concepts. Hypothetical propositions that ordinarily would have been simply assumed were formalized as axioms. It was then possible formally to deduce from our interpretative conclusions a series of statements that could be matched against descriptive statements of observed relationships. If errors or ambiguities were present in our reasoning, they would be easier to detect and to correct if this process of formalization and testing were followed.

Consider first what can and cannot be directly observed in the exposure created by digging a small (1 m) hole next to the walls of a room corner. The orientation of the rocks in three planes is variable and several rock size classes (building stone and chinking spalls) are present. Standing wall remnants can be distinguished from wall fall by the relations the constituent rocks bear to one another: one positioned regularly above or adjacent to the other in a vertical array with layers of mortar between that often contain chinking stones. The principal short-coming of this kind of excavation unit, however, is that the exposure is usually too limited to make sense out of the seemingly chaotic orientation relations among the fallen wall stones. Yet once the stones have been widely exposed laterally, regularities in such relations can often be observed, and it is then possible to determine from which wall each set of stones fell. The sequence of a pueblo's collapse and the character of the processes that contributed to it can then be established. No such model of Grasshopper has been constructed, and given the extensive disturbance caused by the excavation of corner holes, it is doubtful it can be now.

Once wall remnants have been exposed, it is possible to investigate the relations they bear to one another, and whether they are bonded or abutted. With only wall remnants to work with, and lacking the information potentially available in wall fall, statements about the relations between full walls must be inductions based on the relations between the wall remnants. The exposures in corner holes provided only a sample of even the wall remnants. What is directly observable are relations among rocks, spalls, and the mortar in the walls. An *abutment* is a relation between classes of rock, spalls, and mortar in one wall with those in another such that at the intersection of the two walls none of the elements in one overlap any of those in the other (Wilcox 1975). When overlap does occur, the two walls are bonded. How long, and hence how significant, the temporal hiatus was between particular enactments (Krause and Thorne 1971) of rock "deposition" during the construction of a wall, or between the construction of each wall separated by an abutment, is not apparent from the mere fact of superposition or of the abutment. Other data are necessary to determine the order of magnitude of those temporal hiatuses.

The examination of each wall juncture in both its vertical and horizontal planes is necessary in order to determine overlap and nonoverlap relations accurately. Where walls are only one stone thick, examination of one side may be sufficient, but where walls are two or more stones wide, both sides of the wall juncture must be observed. As shown in Figure 4.1, it is possible for a wall to appear beautifully abutted in the exposure of one side and still be completely bonded on the other; cases like this were documented in both the East and West units at Grasshopper Pueblo in 1970 (Wilcox and Collins 1971). Because no systematic reanalysis of all such corner situations has been undertaken to date (1982), serious questions may be raised about all models of the construction sequence based on the current wall-abutment data.

While the value of bond and abutment relations for modeling construction sequences in pueblos has long been recognized (Morley 1908; Roys 1936; Rinaldo 1964a),

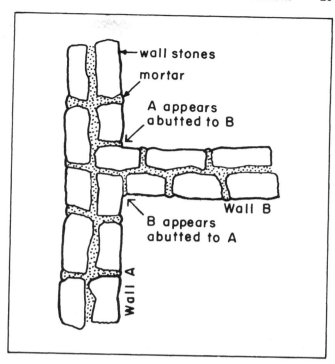

Figure 4.1. Plan view illustrating the complexity of abutment interpretation.

their logical limitations have been less apparent. Analysis of the patterns perceived in the distribution of bond and abutment relations on the work map of the West Unit at Grasshopper Pueblo led to a formal definition of "construction units." Influenced by the enthusiasm at Grasshopper in the late 1960s for the "deductive-nomothetic" approach to research, our definition of "construction units" was reduced to two axioms from which several corollaries were deduced. Basic to both axioms was the concept of a *building episode* (Wilcox 1975; Wilcox, McGuire, and Sternberg 1981): all the goal-related building that occurred relatively continuously in a discrete spatial locus during a short time interval. Building episodes may be distinguished from one another in terms of the hiatuses that intervene between them during which no building took place. Superposition relations are evidence not only of temporal order but also imply temporal hiatuses of different lengths. Before one rock was placed above another, a few seconds probably intervened, while days or weeks might interrupt the completion of a house and years may pass before an addition was made to the house. If the goal of constructing the wall is inferred to be completion of a house, the concept of a building episode refers to the latter activity.

The two axioms that define a so-called "construction unit" are as follows.
1. Continuously bonded walls were constructed during a single building episode.
2. Only fully enclosed spaces were being built.

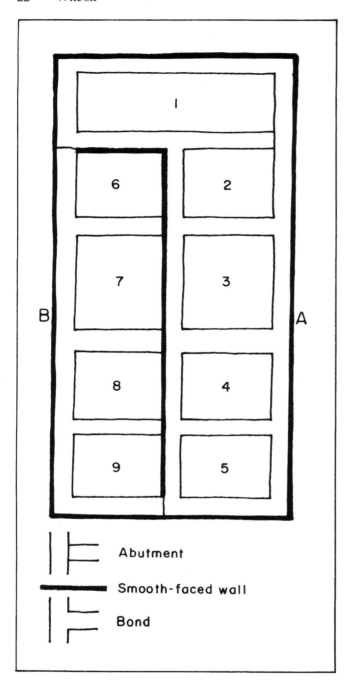

Figure 4.2. Plan view of two construction units and one core structure.

In Figure 4.2 the walls of room spaces 1, 2, 3, 4 and 5 are interbonded, while only some of the walls of 6, 7, 8 and 9 are interbonded. The set of room spaces 1 through 5 is a construction unit and the set 6 through 9 is a second unit that abuts the former. A corollary follows from the two axioms: In any abutment situation, the abutting wall is either later than *or contemporaneous with* the abutted wall. Unit A was built before Unit B or contemporaneously with B. Abutment data alone are not sufficient to demonstrate more than this, even if both axioms are

true. Clearly, a wall may be both continuously bonded and abutted to itself (room space 1, Fig. 4.2). Logically, then, more than the knowledge of wall abutments is necessary to demonstrate a significant temporal hiatus.

The corollary of the axiomatic assumption that only fully enclosed spaces were built is that, in any abutment situation, the abutting wall is not earlier than the abutted walls. In Figure 4.2, B cannot be later than A because its walls do not fully enclose spaces 6 through 9. Thus, a theorem is easily proven: if each of the walls of construction unit B that adjoin the walls of construction unit A abut to that unit, then construction unit B is either later than or contemporaneous with A.

The formal definition of "construction units" has several advantages; one is procedural. To assert that a particular set of contiguous room spaces is a construction unit requires that a particular series of bond and abutment wall relations be present. To test the assertion, each of the corner situations specified should be examined to determine if the deductions are true or false. If any are false, the assertion would be rejected; it they are all true, all subsets of contiguous room spaces within the specified room set would next be systematically tested as possible construction units. If only the set as a whole satisfied the axioms, then the assertion that it is a construction unit may be accepted. Conclusions about the location of construction units in a room block could be objectively evaluated if a full set of the recorded wall relations (and how they were determined) were published with the conclusions.

A second conclusion that an explicit statement of the construction unit axioms makes clear is that while their statement in the context of the cornering project may initially be taken as axiomatic, in the context of the research as a whole the statements are treated as hypotheses to be tested (Wilcox 1970). How can these "axiomatic" statements be tested? Are there alternative axioms that would produce comparable arguments about the location of building-sequence constituents that can be tested more readily?

If the rebuilding of a wall can be demonstrated, the first axiomatic statement can be tested, at least in some number of specific instances. As rebuilding has been found at many pueblo sites (Martin 1936: 38; Judd 1964), including Grasshopper, the critical question is the degree to which it can be confidently asserted that *no* rebuilding has occurred in a particular set of wall junctures. Given the loci of definite rebuilding, the conclusions drawn from the axiom may be revised accordingly in those instances. When the investigator cannot decide whether rebuilding has or has not occurred, the axiom cannot be tested. In some room blocks this may impose a serious limitation on interpretation, but in the absence of evidence for rebuilding, there is no reason to believe it did occur.

While the first axiom has been stated as an explicit assumption by a number of authors (Martin 1936: 38; Rinaldo 1964a: 49), to my knowledge the second one has not been, though it appears to be implicit in the arguments of some workers (Roberts 1931: 92-95). Some walls were built at Grasshopper that did not fully enclose a space (Chapter 3). This finding confirms that the second axiomatic statement can be tested. It also raises a legitimate question as to the heuristic value of the "construction unit" concept. Short of digging a whole room block, how can such walls be identified?

One suggestion has been to reject the second axiom in favor of an alternative and to redefine "construction units" accordingly (Reid 1971). This alternative assumes that the smooth-faced sides of walls with chinking were exterior faces when the walls were built (Rinaldo 1964a: 49). Many walls at Grasshopper show a marked contrast between the two sides—rough and angular on one, smooth on the other. Marion Parker, assistant director at Grasshopper in 1963 and 1964, first pointed out an apparent correlation between the rough side of a wall with room interiors, and the smooth side with former or present-day exterior space. At best, the generalization of this correlation is an inductive inference that needs to be tested. It is also not clear why the smooth-faced side of a wall could not have been built as an interior face, since it is well established by excavation results that they often functioned as interior faces at some time.

The most important result of the logical formalization of the "construction unit" concept was the recognition that it was not a sufficient basis for distinguishing all that was built during a single building episode. Fundamentally, the problem is one of a set and its subsets. Building that occurs *during* a building episode, as specified in axiom 1, is a subset of the total amount of building completed within the limits of that episode. It is the set of *all* building during each episode that naturally forms the basic *unit* required to model building sequences in pueblo room blocks. Our definition of a "construction unit" was derived by proceeding inductively from empirical patterns in the data of wall abutments and bonds. It was thus possible to partition room blocks into a series of "construction units," but how these may have been grouped into a *sequence* of actual construction events could not be determined. Logically, for all we knew, the whole room block may have been built during a single complex building episode, or in a sequence of several building episodes. To move beyond this impasse it was necessary to introduce new theoretical concepts.

A *core structure* is the outcome of all the building that took place in a single building episode and that generated an original room block. An *aggregation unit* is the outcome of all the building that took place in a single building episode and that generated an addition to an existing room block. The collapsed remnants of room blocks observed in the archaeological record consist of one or more core structures and some number (including the number zero) of aggregation units. Armed with these concepts it is possible to gain new insights into the problem of modeling pueblo construction sequences.

The question, "What is the distribution of exterior wall faces?" is equivalent to asking, "Where are the boundaries of aggregation units and core structures?" It can be deduced from the definition of these latter concepts that their outer perimeter at the time of construction faced space exterior to rooms. Similarly, because nonexterior faces are the interior faces of rooms, the distribution of exterior wall faces partitions a room block into sets of contemporaneous, contiguous spaces that satisfy the definitions of aggregation units and core structures. In this light it becomes clear that to test systematically the hypothesis that "smooth-walls-with-chinking" faced exterior space involves more than testing it against axiom 1. The relationships of what were outdoor occupation surfaces to the walls, the distribution of different building techniques and various kinds of wall relations, as well as the clustering of absolute dates within the site's provenience matrix, also bear on this question (Wilcox 1975). Obviously, then, the smooth-wall-implies-exterior-space hypothesis is not a solution to the problem of identifying the components of architectural building sequences. Again, short of digging the whole room block, how can we factor out those instances when the statement is false?

To model building sequences in pueblo archaeology, workers traditionally have used the analysis of the distribution of different building techniques (Martin 1936; Roys 1936; Brew 1946: 193; Roberts 1931: 95, 1939: 196; Judd 1964), stratigraphic relations between walls and occupation surfaces (Roberts 1931: 103, 1939: 196; Judd 1964), and the distribution of tree-ring cutting dates (Haury 1931, 1934), in addition to wall abutment analysis (Morley 1908; Roys 1936: 135). In line with this body of reasoning, a general strategy for deriving building sequences from the set intersection of four broad dimensions of archaeological evidence (stratification, the distribution of building techniques, wall relations, and absolute dates) has been suggested (Wilcox 1975). By implementing a series of approaches under these four categories, a room block may be partitioned into a number of core structures and aggregation units. Each approach provides a way to draw set boundaries that may indicate a significant temporal hiatus between building episodes. The set intersection of these partition classes provides a formal way to factor out the errors engendered by any subset of approaches. Quantitative methods that provide a way to assign probability weights to each partitioning could further strengthen the rigor of this strategy.

PUEBLOS AND DOMESTIC-GROUP DOMAINS

As initially conceived, the cornering project located the points of wall intersection in each room block and partitioned them into quadrilateral spaces. These spaces were numbered, a stratified random sample of them was drawn, and each space in the sample was excavated to subsoil. Such spaces have traditionally been called "rooms," implying that they may yield behaviorally-meaningful information about the domestic groups that once occupied them. In fact, the relationship between what is observed in the archaeological record and past systems of human behavior is far more complex than this facile approach has assumed.

Rooms, Room Spaces, and Quadrilateral Spaces

What is the relationship between a quadrilateral space defined by the intersection of the walls of a pueblo room block with the modern surface and a room lived in by the prehistoric inhabitants of the pueblo? They are not isomorphic. Even in cases where the walls and roof are intact, many floors may be present that have different feature associations and that were occupied by a succession of domestic groups doing different things in what was otherwise the same physical space. Time as well as space must therefore be taken into account if the information observable today in the archaeological record is to be translated in ways informative about past human behavior. A new set of concepts that facilitates such translation is required.

Because people live on surfaces, the primary concept needed is that of a floor. A *room floor* is the ordered set of a single physical occupation surface (formed by plaster or packed earth) that is bounded on all sides by walls and of all the absolutely contemporaneous features (like hearths or mealing bins) directly associated with it (see Dean 1969 for the concept of absolute contemporaneity; see also Wilcox 1975; Wilcox, McGuire, and Sternberg 1981). A *room* is a spatio-temporal and cultural space physically bounded on all sides by walls, above by a roof, and below by a single floor. If a building sequence of features on the same physical occupation surface, or a succession of such surfaces, is present, then each stage of such sequences is considered to be a separate floor and a sequence of "rooms" is recognized. Thus, a sequence of floors *defines* an ordered set of rooms in the same physical space. Those physical spaces may be called *room spaces.* Although the transition from one room to another in the same room space entails the abandonment of the earlier room, the room space may only be vacated, to be used again later as a room, a trash receptacle, or a burial area.

In light of these definitions, and their appropriateness as judged from excavation results, it may be concluded that the quadrilateral spaces determined by the original cornering project possessed six major structural constituents: (1) a portion of some number of preroom occupation surfaces; (2) one or more first story rooms; (3) one or more second story rooms; (4) one or two room spaces; (5) one or two roofs; (6) natural fill.

Activities were carried out on roofs and it is not unusual to find artifacts in the fill that had been left on top of the roof. Thus "roof artifact assemblage" may be considered as a seventh constituent. Roof dirt may contain sherds and other artifacts scooped up when the roof was built, and care must be taken to distinguish these items from the "roof artifact assemblage" and trash. Sometimes this differentiation can be inferred by answering the question: How did the roof fall in? "Trash" is an eighth constituent, and artifacts in the roof matrix, a ninth.

Before a simple random sample can be drawn from a finite universe, all items in that universe must be counted (McCarthy 1957: 272; Parzen 1960: 299; Vescelius 1960: 459). The quadrilateral spaces in a room block and each of the six constituents form finite universes; given only systematic information on the intersection points of standing wall remnants, however, the classes that can be counted are first-story room spaces, and the quadrilateral spaces as wholes. The earliest and latest floors may be the same but often they are not. It should also be observed that all

of the "latest floors" are probably not mutually absolutely contemporaneous. At Grasshopper some room spaces were permanently vacated before the end of occupation at the site, so some of the latest floors in the room spaces may have been abandoned before others. If the data potentially exposed by the cornering project were fully exploited, it might also be possible to count all (or nearly all) second-story room spaces and roofs. In that event, room spaces generally, the sets of rooms from each room space, and roofs could also be randomly selected on an equal likelihood basis. However, more exposure than that provided by digging meter-square corner holes is needed to adequately assess the sequence of floors in any given room space. Excavation results indicate the common occurrence of several floors in Grasshopper room spaces, and it is doubtful that a simple random sample of rooms could be drawn on the basis of information from the cornering project alone.

THE PERCEPTION OF DOMESTIC GROUPS

The sets that can be simply random sampled may also act as groups for cluster sampling of the artifact classes or other items found associated (McCarthy 1957: 272-280). It is necessary to examine the foundations on which any appropriate probability model could be built in this situation and to estimate the potential value that statements derived from such a model might have toward solution of the Grasshopper research problems. In particular, attention is focused on one specific goal:

> to attempt to define and analyze the nature of social groups, residence and inheritance patterns, and means of achieving social integration at the site in an effort to understand the processes responsible for the cultural system of the modern western Pueblo peoples (Thompson and Longacre 1966: 257).

Three facts are now established about the relations of Grasshopper room blocks to the location in them of the domains of socioeconomic groups (Rohn 1965). First, these domains are room sets of one or more rooms; second, the larger room blocks seen today are the result of building sequences; and third, the total occupation span for the site is about one hundred years (plus or minus 30 years; see Chapter 8). Several conclusions may be drawn on the basis of these facts. The distribution of socioeconomic groups across rooms probably changed, perhaps considerably, during the several generations when the site was occupied. New rooms were built and old rooms were abandoned, sometimes to be used again, sometimes not. Room spaces once used by one group quite likely were used later by other groups. Relations of this kind have been documented at a number of pueblo sites (Rohn 1971; Dean 1969) and appear likely at Grasshopper. The activity structures of the groups probably also changed. Developmental cycles in domestic groups alone could produce such change (Goody 1971), as could alterations in the cycles. Furthermore, at any one time the distribution and activity structure of any one group might be greatly different from others, a situation that could be generated by the simultaneous occurrence of groups in different stages of one (or more) domestic cycles. Abandonment and discard activities may not have been the same from group to group (Schiffer 1972, 1976), and this behavior, too, may have changed during the occupation period. The domain of a domestic activity or an ordered set of those activities may be treated conceptually as distinct from a room grid and may be mapped onto a room grid. When this distinction is observed, it becomes apparent that even if two groups practice the same set of domestic activities in the same number of rooms, the location of space allocated to those activities may differ markedly from one group to the other. For example, one group may have ground corn in a room used to store grain, while the other located mealing bins in a room used to cook food. A majority of Grasshopper rooms show multiactivity usage.

The domain of a socioeconomic group may be specified formally as a set of absolutely contemporaneous rooms. In order to study these groups it first must be determined which floors belong and which do not belong in the requisite sets. Once the sets are isolated their spatio-temporal relations to one another and to other factors may be analyzed and their contents may be studied and integrated. In effect, these sets are new provenience units that provide a partial basis for evaluating the comparability of frequency data from individual floors. They provide only a partial basis because items left in a room space are the outcome of abandonment or discard behavior, which could easily vary from group to group with respect to any given class of items (Schiffer 1972). The influence such behavior had on the occurrence of specimens and sample contents in rooms must also be estimated before frequency patterns among the room sets can be properly evaluated. If set inclusion rules for these room sets can be specified and applied, attainment of the research goal cited above would be in sight.

It is obvious that a stratified random sample of room spaces or a cluster sample of rooms or artifact classes by no means assures an unbiased sample of the *room sets* that were the domains of socioeconomic groups. Nor does it provide a way to group the excavated floors into the requisite sets. Because the space allocated to domestic activities, or ordered sets of them, within those domains need not be the same from one domain to the next, and abandonment and discard behavior may not have been identical from group to group (Schiffer 1972), there is no assurance that the frequencies of artifact classes associated on one floor are directly comparable to those on another. The typological concept "room function" masks this problem without solving it. Cluster samples of artifacts in room spaces also do not provide a probability measure of the total frequencies of various artifact classes in a room universe (contrary to J. N. Hill 1967: 154). If the deposition frequency of artifact classes varies from one socioeconomic group to the next, and no assurance can be given that their domains have been representatively sampled or reconstructed, what guarantee is there that the sample frequencies provide a sound basis for estimating the total frequencies? As a method to isolate and study social groups Hill's rule for selecting excavation units has a low potential value.

The second rule considered here is part of what may be called a set-theoretic approach (Wilcox 1975). Archaeological field work is conceived as a complex, creative activity system in which the researchers are continuously asking questions, making interpretations, formalizing both of these into a scientific theory, deriving hypotheses and testing them. By continuously interacting with the field phenomena, the researcher attempts to define formal concepts that appropriately and meaningfully model the field context and contribute toward solution of the research problems. When these new concepts are fed back into the growing corpus of facts, hypotheses, partial theories, and interpretations, new questions may be asked. Research then may turn in new and more relevant directions toward the solution of major problems. The rule for selecting excavation units in this approach is to select those situations that are likely to provide opportunities to study information relevant to answering the current body of questions. As the questions change, new situations may become important, and old situations may need to be reexamined. Revising the aims of the cornering project is an example of how this process works.

The problem of specifying the domains of social groups may be broken down into two components: first, separating the universe of all floors into absolutely contemporaneous sets; and second, partitioning those sets into the requisite social-group domains. If the building sequence at Grasshopper can be determined (not only of architecture but also of all surface modification), along with the sequence of abandonment, then absolutely contemporaneous sets of floors can be isolated in a formal way by intersecting the first sequence of sets with the second. Architectural features, floors, and artifacts coexistent during any given hiatus period between building or abandonment events are called *site structures* (Wilcox 1975; Dean 1970: 143). The set of absolutely contemporaneous floors across a whole settlement is called a "living surface" (Wilcox 1975; Wilcox and Shenk 1977; Wilcox, McGuire, and Sternberg 1981).

The critical relevance of a well-documented interpretation of architectural building sequences to the problem of perceiving social groups is apparent, and the value of the second rule for this purpose has been indicated. Information regarding floor succession, abandonment events, and partial abandonment sequences may also be derived from the same excavation units, and when these data are integrated it may be possible to estimate the overall abandonment sequence. Certainly many specific questions are brought into focus that are useful in deciding where next to dig in order to test building-abandonment sequence hypotheses.

Living surfaces are the stages on which human actors at the pueblo acted out their roles. To the extent that living surfaces can be discerned, they can be used as provenience grids to document what people did and how their activities changed. The kind of statements required (Wilcox 1975) are ones that specify an action or action sequence, making interpretations explanatory on one hand, and subject to uniform experiment on the other (because we could repeat the actions and control their contexts). Thus, an *enactment* (Krause 1971: 240; Krause and Thorne 1971; Wilcox 1975) is any minimal behavioral operation (for example, striking a blade off a core, twisting a post into the ground). An *activity* is an ordered series of enactments, and an *activity system* is an ordered series of activities and enactments. Specifying enactments, activities, and activity systems is simply a formal way of showing what prehistoric people were doing. On the basis of this approach, a *social group* may be formally defined as any population set responsible for an activity, an activity system, or a set of activity systems and activities for which the location on a living surface is known (Wilcox 1975; see also Freeman 1968: 266). This definition is an adequate solution to the problem of partitioning the rooms in a site structure into "the domains of social groups" as discussed above.

Enactments, activities, and activity systems and ordered sets of them all entail behavioral boundaries that show up in the archaeological record as discontinuities in the spatial and temporal distribution of qualitative and quantitative evidence for the behaviors (Krause and Thorne 1971: 253). The edges of core structures and aggregation units, for example, mark the temporal discontinuities generated by distinct building activities and activity systems. To the extent that enactments, activities, and activity systems can be identified and documented, behavioral boundaries and their consequent discontinuities in the archaeological record can be determined. Analysis of the interrelations and overlap of all these behavioral domains probably will reveal clustered domains that are either identical in content or are functionally analogous. Such clusters are already well known to southwestern archaeologists (Prudden 1903, 1914, 1918; Roberts 1931, 1939; Brew 1946: 193; Rohn 1965; Dean 1969); what is suggested here is an objective way to approach their formal definition and study.

The fundamental importance of detailed stratigraphic analysis and the painstaking collection of all specimens and samples in terms of behaviorally-meaningful provenience units is readily apparent. If we are to obtain collections that constitute behaviorally-meaningful sets, it is not enough to write on the bag or in notes from what room space, or even what floor, a specimen or sample came. It is essential to record what relations the specimen or sample had with the floor, with other specimens, and with features that are also part of the floor, as well as what relations the ordered floor set had with other sets such as the collapsed roof, trash, or other floors. By "relations" I do not simply mean spatial coordinates but also relations that document inclusion of a specimen or sample into a behaviorally-meaningful set and the relations of those sets to one another, spatially and otherwise. An ash lens, firepit, or pot cluster are such sets, as are secondary roof beams, chipping debris, or roof artifact-assemblages. To say a tree-ring specimen is a "secondary roof beam" is an interpretation, but no less so is the statement that a burned potsherd is *in* an ash lens. In each case, based on initial impressions and observed facts, specific questions can be raised and answered.

Once the questions are stated, research activity can be focused into a systematic investigation of the possibilities. Is there ash *under* the burned potsherd or does it lie *half buried* in the floor *below* the ash lens? How did the ash lens get there? Where did it come from? Does the tree-ring specimen lie in the same geological context *across* another specimen and *at right angles* to it but *below smaller* specimens also *at right angles* to it? Is there burned roof clay *above* but *in contact with* the burned wood? How did the roof collapse? Italicized words or phrases each specify a relation. Once a behaviorally-meaningful set is recognized, its relations with other sets may also be systematically investigated. In this manner a coherent body of theory and documentation can be built to the point that we can determine where core structures and aggregation units are, what the sequences of abandonment were, and something of how people behaved in site-structure settings.

Two further conclusions about method may be stated. The only situation in which the kind of relations indicated above can be objectively and systematically studied and determined is in the field. Second, only in the field, again, can we learn to ask appropriate *specific* questions and execute the process of developing arguments to adequately answer them. Past experience may make apparent the *form* of many relevant questions, their hierarchical relations to other questions and to research goals, and classes of observation that would help answer them. Such knowledge may have an extremely useful heuristic value for figuring out what happened in particular excavation contexts. It must be remembered, however, that the appropriateness of all questions is contingent on finding something in the field. Furthermore, as an argument proceeds, it is not unusual to think of new questions never contemplated before, but whose relevance to solution of the research problems is suddenly apparent. When a process of formalization is followed, new concepts are often generated and thus new questions employing these concepts can immediately be asked.

These considerations show that a set-theoretic approach to the selection of excavation units has a high potential value as an effective method for achieving the Grasshopper research goals.

CONCLUSION

"Comparable data" is a relative concept; it is relative to particular research goals. Questions are posed in terms of the goals, and two or more data sets are comparable only if they each provide a necessary and sufficient documentation to adequately answer the questions, and thus to attain the goals. There may be comparability of answers to the same questions, but data sets are "comparable" only insofar as the answers they document are comparable. Following the same mechanical collecting procedures or filling out the same check list from situation to situation does not in itself guarantee comparable data and may even assure the opposite. It is necessary to ask the same question each time and to collect or record the data in every excavation context that document adequate answers.

Comparability of data, therefore, cannot be legislated ahead of time, prior to field research. The problem of how to set up and select excavation units that will yield sets of comparable and representative data may be solved (to the extent the record allows) in six steps. The first step is to state the major goals orienting the research. Second, in light of these goals and what is already known about the site, many general research questions may be asked, and preliminary strategies for reaching the goals may be built from these questions. Third, depending once more on how much is already known about a site, after research questions have been posed, situations may be specified that have the potential to yield data useful in answering the questions. In pueblo sites, for example, the wall-corner situations are known to have a high data potential for studying building and abandonment sequences. Step four is to select a set of these situations for excavation. Together, these four steps constitute a "discovery strategy."

Once excavation is underway, it is time to attempt to answer the questions and to test them against the phenomena at hand and against alternative answers (step five). Asking specific questions is part of this process. The most fruitful and objective way to structure an answer is to treat it as a logical argument. Collections and notes, then, should document a repeating process of initial interpretation, formalization, argumentation, and testing. At the end of the field work collections and notes should include the evidence to substantiate or refute a series of alternative answers to the full range of research questions. As new information is received, step six involves continuous reevaluation of the earlier statements of goals and questions, specifications of situations, and formulations of arguments. The continual evaluation procedure may result in the restructuring of

excavation formats (situations), of research procedures (answering questions), or of collecting and recording policies (documentation), and also it will provide a running check on the extent and limits of comparability among the recorded data sets. New research may be planned as needed.

Statistics, while they are undoubtedly valuable tools for revealing useful information, do not provide an adequate language for general theory construction (R. A. Thompson 1971: 390). By itself, a random sampling approach to archaeological field work (Binford 1964) can only provide a set of statistical statements. These statements may serve as indicants of theoretical constructs, but until they can be translated into a qualitative language of theoretical concepts appropriate to modeling archaeological phenomena, they are of little value in explaining aspects of archaeological phenomena or sociocultural behavior. Ethnographic analogies also may have some heuristic value as indicants, but they are neither logically necessary to, nor sufficient for solution of, the translation problem. It is still necessary to identify the analogical concepts in the context of archaeological phenomena (Tuggle 1970).

Within the context of a continual process of questioning, formalization, argumentation, and testing, probability sampling may be used as a technique to help implement certain excavation decisions. Sampling designs should be subordinate parts of field strategies. If not all specified excavation situations can be dug, a random selection of them may help to assure that a maximum of data potential will be tapped with the least cost of time and money. Because comparability of data does not depend on the structure of such probability samples but on the comparability of answers found for the research questions, if evaluation of new data indicates a different picture for the distribution of data potential than first thought, a new probability sampling procedure can be implemented without jeopardizing the comparability of resulting data.

5. ARCHAEOLOGICAL SEDIMENTS: DISCOURSE, EXPERIMENT, AND APPLICATION

Stephanie M. Whittlesey, Eric J. Arnould, and William E. Reynolds

Archaeological deposits are formed and modified by complex natural and cultural processes that mold the material output of past behavior. The principles that model these processes specify both the ways in which a cultural system produces the material outputs observed archaeologically and the interaction between these materials and variables active in the natural environment (Schiffer 1976: 14-16). By understanding such principles it is possible to state combinations of behaviors that contributed to the formation of any archaeological deposit. It then becomes necessary to formulate a framework for interfacing the material remains recovered and the behaviors they represent. Interpreting past human activities as they are reflected in the archaeological record is a particularly difficult task because natural processes may reduce the deposited yield of human behavior to a vague approximation of its original state, while adding still more material.

Archaeologists justifiably concentrate on artifacts, but while striving to understand their deposition and subsequent disturbance, some nevertheless maintain at best a thinly disguised hostility to the sediment in which these artifacts rest. By ignoring this sediment a potentially vast reservoir of information is bypassed. The emerging study of geoarchaeology strives to rectify this neglect of the physical context of artifacts by integrating the special knowledge and techniques of both archaeology and geology. It is a field that in sophistication of application has progressed immeasurably from the first attempts of archaeologists to borrow geomorphological or pedological concepts (for example, compare Davidson 1973 with Cook and Heizer 1965). Although geoarchaeology is defined in several different ways (Gladfelter 1977, Davidson and Shackley 1976, Hassan 1979, Butzer 1977), it remains a discipline emphasizing "the earth or 'geo' component of the archaeological record" (Gladfelter 1981: 344). The study of archaeological deposits, however, is best approached by keeping the behavioral element peculiar to their formation foremost in our minds. To demonstrate the potential of such an archaeologically-specific study of sediments, a typology of archaeological sediments is proposed that has proved useful at Grasshopper Pueblo in recognizing the role of behavior in archaeological sediment deposition.

A TYPOLOGY OF ARCHAEOLOGICAL SEDIMENTS

Archaeologists exhibit widespread confusion in their use of the term "soil," despite the early distinction between soils and sediments made by Butzer (1964). The dichotomy is maintained in this paper, following Shackley (1975). Accordingly, soils are deposits physically and chemically altered in situ, and correspondingly they display the vertical horizon development produced by chemical movement. Sediments, on the other hand, are collections of mineral particles that have been weathered from an original source and redeposited; they do not necessarily display morphological development (Shackley 1975: 1, 3). All soils are sediments, but not all sediments are soils. Also there is a distinction between depositional processes and developmental processes. The former are processes of accumulation of materials; the latter are pedogenetic processes transforming sediments into soils.

All sediments display a "life history," and several models have been developed by geoarchaeologists to discuss this history. Hassan (1978: 198), for example, views sediment life history in terms of three stages: weathering, transportation, and deposition. Stein (1980) sees four variables as important in sediment life history: (1) source material, (2) transport medium, (3) environment of deposition, and (4) postdepositional changes. In this chapter the focus is more narrowly on the critical factor in deposition of archaeological sediments—the distinction between human and natural agents of deposition.

True Soils and True Sediments

One deposit encountered in archaeological sites is the kind in which human agents played no role in either its deposition or subsequent disturbance. It is produced in situ by natural formation processes of physical and chemical weathering on the parent material. True soils possess horizon development and structural properties. They may be buried beneath a site or accumulate following site abandonment. Frequently they are paleosols—soils formed in the landscape of the past (Yaalon 1971).

In environments protected from weathering, such as caves, the archaeologist may deal with a true sediment (Butzer 1964). Lacking the horizon development of soils, true sediments may be deposited as specific events within, below, and above archaeological sites. In the analysis of true sediments, pedological and sedimentological techniques are applicable as long as morphology is undisturbed by human activity. Analyses of true soils and sediments may aid paleoenvironmental reconstruction and chronological assessment of the site associated with them (Hassan 1978). These kinds of sediments have been studied by Butzer (1974), Hay (1976), Shackley (1976), Haynes (1975), Jaehnig (1971), and Malde (1972). Earlier studies include those by Harradine (1953) and Storie and Harradine (1950).

Behaviorally-altered Soils and Sediments

Another kind of sediment represents a combination of natural formation processes and subsequent human disturbance. When true soils or sediments underlying or adjacent to a site are disturbed by human activity, they become behaviorally altered. Digging burial pits or irrigation canals, building mounds and earthworks, and procuring pottery clays are examples of activities that disturb, intermix, and redeposit sediments. The original character of the sediment is altered; soil morphology is destroyed and natural chemical properties may be modified.

Such sediments are frequently encountered in archaeological contexts (see Parsons 1962; Cook and Heizer 1962; Dietz 1957; Farrand 1975; and Hughes and Lampert 1977).

Pedological and sedimentological techniques of analysis cannot be applied indiscriminately to them, but must be supplemented with techniques suitable for the interpretation of behavior.

Sediments Deposited by Human Activity

A third sediment encountered in archaeological sites is deposited as a primary byproduct of human occupation. These deposits have been termed anthrogenic sediments (Whittlesey, Arnould, and Reynolds 1976), anthropic soils (Sjöberg 1976), and anthropogenic sediments (Hassan 1978). The anthrogenic sediment is distinguished most critically from natural sediments by the agent of deposition. During human occupation, organic and nonorganic refuse accumulates. Natural processes of sedimentation may be interspersed with episodes of cultural deposition, and decomposition of organic material further alters chemical properties.

Anthrogenic sediments are also altered by transport mechanisms (Stein 1980), either natural or human. Construction of houses and features, architectural remodeling, refuse dumping, refuse filling to level floors, and sweeping of house floors are familiar activities that transport and redeposit anthrogenic sediments.

Following site abandonment, other factors alter the anthrogenic sediment. Architectural materials—masonry or adobe walls, wall and floor plaster, jacal—collapse and weather, adding more sediment that is cultural in origin but deposited by natural agents. Collapse of architecture may bury anthrogenic sediments, protecting them from weathering. In open areas, anthrogenic sediments

may undergo pedogenetic development. Wind and water continuously work to mix culturally derived sediment with naturally derived material and redeposit the mixture in another location. Decomposition of organic materials continues. Postdepositional disturbance processes may alter the original deposits further (Wood and Johnson 1978, Gifford 1981, Karcz and Kafri 1978, Hanson 1980).

Since natural environmental and behavioral variables may alternate or combine in many ways to create sediments with endlessly different life histories, each deposit is potentially unique, with enormous variability even within a single site. The archaeologist must identify the discrete deposits of sediments found within each site and the processes that have produced and altered them. It is crucial that those sediments that have been produced and altered by human behavior be identified. Archaeologists have traditionally distinguished deposits within archaeological sites from naturally deposited sediments only by the presence of artifacts embedded in them (Cornwall 1960, R. B. Parsons 1962, Krieger 1940, Pyddocke 1961, Buehrer 1950). When anthrogenic and natural sediments are equated, the inferential power of archaeological sediment analysis is reduced. As Hassan (1979: 269) writes, "geological investigations should be integrated with archaeological work to be truly geoarchaeological."

ARCHAEOLOGICAL SEDIMENTS: THE GRASSHOPPER PLAZAS

Experimental studies have a long history in geoarchaeology, but, not unexpectedly, they have been used for purposes that closely reflect the traditional view of archaeological sediments as natural bodies rather than as cultural artifacts. Experiments have focused on processes of erosion and on deposition and disturbance of artifacts by natural agents (Jewell and Dimbleby 1966; Isaac 1968; Wood and Johnson 1978). Taphonomists and palaeoecologists have been more advanced in seeking cultural as well as natural factors in site formation (for example, Gifford 1977, 1978, 1980; A. P. Hill 1979; Hanson 1980; Walker and Long 1977). More recent geoarchaeological studies have attempted to isolate the cultural and natural factors affecting the developmental history of a site (Davidson 1973, Lubbell and others 1976). Experiments designed to identify formation processes of anthrogenic sediments are conspicuously absent, yet here is where our comprehension is most inadequate. At Grasshopper the experimental study of sediments aided not only in understanding their deposition but also helped to solve specific interpretive problems.

Research on Outdoor Activity Areas

Intensive investigation of outdoor activity areas at Grasshopper was launched in 1974 when Whittlesey began excavation of Plaza II. A critical concern was to determine how the plazas were used by comparing the types and distribution of features. The ultimate aim was to contrast community and household activities.

Two patterns in the use of plaza space emerged from this work. Plaza III was intensively used for domestic purposes. Hearths, firepits, and other facilities were densely distributed, and little refuse deposition took place. The opposite pattern prevailed in Plaza II, where features were sparse and refuse deposits thick. The plazas were similar only in size and in their usage as areas for burial of the dead.

Excavation of Plaza I in 1975 was designed to test hypotheses that might explain these observed differences. A stratified sampling procedure divided Plaza I into open central areas and areas adjacent to walls. Fifteen excavation units were selected from these strata. A backhoe was also used to reexcavate two test trenches dug in 1965 and 1969 (Fig. 5.1).

It became clear early in the season that the distribution of activity residues in Plaza I was unique. Instead of conforming to one of the patterns seen in Plazas II or III, it was characterized by marked internal variability. The eastern and western sides of the plaza contrasted so much that they could have been located in totally different parts of the site. Abundant refuse dominated the eastern portion, while most features were located near the western wall. Stratigraphic differences matched the east-west dichotomy in feature distribution. While the eastern plaza units displayed complex stratification, western deposits appeared almost entirely homogeneous. The depth of cultural deposits ranged from 2 m on the east to less than 40 cm on the west. Even the sediment matrix itself differed, representing a brown sandy loam in the east and a red clay in the west.

Adding to this growing list of enigmas was the uneven distribution of water-deposited laminated sediments. Ranging from small lenses of several centimeters to deep bands extending 4 m in length and 20 cm thick, laminated sediments were present everywhere within the plaza deposits except in the extreme west.

To solve these puzzles a familiar model of deposition within pueblo rooms was initially used. In this model, laminated sediments on room floors represent the effect of rainwater filtering through the collapsed walls and roof of an abandoned room, eroding and picking up material from building stone, wall and roof plaster, and the room floor and depositing it in bands on the final occupation surface. While laminated sediments were abundant in Plaza I, nothing resembling a discrete occupation surface was present—another source of puzzlement. Because it did not seem justifiable to extend to plaza deposits the inference that laminated sediments represented abandonment of the occupational surface on which they were deposited, we attempted to define the processes that were responsible for their deposition. An experimental study was designed to duplicate the general processes by which laminated sediments were formed in order to determine what factors might influence the horizontal and vertical extent of sediment deposition during a short interval of time.

The Deposition Experiment

The locale selected for the experiment had to meet two requirements: (1) to recreate cycles of water accu-mulation and evaporation action on (2) an enclosed surface. We chose a completed recovery unit in Plaza I that measured 2 m by 2 m. Section 507 had been excavated to sterile material and averaged from 30 cm to 60 cm in depth.

To initiate the experiment, a 55-gallon drum of water was poured into the empty pit on June 29, 1975. Subsequent rainfall kept it almost continually wet until the end of the field season. Thirty-one days of rain were recorded in July and August, varying from 0.02 to 0.55 inches per day, with a total accumulation of 7.84 inches (19.91 cm). We returned to the site on October 11, 1975, and excavated a trench in the accumulated fill of Section 507. Profiles and photographs demonstrate that in the period from June 29 to October 11, 10 cm of banded sediments accumulated in the lower half of the test pit (Fig. 5.2). We infer that simple processes of sediment deposition explain their nature.

First, the erosional action of moving water working on the pit edges and surfaces produces a sediment-water solution. Differential settling rates of the sand, silt, and clay fractions of the solution produce the lenses. The large, heavy particles settle out quickly in the initial spill area. Above the sand are thinner, light-colored lenses that represent the silt fraction. Clay particles are the last to settle out of suspension, forming thin, greasy dark lenses above the silt. Each set of lenses thus forms a single depositional event.

The characteristics of the experimental laminae indicate further that water velocity and volume of source material affect the depositional process. Sand lenses are visible near the locus of initial dumping (see Fig. 5.2); elsewhere, silt and clay lenses alone alternate. We infer that sand will be deposited only where the velocity and volume of water are sufficient to form a sediment solution containing a sand fraction, as in the initial dumping event or an extremely heavy downpour (and where, of course, soil or sediment composition includes a sand fraction).

The experiment indicates that slope is also a factor. No clay laminations were deposited on the highest portion of the test pit surface. Heavy particles are precipitated more rapidly than clay and as a result are deposited across most of the test pit surface. The clay fraction remained suspended in solution for a longer period of time, and the solution quite naturally was located in the lowest portion of the pit.

This experiment served to demonstrate empirically much intuitively recognized knowledge about water-deposited sediments. Most importantly, it showed that thick lenses of these sediments can be deposited within a very brief period of time. Since the number of laminations and the thickness of the deposit are dependent on the number and nature of depositional events, neither time nor abandonment are necessary factors in producing water-deposited sediments. These sediments will be deposited according to the following conditions:

1. Sediment, especially silt and clay, will be deposited in the low-lying portions of outdoor areas.
2. The quantity of water and the number of flooding events determine the number and thickness of lenses.

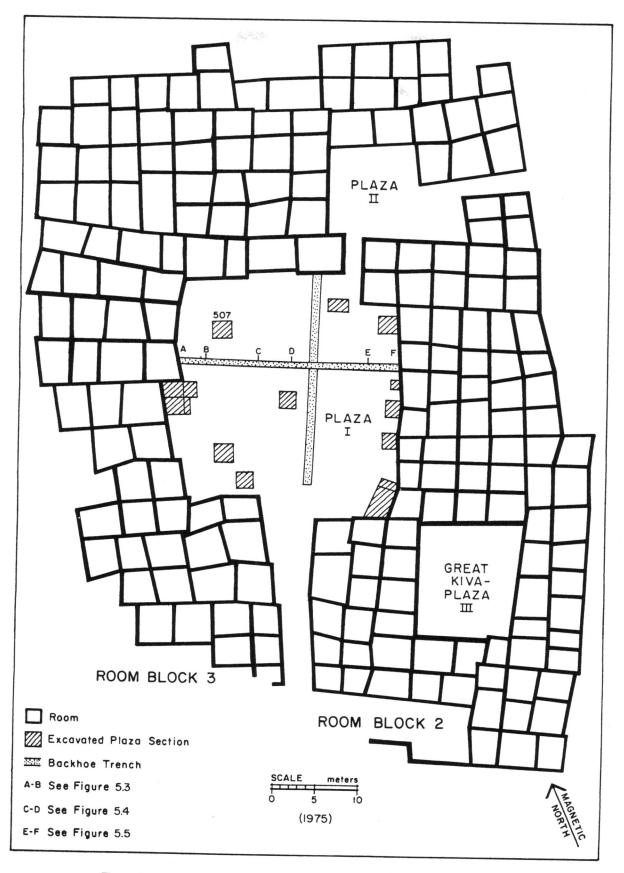

PLAZA
II

507

A B   C   D   E F

PLAZA
I

GREAT
KIVA-
PLAZA
III

ROOM BLOCK 3

ROOM BLOCK 2

☐ Room

▨ Excavated Plaza Section

▨ Backhoe Trench

A-B See Figure 5.3

C-D See Figure 5.4

E-F See Figure 5.5

SCALE   meters

0   5   10

(1975)

MAGNETIC
NORTH

Figure 5.1. Excavation units and test trenches in Plaza I, Grasshopper Pueblo.

Figure 5.2. North profile of Section 507, Plaza I test pit.

3. The velocity of runoff, the composition of source material, and the slope of the surface on which runoff flows will affect the number of aggregate layers deposited.

In addition, human activity and fine-grained sediment deposition rarely occur together. Fine-textured material will be deposited in low-lying areas where water collects and evaporates without disturbance. Human activities will be carried out elsewhere to avoid water, and may only be performed in low-lying areas on a seasonal basis when the ground is dry. Such activity will disturb and alter the original character of water-deposited sediments.

The information gained from the experiment can be used to predict where laminated sediments will and will not form in an outdoor area. The important consequence of this predictive ability is that the archaeologist can reconstruct the prehistoric topography of an outdoor activity area, regardless of its subsequent activity history, and can trace alterations of that topography. By applying the experimentally gained knowledge concerning processes of laminae deposition to the stratigraphic profiles of the plaza backhoe trenches, it was possible to solve what had previously been vexing depositional puzzles. The presence or absence of waterlain sediments in plaza deposits proved to be a reliable indicator of the nature of those deposits and the activities that produced them.

Interpretation of Plaza Stratigraphy and Activity History

The most critical variable in understanding what happened in Plaza I is topography. The east-west backhoe trench revealed its dramatic slope; bedrock is only 50 cm below the modern surface of the plaza in the northwest, but is overlain by several meters of sterile deposits in the east. Runoff from the elevated areas was channeled directly into the low-lying portions of the plaza.

Topography, in combination with the construction history of Plaza I, determined how that area was used. Early in the occupation of Grasshopper Pueblo, Plaza I was largely an open space west of the central core unit of Room Block 2 and south of the core construction units of Room Block 3. At that time the plaza had not been entirely enclosed by room construction. The pueblo occupants used the low, no doubt muddy, area of the plaza near what later became the east plaza wall (the west wall of Room Block 2) as a refuse dump, as indicated by complexly stratified deposits (see Fig. 5.5). Numerous bands of laminated waterlain deposits intermixed with the refuse, produced by downslope runoff from the northwest, indicate the wet and undisturbed nature of the deposit.

In the central part of the plaza, the natural topographic depression was accentuated by the refuse sloping up against the west wall of Room Block 2 (Fig. 5.4). Sediments deposited here by runoff were not disturbed by

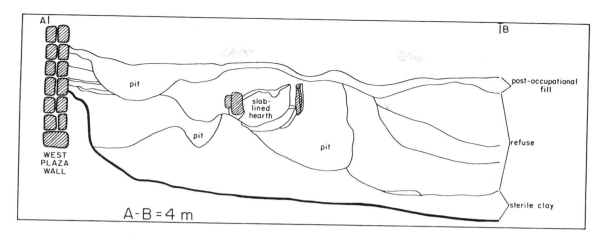

Figure 5.3. Test Trench 1 of Plaza I, section near west plaza wall.

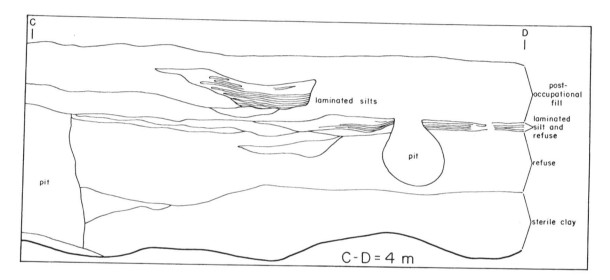

Figure 5.4. Test Trench 1 of Plaza I, center section.

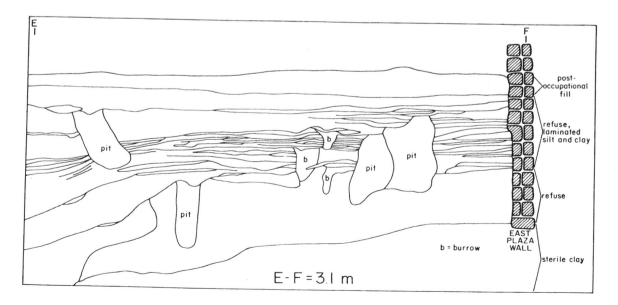

Figure 5.5. Test Trench 1 of Plaza I, section near east plaza wall.

traffic, resulting in thick, wide deposits. In contrast, no laminae formed in the western portion of the plaza area because of its higher elevation. At this early stage, then, this area was little more than an open backyard dump.

This picture changed as construction in Room Block 2 and especially in Room Block 3 accelerated. At this time, the high and dry portion of the enclosed plaza now adjacent to Room Block 3 was used for domestic activities (see Fig. 5.3). Pueblo occupants continued to dump refuse into the eastern portion of the plaza. Sometime later, probably near the maximum population and construction peak, both human and natural activities combined to level the slope of the plaza. Because runoff into low-lying areas within the plaza no longer created such a problem, activities extended into previously unused areas. Ramadas were constructed in the central and eastern portions, hearths were built there, and refuse ceased to be deposited. We infer these changes from sudden differences apparent in the stratigraphic profiles. In profiles representing the central parts of the plaza, laminae are absent above a certain depth. Simultaneously, the complex series of deposits representing refuse in eastern plaza profiles were cut into by postholes, pits, and other constructions.

In the western and central parts of Plaza I, continuous interment of human burials and intense cultural activity operated to homogenize the deposits, producing stratigraphically undifferentiated profiles. Some refuse also was deposited in this area. It was visible near the western plaza wall as thin stratified deposits resembling deposits near the eastern wall but lacking laminated sediments, suggesting that refuse deposition occurred here toward the end of occupation at the Pueblo.

When the appropriate distinctions were made among factors influencing sediment deposition in Plaza I, the different characteristics of the eastern and western deposits became less puzzling. Deposits in the eastern part represent anthrogenic sediments—the product of refuse accumulation interspersed with waterlain deposits of sediments channeled to the area by wall construction and topography. The whole is a complex sedimentological artifact attributable to primarily human variables of deposition.

In contrast, deposits in the western and central plaza areas began as something akin to true soils. Before Grasshopper Pueblo was established, natural weathering processes worked on the substrate. These weathered deposits remained until Plaza I was completely enclosed and the western portion became the focus of human activity. Then, construction of hearths, digging of burial pits, and daily traffic modified these deposits into what we have termed behaviorally-altered sediments.

Following the abandonment of Grasshopper Pueblo, the unprotected deposits in Plaza I were subject to weathering and pedogenetic development. Water runoff containing a mixture of cultural materials and weathered local sediments covered the existing deposits to variable depths. Incipient horizon development began to take place in all deposits, regardless of their origin. Architectural debris was intermixed with deposits near the plaza walls.

Implications of the Deposition Experiment

A number of wider implications stem from the sedimentation experiment and the application of its results to stratigraphic interpretation. First, we have demonstrated how an understanding of sedimentation processes can be significant to behavioral interpretation. When the processes responsible for laminated sediments in outdoor areas were clarified, the distribution of these deposits became a useful predictor of activity loci. Knowing that in Plaza I the distribution of permanent facilities such as hearths was linked to the presence of usable, dry ground permitted us to make more appropriate interpretations of plaza function. Had feature distributions alone been considered, we probably would have concluded that Plaza I was used only sporadically or briefly, especially in contrast to the intensively-used Plaza III. Plaza I was used continuously throughout the occupation of Grasshopper Pueblo, but for different purposes at different times. Without the deposition experiment we might have misunderstood the significance of the changes in activities through time. Some changes, specifically the contrast between refuse disposal and domestic tasks such as food preparation, were keyed not so much to a shift in plaza function as to changing plaza topography and construction activities. Other changes do seem to indicate fluctuations in plaza function. Late in its use-history, domestic facilities were no longer constructed in Plaza I and many existing facilities were deliberately dismantled. Yet the deep layers of refuse deposited in Plaza II after it, also, had ceased to be used for domestic purposes are absent from Plaza I, implying that it was deliberately kept clear for some as yet unknown purpose. Thus, stratigraphic information considered in conjunction with the pueblo growth sequence (see Chapter 3; Reid 1973, 1978) forms a comprehensive package for interpreting plaza activity history, information not readily available if Plaza I were considered only as a stratigraphically and chronologically undifferentiated unit.

Inferences made concerning Plaza I may be extended to interpret activities in the other Grasshopper plazas. Feature distribution in both Plazas II and III is also explained as a function of their unique topographies. Plaza II is similar to Plaza I with a pronounced north-south slope, and its feature distribution is parallel. Features were discovered only in the northern and western boundaries of Plaza II, while deep refuse deposits distinguish the southern portion. Plaza III, on the other hand, was a relatively level area and therefore free from topographic constraints. The dense distribution of cooking and manufacturing facilities in all parts of Plaza III reflects in part the absence of such constraints. The contrast between activity levels in Plazas I and III also becomes less peculiar; in part the latter was used more intensively because there was little usable space in the former.

Interpretations of Plaza I use-history illustrate the necessity for dealing with archaeological sediments as variable phenomena. Even within this single space, sediments differed vastly in origin and resulting characteristics. While this means that the archaeologist must approach each deposit as a unique unit of study, it also brings the reward of permitting the design of more effective sampling strategies for both excavation and analysis. For example, if we wished to continue investigating the Grasshopper plazas, we now have the information to employ a sampling design far more efficient than our original use of stratified random sampling. We also have data important to the design of an appropriate technique for collecting sediment samples for laboratory analysis. Chemical analyses of samples taken from the deposits in the eastern portion of Plaza I could confirm that these indeed represent refuse, and also suggest their source. While it might be profitable to compare analytically samples of refuse from plazas, extramural areas, and abandoned rooms to determine if preferential disposal practices existed, it would be uninformative to include samples from the central portions of Plaza I in such a study. The general results of this experiment underscore the necessity for investigating the human element in archaeological sedimentation as well as the action of natural processes.

CONCLUDING REMARKS

The process of rethinking the study of sediments in archaeological sites means sedimentological and pedological concepts and technological methods must be matched with the products of human behavior. Geoarchaeological studies should not simply borrow and apply concepts derived from a nonbehavioral science to one whose essence is behavior. Anthrogenic sediments should be viewed by archaeologists as cultural artifacts whose information potential may exceed, in some cases, more traditional data categories. The sediment typology proposed here provides a conceptual framework for catego-rizing formation processes of archaeological sediments. It further serves as an effective aid in the design of adequate sampling and analysis strategies.

One implication of this behavioral perspective to geoarchaeological studies is perhaps obvious, but important enough to state again. Programmatic applications of sedimentological techniques will prove fruitless; what is appropriate for a Paleolithic rock shelter will not suffice for a Mogollon pueblo. The techniques used will also be dictated by the kinds of questions about past behavior asked by the archaeologist. And both will be linked to research design. These aspects of site-problem match (see Reid 1975) become especially critical when designing research requiring laboratory analysis. It is necessary to ensure that the cost of analyzing specimens is equaled by the information return. Otherwise, the design may become prohibitively expensive and, in addition, possibly uninformative.

Archaeologists once viewed their data as distorted, incomplete, and capable of providing only limited information about past human behavior. The tendency in more recent years has been to realize that archaeological data is endlessly informative, limited only by the techniques and theory of archaeological science. It is curious that both then and now the approach to interdisciplinary cooperation has been similar—a rather uncritical acceptance of borrowed techniques. Just as the truth about archaeological data lies somewhere between the above extremes, so should the archaeological use of specialized techniques hold an intermediate position. Archaeologists should selectively choose those methods that suit particular purposes, even to the extent of becoming specialists, in order to harness technical approaches to behavioral problems. The result will be a rich harvest of behavioral information.

6. BIOSOCIAL INTERPRETATIONS FROM CRANIAL NONMETRIC TRAITS OF GRASSHOPPER PUEBLO SKELETAL REMAINS

Walter H. Birkby

Analyses of major Southwestern archaeological site skeletal material generally have relied on metric and morphological data for interpopulational comparisons (see especially Bennett 1973; Butler 1971; Wade 1970). Unfortunately, both kinds of data suffer in the statistical processing for obvious and various reasons: (1) the vast majority of Southwestern crania are artifically deformed so that many cranial measurements cannot be compared; (2) usually the number of metric observations is severely limited because of poor preservation, faulty recovery of the remains, or both; and (3) normal sexual dimorphism requires that the data be segregated prior to comparison, considerably reducing the size of the samples even where a site population might be numerically large.

A somewhat newer, although still controversial, approach to the study of skeletal populations utilizes nonmetric or discontinuous traits. These traits are scored simply as present or absent and, unlike osteometrics, do not require (1) intact or measurable skeletal elements (Buikstra 1972), (2) a segregation of the sexes (Berry 1968; Ossenberg 1970), or (3) nondeformed crania for purposes of comparative analyses (Birkby 1973). The history for the reporting of these traits is summarized by Brothwell (1965: 9-10) and by Berry and Berry (1967: 361-362).

Various publications (Kellock and Parsons 1970a, 1970b; Pietrusewsky 1970, 1971a, 1971b) and dissertations (Jantz 1970; Finnegan 1972; Birkby 1973) have appeared covering local and regional skeletal populations wherein divergence analyses have been employed. These "distance" studies generally have shown that the variation exhibited in prehistoric crania conforms to what is suspected archaeologically about the relationships of most of the populations. Additionally, Lane and Sublett (1972) have demonstrated with a divergence statistic that residence patterns can be reflected by an analysis of nonmetric cranial traits in *historic* cemetery skeletal material. Using the archaeologically well-documented osseous remains from the ruin at Grasshopper, attempts are made to interpret social factors from discontinuous morphological traits.

MATERIAL AND METHODS

While more than 600 adult and nonadult interments have been removed from the large multiroom ruin at Grasshopper only 459 individuals were available for analysis at the time the present study was undertaken. From this latter number, 163 adult crania were selected for the nonmetric trait analysis. Selection was based solely on whether the individual had reached at least 16 years of age prior to death. The seemingly small proportion (163 of 459) of the total crania available results primarily from the large percentage (greater than 60 percent) of "prereproductive age" deaths at the site (Birkby 1972). It should be noted for the record, however, that as in most prehistoric American Indian populations, the greater portion of this early loss occurs at the critical ages of life prior to approximately 5 years of age.

Where skeletal material was adequate, a total of 54 different nonmetric traits (Table 6.1) were recorded for the cranium and mandible. Forty-eight of the traits occur bilaterally and six occur in the midline of the cranium. Therefore, it is possible for an intact skull to have a maximum of 102 separate recorded observations when the two sides are considered. Statistically, it would be ideal to use only those crania that were completely intact or that otherwise provided all 102 observations. The ideal can seldom be realized, however, with archaeologically recovered skeletal material. The number of trait observations decreases as less and less of the cranium is available. In reality, there were few crania from this study on which at least 30 percent (16/54) of the traits could not be observed and recorded.

The traits were scored as either present, absent, or not observable. The latter category was used where observations could not be made because of the actual absence of bone or where traits were obscured either through advanced skeletal age (for example, obliteration of sutures) or through a pathology. This "have or have not" scoring readily lends itself to the mean measurements of divergence (biological "distance") statistics developed for nonmetric data.

The trait frequency tabulations were generated on the CDC 6400 Computer at the University of Arizona Computer Center using a canned SPSS (Statistical Package for the Social Sciences) program. The mean measures of divergence and the variance formulations were programmed for the computer by David Taylor, Department of Anthropology, University of Arizona.

DISCUSSION

For purposes of this study, a "cemetery" status was assigned to each of two major habitation features—the east and west construction units of the site—that were physically separated from each other by a stream channel (see Figs. 1.2, 1.3). As a point of departure for the

[36]

TABLE 6.1

Cranial Nonmetric Traits
used in the
Analysis of Skeletal Remains from Grasshopper Pueblo

Trait Number	Trait	Trait Number	Trait
1	Auditory torus	28	Mastoid foramen extrasutural
2*	Palatine torus	29	Zygo-root foramen
3	Mandibular torus	30	Posterior condylar canal
4*	Bregmatic ossicle	31	Hypoglossal canal double
5	Coronal ossicle	32	Dehiscence (Foramen of Huschke)
6*	Ossicle at Lambda	33	Pterygo-spinous foramen of Civinini
7	Lamboidal ossicle	34	Pterygo-alar foramen of Hyrtl
8*	*Os Inca*	35	Foramen spinosum open
9	Riolan's ossicle	36	*Canaliculus innominatus*
10	Asterionic ossicle	37	Foramen Ovale incomplete
11	Parietal notch bone	38	Posterior malar foramen
12	Temporo-squamosal bone	39	Accessory lesser palatine foramen
13	Epipteric bone	40	Carotico-clinoid foramen
14	*Os japonicum*	41	Clino-clinoid bridge
15	Lacrimal foramen	42	Mental foramen double
16	Posterior ethmoid foramen	43	Accessory mandibular foramen
17	Anterior ethmoid foramen extrasutural	44*	Metopic suture
18	Accessory infraorbital foramen	45	Fronto-temporal articulation
19	Zygo-facial foramen	46	External frontal sulcus
20	Accessory zygo-facial foramen	47	Sutures into the infraorbital foramen
21	Supraorbital foramen	48	Petrosquamous suture
22	Supraorbital notch	49	Spine of Henle
23	Supratrochlear spur	50	Double condylar facet
24	Frontal notch	51	Pre-condylar tubercle
25	Frontal foramen	52*	Pharyngeal fossa
26	Parietal foramen	53	Para-mastoid process
27	Mastoid foramen	54	Mylo-hyoid bridge

*Medially appearing traits.

intrasite comparison, all interments within and in the vicinity of each unit were classified as coming from one of these "cemeteries." The assumption made here was that if there were discrete breeding groups within the site, the groups conceivably could have been utilizing their own immediate habitation areas for the disposal of their dead.

The divergence statistic selected for the analysis requires that the percentage frequency (p) of each trait be transformed into an angular value (Θ), measured in radians, that corresponds to the trait frequency such that:

$$\Theta = \sin^{-1}(1-2p).$$

The difference between two populations or groups (1 and 2) with respect to any trait is $(\Theta_1 - \Theta_2)^2$, where Θ_1 and Θ_2 are the angular transformations of the percentage occurrence of the trait in populations 1 and 2 respectively. The mean measure of divergence (MD) between the two populations for the whole array of traits is calculated from the formula:

$$MD = \frac{\sum \left[(\Theta_1 - \Theta_2)^2 - (1/n_1 + 1/n_2)\right]}{N}$$

where N is the number of traits classified and n is the number of individuals in each population. The term $1/n_1 + 1/n_2$ is the variance of the differences due to random sampling fluctuations. The estimate of the variance (V) of the MD for any pair of populations classified for N traits is computed as:

$$V = 4\frac{\sum \frac{(1/n_1 + 1/n_2)}{N}\left[(\Theta_1 - \Theta_2)^2 - (1/n_1 + 1/n_2)\right]}{N^2}$$

The mean measure of divergence (MD) will be significant at the .05 level of probability when it is twice as large or larger than its standard deviation (the square root of the variance V). Both formulae differ somewhat from those that have been used in previous analyses; the ones presented here were developed by Constandse-Westermann (1972).

The basic assumption of the MD measure is that all the traits under consideration have an equal genetic expression in the phenotype, that they are uncorrelated or independent of each other and that, for these reasons, they can be summed. While there are some indications this may not be an entirely accurate assumption, the correlations found to date among such traits have been quite small. Truslove (1961) found that nearly all of the traits she examined in mouse populations were uncorrelated. Berry and Berry (1967) found only 10 pairs out of 378 that were significantly correlated. Hertzog (1968) found 10 out of 21 2-by-2 comparisons significant in his samples, which suggested that some are highly correlated. However, Benfer (1970) reevaluated Hertzog's data and found that the appearances of these traits were, in fact, independent of each other.

No attempt was made to determine whether the 54 variants were correlated in this preliminary study of the Grasshopper remains. I assume that the traits, on the basis of the above studies from other investigators, are uncorrelated or only weakly correlated and therefore will not alter appreciably the results of the distance measures.

A previous study (Birkby 1973) on skeletal populations from Grasshopper and three other southwestern sites has shown that the trait frequencies are not adversely influenced by either sex or cranial deformation. Thus, these factors were ignored when the adult crania from the two selected "cemeteries" of the ruin were compared. The elimination of these two segregating categories, normally employed in metric comparisons, allowed all of the 75 crania from the east unit "cemetery" and the 88 crania from the west unit "cemetery" to be used in computing the mean measure of divergence (MD) between the two groups.

The MD generated from the cranial data of these two populations produced a biological distance of 0.01369 units. This figure indicates that, for whatever reason, the interments from these two habitation complexes were significantly different from each other because the divergence was greater than twice its standard deviation of 0.00106. Therefore, on the basis of the MD statistic, it would appear that there were at least two different intrasite breeding groups at the Pueblo, each of which had preferred burial areas in and around the two major habitation features. It is doubtful that these intrasite groups varied significantly due to any temporal differences between the two habitation centers since the site itself was probably occupied for a period of less than a hundred years.

There are several different factors that may explain the observed differences between the inhabitants of the two units at the site: (1) the community was initially populated by several different founding groups, each of which established its own separate habitation complexes; (2) a somewhat later and possibly migratory group joined the already established community and constructed its own habitation units; (3) the two habitation features were peopled by members of different "social units" as McKusick (1972) has suggested. Since the divergence generated between the east unit and west unit populations is small, it is doubtful that disparate groups could have been involved in either the first or second explanation. The measure would best fit the third proposal, which does not call for large or major influxes from outside groups.

In order to test the three proposed explanations, however, determinations were made for possible differences or similarities between the sexes in the suspected breeding groups of the two units. That is, the divergence between the sexes of the two habitation units should show, when using the MD statistic, whether the males were more similar to the males than to the females or vice versa, or whether differences occurred in all possible sex comparisons.

If the first two explanations for the observed intrasite divergence were true, then we would expect to find that both the males and the females differed markedly from their counterparts at the opposite habitation unit, and that between these units the males differed from the females in a similar manner. If the third explanation accounts for the observed divergence, then we would expect to find little or no difference in only *one* of the same-sex comparisons between the east unit inhabitants and those from the west unit. At the same time, the other same-sex comparison should appear markedly different as would the comparison between the opposing sexes of the two units.

The cranial trait frequencies and their angular transformations that were used in computing the measures of divergence (MD) between the sexes of the two habitation units are presented in Table 6.2. The MD and the standard deviation for each distance generated between the units for each sex are presented in Table 6.3.

The data presented in the latter table show that: (1) all of the subgroups differ significantly both within and between the habitation units of the site; (2) the divergence between the east and west unit males (0.09918) is greater than that for the females of the two units; (3) the generated distance between the females of the east and west units (0.02734) is less than any of the other distances either within or between units; (4) the male-female divergences within the east and west units (0.08254 and 0.08365 respectively) have the second highest values and are nearly equal numerically; (5) male-female distances between the east and west units (0.06998 and 0.04014 respectively) are less than the distance found between the males alone, but are greater than the distance seen between only the females of the two units.

These findings would exclude the possibility that either one or both units were initially inhabited by different founding or migratory groups. However, the data *would* support the earlier suggestion that the two units were habitation areas for different "social units" inasmuch as the females, although differing significantly, are much more homogeneous than are the males. Further, one may infer from these data that these social units were practicing male exogamy and that the residence pattern was probably uxorilocal. Such residence patterns and mating rules are certainly observed among the probable descendents of the late Mogollon, that is, the Western Puebloans such as the Hopi (Dozier 1965). The inference posed here for the comparable systems at Grasshopper Pueblo is based on the greater heterogeneity in the males as revealed by the male-male divergence between the east and west units.

TABLE 6.2

Percentage Frequency (p), Sample Size (n), and Angular Transformation (Θ) for Each Cranial Trait and Each of the Sexes in the East and West Construction Units at Grasshopper Pueblo

Trait	East Unit Males			West Unit Males			East Unit Females			West Unit Females		
	p	n	Θ	p	n	Θ	p	n	Θ	p	n	Θ
1	.000	26	1.5708	.000	30	1.5708	.000	48	1.5708	.000	57	1.5708
2	.000	16	1.5708	.080	25	.9973	.057	35	1.0886	.000	42	1.5708
3	.292	24	.4290	.379	29	.2444	.268	41	.4825	.269	52	.4802
4	.000	20	1.5708	.000	25	1.5708	.000	32	1.5708	.000	43	1.5708
5	.000	23	1.5708	.000	28	1.5708	.000	37	1.5708	.045	44	1.1433
6	.105	19	.9108	.160	25	.7478	.293	41	.4268	.311	45	.3876
7	.417	24	.1668	.400	25	.2014	.634	41	.2713	.511	47	.0220
8	.037	27	1.1837	.000	29	1.5708	.000	48	1.5708	.000	56	1.5708
9	.375	24	.2527	.458	24	.0841	.417	36	.1668	.245	49	.5352
10	.280	25	.4556	.185	27	.6815	.205	44	.6311	.357	56	.2900
11	.080	25	.9973	.154	26	.7643	.085	47	.9791	.121	58	.8602
12	.150	20	.7754	.040	25	1.1681	.045	44	1.1433	.060	50	1.0759
13	.000	16	1.5708	.100	20	.9273	.107	28	.9043	.143	42	.7952
14	.000	26	1.5708	.000	30	1.5708	.000	43	1.5708	.020	51	1.2870
15	1.000	18	1.5708	.895	19	.9108	.806	36	.6586	.889	45	.8915
16	.923	13	1.0084	.955	22	1.1433	1.000	26	1.5708	1.000	39	1.5708
17	.800	5	.6435	1.000	7	1.5708	.929	14	1.0314	1.000	20	1.5708
18	.045	22	1.1433	.160	25	.7478	.135	37	.8183	.111	45	.8915
19	.962	26	1.1784	1.000	30	1.5708	.978	45	1.2730	.926	54	1.0198
20	.650	26	.3131	.700	30	.4115	.659	44	.3236	.725	51	.4668
21	.556	27	.1122	.679	28	.3661	.636	44	.2755	.636	55	.2755
22	.923	26	1.0084	.643	28	.2900	.756	41	.5375	.865	52	.8183
23	.526	19	.0520	.524	21	.0480	.457	35	.0861	.538	39	.0761
24	.542	24	.0841	.615	26	.2321	.462	39	.0761	.340	47	.3257
25	.519	27	.0380	.414	29	.1729	.533	45	.0660	.472	53	.0560
26	.720	25	.4556	.741	27	.5029	.870	46	.8331	.836	55	.7369
27	.962	26	1.1784	1.000	30	1.5708	.933	45	1.0471	.948	58	1.1107
28	.840	25	.7478	1.000	30	1.5708	.857	42	.7952	.737	57	.4938
29	.440	25	.1203	.667	30	.3405	.688	48	.3855	.724	58	.4645
30	1.000	22	1.5708	.966	29	1.1999	.974	39	1.2469	1.000	48	1.5708
31	.280	25	.4556	.207	29	.6261	.205	44	.6311	.314	51	.3812
32	.370	27	.2630	.207	29	.6261	.333	48	.3405	.228	57	.5752
33	.000	12	1.5708	.000	11	1.5708	.043	23	1.1530	.000	24	1.5708
34	.100	20	.9273	.037	27	1.1837	.029	35	1.2285	.043	46	1.1530
35	.000	20	1.5708	.143	28	.7952	.100	40	.9273	.000	49	1.5708
36	.050	20	1.1198	.286	28	.4423	.268	41	.4825	.160	50	.7478
37	.000	22	1.5708	.000	27	1.5708	.000	44	1.5708	.000	53	1.5708
38	.808	26	.6636	.552	29	.1042	.568	44	.1364	.558	52	.1163
39	.850	20	.7754	.714	28	.4423	.765	34	.5586	.750	44	.5236
40	.190	21	.6687	.118	17	.8695	.138	29	.8096	.229	35	.5728
41	.158	19	.7532	.000	18	1.5708	.129	31	.8360	.146	41	.7867
42	.077	26	1.0084	.100	30	.9273	.089	45	.9649	.056	54	1.0930
43	.630	27	.2630	.724	29	.4645	.659	44	.3236	.706	51	.4246
44	.000	26	1.5708	.000	30	1.5708	.000	47	1.5708	.018	56	1.3017
45	.000	17	1.5708	.042	24	1.1580	.000	33	1.5708	.022	45	1.2730
46	.192	26	.6636	.393	28	.2157	.467	45	.0660	.404	57	.1932
47	.130	23	.8331	.440	25	.1203	.553	38	.1062	.442	43	.1163
48	.259	27	.5029	.233	30	.5633	.104	48	.9141	.145	55	.7895
49	.852	27	.7810	.800	30	.6435	.362	47	.2796	.379	58	.2444
50	.000	21	1.5708	.000	27	1.5708	.000	40	1.5708	.000	46	1.5708
51	.045	22	1.1433	.000	24	1.5708	.079	38	1.0010	.136	44	.8154
52	.333	24	.3405	.200	25	.6435	.351	37	.3026	.364	44	.2755
53	.267	15	.4848	.133	15	.8242	.038	26	1.1784	.071	28	1.0314
54	.240	25	.5468	.241	29	.5468	.136	44	.8154	.137	51	.8125

TABLE 6.3

**Mean Measures of Divergence* by Sex
(with Standard Deviations)
Between the East and West Construction Units
at Grasshopper Pueblo**

	West Unit Males	East Unit Females	West Unit Females
East Unit Males	.09918	.08254	.06998
	(.00391)	(.00299)	(.00313)
West Unit Males		.04014	.08365
		(.00202)	(.00260)
East Unit Females			.02734
			(.00147)

*Distances are significant at the .05 level of probability if they are equal to or greater than twice their standard deviations.

To speculate further—realizing how tenuous such speculation may be—I suggest, based on the data from Table 6.3, that a rule of exogamy extended to the males of the Pueblo as a whole. Male exogamy for the social units *and* the village would be like the classic case for the Iroquois clans. And, while specific data are lacking for a similar cross-village mating system operating among the historic Western Pueblos, the Hopi nevertheless have a requisite clan grouping wherein these units also occur simultaneously in the villages on the three mesas (Eggan 1950). I also suggest that a similar distribution of "clans," or some other biologically-based social units, could have existed prehistorically among the late Mogollon. This idea stems from the greater degree of heterogeneity in the male-female divergences than in the female-female comparison. For example, the two male-female *within-unit* distances differ but little from the highest value obtained for the males alone (0.09918). Simultaneously, the two male-female *between-unit* divergences are greater than that for the females alone (0.02734). It would appear, therefore, that the males of one unit are not much more "related" to the females from the opposite unit (although allegedly from the same social unit as the males) than they are to the females with whom they mated and who should be of a different "social unit." If truly reflective of mating patterns, these findings would support a contention that male exogamy may have been practiced to a major extent for Grasshopper Pueblo.

I further suggest that the same male exogamous social units that existed at Grasshopper may have existed also at various coeval peripheral sites as well. Inasmuch as it would be necessary for each male to mate outside his own habitation area *and* outside his village as well, the only females available as mates would come from the opposite prescribed social unit at another village. Thus,

with a structured mating system such as this, male exogamy, coupled with a uxorilocal residence rule, would have created strong social solidarity between Grasshopper Pueblo and the various surrounding villages in the region.

The foregoing assumes, of course, that the male exogamous social units were indeed a prehistoric reality and that the distances generated for the males in Table 6.3 are not greater than they would have been had their sample sizes been more adequate. If the quantity of male crania were increased to something numerically comparable to the female crania, it is possible that any of the comparisons involving the former would have produced smaller divergences. However, I doubt that such altered distances would have approached those produced between the females alone for the two construction units.

Admittedly, these speculations and suggestions are based on rather scanty data or are, in the case of comparable social units existing between various coeval villages, fabricated on a complete lack of skeletal populations from ruins within the immediate area of the Grasshopper site. As human skeletal remains are collected from pot-hunted sites in the region, the assumptions expressed here may be more adequately supported or rejected through subsequent osseous and auxiliary studies.

CONCLUSIONS

The foregoing analysis is an attempt to show the feasibility of using cranial nonmetric traits to (1) define or delineate prehistoric populational subgroups and (2) reconstruct some aspects of the social organization of these subgroups using a mean measure of divergence statistic. Results can be summarized as follows:

1. Cranial nonmetric traits are useful in demonstrating possible prehistoric "cemeteries" or "burial plots" within an archaeological site.

2. Data derived from intrasite "cemetery" comparison at Grasshopper suggest that two differing social units existed in the prehistoric community, each inhabiting one of the two major habitation features.

3. A male exogamous mating pattern is indicated for the proposed Grasshopper Pueblo social units. Similarly, for the same population, an uxorilocal residence rule is suggested as a corollary to the mating pattern.

4. Mean measures of divergence generated between burial areas at Grasshopper suggest that not only did the two proposed social units practice male exogamy, but the community population as a whole was male exogamous as well.

The hypothesized social units (whether "clans" or other biological-based units) and village male exogamy, and the solidarity between villages that such a system could promote, may explain the lack of fortified sites in the late Mogollon period and the dearth of skeletal remains that exhibit evidence of any violently induced traumata. The period A.D. 1250 to 1450 was apparently a time of peaceful coexistence between contemporaneous and spatially close sites, even though there must have been ever-widening circles of hunting and gathering as the immediate areas around the larger villages became more and more depleted of animal and fuel resources.

Because each village may have been composed of males from various pueblos, and because the males were probably the political and religious leaders as well as the hunters for each village, close personal ties between the males and across various villages may have reduced potentially explosive intervillage discord or may have created a strong alliance against possible intermittent migrating territorial intruders. It is also possible that this same cohesiveness would have proven advantageous when large numbers of workers were needed periodically for projects such as the expansion of habitation units, as suggested by the so-called "building spurts" detected archaeologically at Grasshopper.

While this summary attests to the usefulness or potential usefulness of nonmetric variants in a distance analysis of a Southwestern prehistoric population, there are several considerations that should be mentioned with respect to future research. Foremost is the fact that little is known about the mode of inheritance for the majority of the 54 cranial traits. It would be useful, therefore, to determine statistically which variants contribute most to the distance measures and which contribute little. If such determinations are possible for the discrete traits,

as they now are for metric data, it may well be that by selecting only the most distinguishing characters for regional populations, different conclusions would be drawn from the skeletal material of the present study.

Second, there are several other distance programs now in existence that might produce other, or perhaps better, results than the statistic selected in this study. In a similar vein, there are other archaeological burial data that may be employed as a basis for segregating the human skeletal population into subgroups for comparison. Such data might include burial orientation, head direction of the interment, degree of flexure, or the amount or kinds of grave furniture in association.

Third, nonadult skeletal material is often not considered when dealing with discontinuous data; certainly this has been the case in the present study. However, we may be missing potentially valuable information with regard to selection at very early ages for certain nonmetric traits. Whether these traits are pleiotropic with some other phenotypic condition is a moot point for the present.

Finally, consideration should be given to post-cranial discrete traits in future studies of any major Southwestern skeletal collection. These traits, coupled with the cranial variants *and* osteometric data, may allow an investigator to pose some cogent speculations on the biological relationships of regional, and perhaps even more widely dispersed, skeletal series.

7. GEOLOGY AND LITHIC RESOURCES OF THE GRASSHOPPER REGION

Larry D. Agenbroad

Topographically, the Grasshopper region is located within the Transition Zone of the physiographic provinces in Arizona (Fig. 7.1). The northern boundary of the Apache reservation coincides with the Mogollon Rim, which is also the southern boundary of the Colorado Plateau province. The Transition Zone is a geologically and structurally complex area of mountains and canyons ranging from 2700 feet (823 m) to 11,590 feet (3532 m) above sea level, bounded on the south by the Basin-and-Range province. The site is at an elevation of about 6000 feet (1829 m). Geologic units in this region date from older Precambrian to Recent in age.

The western portion of the Fort Apache reservation has been subdivided into physiographic subprovinces (Moore 1968). The area west of the Canyon Creek drainage is designated as the Canyon Creek-Salt River Canyon Area. The region east of the drainage is known as Carrizo Slope (Fig. 7.2), composed of cliff, bench, and canyon lands.

The stratigraphic sequence is Mississippian to Recent in age, including predominantly marine sediments with scattered Tertiary-Quaternary basalt exposures. The Canyon Creek-Salt River Canyon subprovince is an upthrown fault block revealing complex Precambrian igneous, metamorphic, and sedimentary units intruded by a younger diabase. Local exposures of Tertiary gravels cap some of the higher ridges and buttes.

The site of Grasshopper is located at the contact of the Pennsylvanian Naco Formation and the Pennsylvanian-Permian Supai Formation. The area is characterized by low relief with small ridges formed by more resistant limestone and sandstone, and "flats" or parks in the less resistant shale outcrops. The pueblo is on a small ridge that has been dissected by Salt River Draw, creating an open park or meadow.

PREHISTORIC LITHIC RESOURCES

The prehistoric inhabitants of Grasshopper Pueblo apparently had a great deal of knowledge concerning the physical qualities and characteristics of various geologic resources, and the source areas for these raw materials.

Utilitarian Materials

A variety of igneous, metamorphic, and sedimentary materials were used in the production of tools, and to a certain extent, their source areas can be identified. Separating tools into the two major categories of ground stone and chipped stone also serves to subdivide the geologic raw materials.

Ground (pecked) stone tools rely on the crystalline, granular nature of the stone for strength and durability. Axes, commonly of diorite, metadiorite, or granite, are common in room excavations within the ruin complex. The source areas for all these kinds of rock are five to six miles west of the ruin in the Oak Creek-Canyon Creek drainage. Granite occurs near the confluence of Canyon Creek and the Salt River. Cobbles of these materials from the stream beds were used often as manos. Other properties, such as the abrasiveness of vesicular basalt and sandstone or quartzite, were desirable for specific tasks like grinding. The sandstone and quartzite source areas are essentially the same as those for diorite and granite. Vesicular basalt occurs on Blue House Mountain, Bear Butte, and in a northeast-southwest trend along Highway 60-77 from Salt River to the head of Corduroy Canyon. The closest occurrence of basalt is approximately seven miles southeast of the ruin.

Chipped stone (flaked stone) tools require high silica content and amorphous or cryptocrystalline properties. Dominant rock types in this category recovered from the site are chert, jasper, chalcedony or agate, silicified wood, and obsidian. Occasionally, quartzite was also used for chipped stone tools. Cherts found at the ruin are predominantly light brown to gray and are apparently derived from nodules within the Mississippian Redwall Limestone exposed along the east wall of Oak Creek Canyon, approximately two to three miles west of Grasshopper. The chert from this source is of excellent quality, abundance, and size for the manufacture of chipped stone tools. Jaspers, chalcedony, agate, and silicified wood occur throughout the geologic section as float, in place, and in stream beds. Obsidian is fairly abundant in tool and waste flake inventories at Grasshopper. The closest known source of quantity and quality is near Superior, Arizona, nearly a hundred miles southwest of Grasshopper.

Ornamental and Ritual Materials

Serpentine (Soapstone)

Deposits of serpentine and asbestos are common in the Mescal Limestone (Precambrian) along Canyon Creek and Salt River Canyon, as well as in areas to the west.

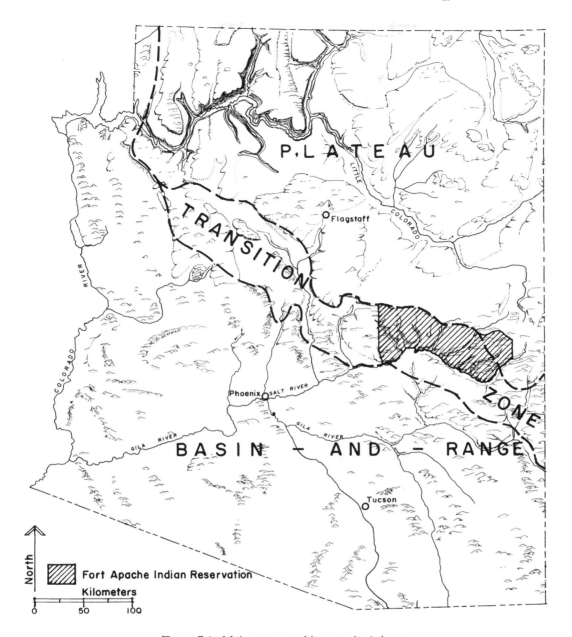

Figure 7.1. Major topographic areas in Arizona.

The occurrence of these minerals is due to metamorphism of limestone by intrusive dikes and sills of diabase. Serpentine has a greasy, waxlike luster in massive deposits, its hardness varies from 2 to 5 on Mohs' scale, and its color is generally variegated or mottled shades of green. These physical properties, plus its local abundance, made it a desired ornamental stone. Cruciform and zoomorphic objects, beads, and grooved stones of serpentine have been recovered from excavations in the Grasshopper site area.

During the 1965 season I visited a quarry associated with a nearby surface site containing Pinedale Polychrome pottery. The site had been used as a workshop area for the production of serpentine beads, and the manufacturing procedure was reconstructed from the materials recovered on the site. Thin slabs of serpentine were sawed and abraded into strips approximately 1.5 cm by 9 cm. The strips were in turn partially sawed, at right angles to the length, to produce squares of serpentine that were then snapped free and perforated in the center. The corners of the serpentine square were broken off, strung on a cord (presumably), and rolled back and forth over some abrasive material such as sandstone until the desired size and smoothness were obtained.

Figure 7.2. Western portion of the Fort Apache Indian Reservation showing physiographic regions.

Turquoise

Turquoise has been recovered in great abundance at Grasshopper. Usually it occurs as pendants with a perforation allowing suspension around the neck or as an earring. Well worked turquoise earrings, in position beside the skulls, have been associated with several burials.

The one source of turquoise known in the vicinity of Grasshopper occurs about one mile northeast of the confluence of Canyon Creek and the Salt River. The deposit consists of two shallow quarries containing small blebs and coatings of the mineral in fractures and bedding planes of the Dripping Springs Quartzite (Precambrian Lower Apache Group; Moore 1968; Haury 1934). The deposit was worked in prehistoric times and Gene Sealey, rancher for the Apache Tribe, visited the site and collected stone picks used in this deposit by prehistoric miners.

Hematite

The use of hematite for pigmentation and possibly for burial offerings was common at Grasshopper. Abraded pieces of hematite, both the massive and specular varieties, are common. A metate still containing a large quantity of powdered hematite was recovered from Room 121 at the southwest corner of the Great Kiva.

Hematite is abundant as both surface outcrop and float material in the Chediski Butte area near the head of Oak Creek, the upper regions of Canyon Creek, and the head of Gentry Creek. The origin of the deposits appears to be a contact metamorphic or pyrometasomatic deposition, the Mescal Limestone, caused by the diabase intrusion (Moore 1968).

Malachite

Evidence for use of malachite as pigmentation was also recovered from Room 121, where a metate containing powdered malachite was found in association with the hematite-stained metate.

Copper mineralization in the Grasshopper area is restricted to small quantities occurring in the intrusive diabase and with the hematite-diabase contacts described above.

Quartz Crystals

Unusual quartz crystals were recovered from the Great Kiva at Grasshopper. The crystals are internally fractured so as to give a "play of colors" on movement in sunlight, presenting the spectrum. The presence of such crystals in the kiva fill suggests possible ritual use. According to Eugene Sealey, the source area for these crystals is Diamond Peak in Gila County, where mineral collectors have now nearly exhausted the supply.

STRATIGRAPHIC TEST TRENCHES

During the 1965 field season, backhoe trenches tested the stratigraphy of areas adjacent to the ruin cluster. The initial backhoe trench (TT-35) extended in a southerly direction from Room 127. Since that time more than 30 trenches of various lengths and depths have been excavated in numerous locations. In addition to the backhoe trenches, 19 hand-dug trenches have been excavated since 1963.

The deepest fill was found in the area north of the ruin, where sedimentary deposits were formed by the silting-in of a pond produced by a historic dam built across Salt River Draw. Nearly 4 m of stratigraphy have been mapped here, and up to 2.5 m of this depth represent silting of the pond (Fig. 7.3a). The impoundment of Salt River Draw, associated with silt deposition, and the subsequent break in the dam have resulted in a new channel cut approximately 40 m east of the original channel.

The ruin and the open park south of the site are considered one area. The stratigraphic sequence is less complex, represented by approximately 2 m of fill resting on the Pennsylvanian-Permian limestone of the adjacent ridge (Fig. 7.3b).

In both the north and south areas, burials were encountered near the base of the trashy fill, usually at contact with dark gray clay. Subfloor burials in the Great Kiva were usually interred in this clay.

Interpretation of the stratigraphic sequence indicates a preoccupation period of marsh land or lake bed environment resulting in the deposition of the dark gray-brown clay. Wet ground conditions may have persisted until the area was occupied by the people who constructed Grasshopper Pueblo. The stratigraphic levels above the dense clay are disturbed, stained with charcoal and other organic material, and contain potsherds, lithic debris, and human and animal remains. Postoccupational deposits include silt, probably of aeolian origin, and the surface soil zone. North of the ruin deposits include the historic sediments of the pond area.

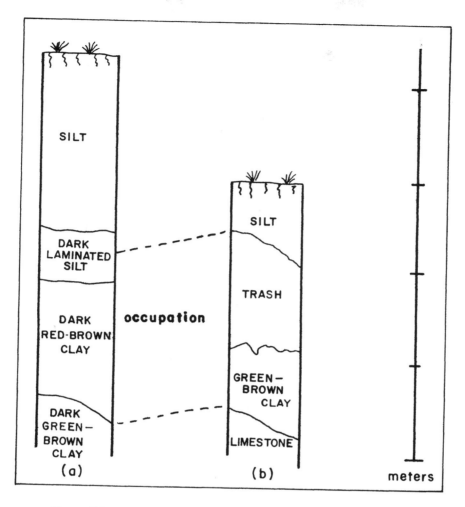

Figure 7.3. Generalized stratigraphy of trenches at Grasshopper Pueblo: *a*, north of the main ruin; *b*, south of the main ruin.

8. DENDROCHRONOLOGY OF GRASSHOPPER PUEBLO

Jeffrey S. Dean and William J. Robinson

The Laboratory of Tree-Ring Research and the Archaeological Field School of the University of Arizona have been closely associated since Byron Cummings established formal field training at Kinishba in 1934. Absolute dating of Kinishba was accomplished by Baldwin (1935) and Senter (1938), who were students in archaeology and dendrochronology. This association was solidified when the Field School operated in the Forestdale Valley beginning in 1939 under the direction of Emil W. Haury. Dating of the Forestdale archaeological manifestations was undertaken by A. E. Douglass (1941, 1942, 1944), the innovator of dendrochronology, and by Haury himself (1940b) who had been trained by Douglass. After the Second World War, when the Field School was moved to Point of Pines, the recovery of tree-ring samples was fully integrated into the excavation program and dating was accomplished within the program of the Laboratory of Tree-Ring Research (Parker 1967; Smiley 1949).

With the establishment of the Field School at Grasshopper in 1963 (Thompson and Longacre 1966), the relationship continued along traditional lines. Tree-ring samples were recovered each season during excavation and submitted to the Laboratory for processing and analysis. Derived dates were reported back to the Director of the Field School on completion of analysis, usually before the beginning of the next field season.

Although we both visited the Field School at Grasshopper nearly every year and discussed methods and applications of tree-ring dating, the analysis presented herein is confined to the kinds of information that can be extracted from the tree-ring collection in the laboratory. We do not have sufficient knowledge of architectural or artifactual details of Grasshopper Pueblo to attempt a detailed intrasite chronology. This aspect of analysis is best handled by the archaeologist equipped with dendrochronological data.

The analysis of a tree-ring collection falls naturally into three categories. First, examination of samples is traditionally performed to derive absolute dates and is often the only analysis undertaken. This category originally brought tree-ring dating into the field of archaeology and has provided thousands of dates for the chronological placement of events in Southwestern prehistory. The second category perhaps should be called simply archaeological analysis. It is based on the view that the recovered tree-ring sample in its context is as much an artifact as a stone tool or ceramic pot. As artifacts, tree-ring specimens possess attributes whose distribu-tions in time and space and context allow inferences to be drawn regarding the behavior of the users. Third, dendroclimatic techniques developed by the Laboratory of Tree-Ring Research can be applied to prehistoric tree-ring series to extract paleoclimatic information.

ABSOLUTE CHRONOLOGY

More than 2000 tree-ring samples have been recovered during excavations at Grasshopper since 1963. A number of projections can be made using this figure. About 20 percent of the Grasshopper site has been excavated, so the estimated total tree harvest during the prehistoric occupation exceeds 10,000 trees. From another point of view, the collection represents 69 architectural units. There are approximately 500 units in the ruin (Longacre and Reid 1974); thus, again, a harvest of 10,000 to 12,000 trees is indicated. Admittedly, these projections are based on constants that may be unreal and assumptions that are not testable, but some measure is required to place wood-use in its numerical context at communities such as Grasshopper.

The collection of more than 2000 samples yielded only 164 dates (Table 8.1). This dating average of less than 10 percent is small compared to many other areas in the Southwest, and it can be attributed to a number of factors. First, preservation at Grasshopper is generally poor, due, we suspect, to unfavorable soil and drainage conditions. Second, many of the ring series are extremely short and possess too few rings to permit dating. Although this may be in part a function of poor preservation, it also seems to reflect the extensive use of small trees, especially with pines. Finally, the builders of Grasshopper used some species that defy the dendrochronologist's skills (oak) and they made extensive use of others that are among the hardest to examine (juniper).

The most difficult interpretive aspect of the dates derived for Grasshopper Pueblo is the lack of cutting dates. Incredibly, only one of the 164 dates is an unequivocal cutting date; all the rest must be interpreted using date clusters (Bannister 1962).

Although individual dates from Grasshopper range from A.D. 1090vv to 1373vv, no architectural unit can be confidently placed much earlier than A.D. 1300 by tree-ring dates. Thus, over all, Grasshopper is generally contemporaneous with other well-known late pueblo communities such as Pinedale and Showlow to the north (Bannister, Gell, and Hannah 1966) and Kinishba and the Sierra Ancha Cliff Dwellings to the east and south (Bannister and Robinson 1971). Canyon Creek Pueblo and the smaller Red Rock House represent contemporaneous or slightly later canyon-located communities within a few miles of Grasshopper.

There are a few comments that can be made concerning the distribution of dates within Grasshopper Pueblo. An examination of Table 8.1 indicates only seven architectural units where the *latest* date falls earlier than A.D. 1300. Because the dated units represent almost all major sections of the ruin, it would seem that the visible architecture all postdates A.D. 1300. The apparent pre-1300 dating of seven rooms may be the result of the small sample of dates from each; none of the seven has more than three dates, most have one or two. If, however, these early dates are meaningful, then it is interesting that three of the seven early units are located in the extreme northern part of the east pueblo. It is possible that this is an older section of the pueblo, but the reuse of timbers may account for early dates in later construction.

The latest dates are associated with the Great Kiva and rooms adjacent to it. Thus the construction of the Great Kiva and the conversion of a part of the plaza into this ceremonial precinct (Thompson and Longacre 1966) is the latest dated event in the life of Grasshopper Pueblo.

Dates from the corridor, a narrow passageway opening south out of the central plaza of the west pueblo, illustrate the date cluster concept. The dates are scattered at the beginning of their total range and they tend to cluster more closely before terminating rather abruptly at A.D. 1320, suggesting that the corridor roof was either constructed in A.D. 1320 or within a few years thereafter. A single later date (1333) is best explained as a repair timber.

ARCHAEOLOGICAL ANALYSIS

Certain attributes of tree-ring materials—species of tree, nature of terminal ring, and technology—may be analyzed using the basic parameters of time, space, and context. Preliminary studies (Dean 1969; Robinson 1967) indicate that this direction of inquiry allows inferences concerning the cultural behavior of the users of the material. Unfortunately, only a single attribute can be observed in the collection of tree-ring material from Grasshopper. Technological alteration of the wood has been obscured by burning and poor preservation, and the nature of the terminal ring is observable only, of course, when the terminal ring is preserved. Thus, only the remaining attribute, species of tree, is available for analysis. The collection includes five arboreal species that are easily observed and they represent more than 95 percent of the recovered sample. These are (not in order of frequency) Douglas-fir (*Pseudotsuga menziesii*), ponderosa pine (*Pinus ponderosa*), pinyon (*Pinus edulis*), juniper (*Juniperus* sp.), and oak (*Quercus* sp.). These species used by the fourteenth century residents of Grasshopper are all present in the contemporary environment of the ruin.

Only one architectural unit contained more than an occasional specimen not of the five most common species. Room 100, near the southeast corner of the east pueblo, contained a few samples of oak and a preponderance of an unidentified, nonconiferous species. Although the late date of the room, as determined by architectural sequence, might suggest unavailability of coniferous trees for construction, this unique assemblage of species remains to be explained.

Three examples in the distribution of species within the Grasshopper ruin suggest the prehistoric occupants recognized the inherent qualities of wood (Robinson 1967). The Great Kiva, mentioned above as a late feature in the architectural history of the pueblo, was constructed from a prior plaza area. The size of the area enclosed by the Great Kiva required a number of upright posts to support roofing cross-members. All twelve posts were juniper, whereas the amount of ponderosa pine in the fill of the kiva indicates that the cross-members were pine. The recognition of the decay-resistant qualities of juniper at Grasshopper parallels similar use patterns found throughout the Southwest. In fact, juniper, often called cedar, is preferred in the contemporary West for fenceposts and other construction where decay is a hazard.

During excavations at Grasshopper, two series of contiguous pit ovens were located. Both are situated outside the room blocks, one east of the east pueblo and the other south of the west pueblo. Each series of ovens had a distinct assemblage of wood species. The ovens east of the east pueblo contained pinyon charcoal almost exclusively. In contrast, the ovens south of the west pueblo were filled with oak charcoal. Both species have qualities of intense heat and pleasant fragrance. Perhaps the use of these species in roasting ovens relates to the same motivation that leads to their preferred use in cooking campfires today. Whatever the explanation, the distribution of species in such functionally-specific areas as pit ovens would seem to reflect behavior patterns involving wood use.

In addition to its occurrence in one set of pit ovens, oak is abundant only in rooms at the southwest corner of the west pueblo and in the fill of a hearth in Room 40, at the extreme northern edge of the east pueblo. Oak occurrence elsewhere in the ruin is sporadic. Since the rooms involved are late in the history of the community, as determined by architectural sequence, the distribution of oak may reflect a change in the arboreal community in the immediate neighborhood of Grasshopper. However, even if true, such distribution could be induced either by climate or human disturbance.

A provocative study was conducted by Alan P. Sullivan using all tree-ring samples recovered during the first nine years of work at Grasshopper, including materials that were collected for species identification only and not permanently placed in the study collection. His aim was to examine the spatial and temporal distributions of tree species in order to reveal patterns that would reflect cultural behavior, or, in the simplest term, how the inhabitants of Grasshopper selected certain species for particular functions.

TABLE 8.1

Tree-ring Dates from Grasshopper Pueblo, Arizona

Room 8	1281p – 1306vv	1309p – 1332v	Room 279	1274fp – 1314vv
1254fp – 1309vv	1248fp – 1310vv	1311p – 1332v	1209fp – 1265+vv	1243fp – 1315vv
			1275fp – 1303vv	1262fp – 1315vv
Room 11	Room 39	Room 195	1278fp – 1308vv	1287 – 1317vv
1275fp – 1333vv	1154fp – 1181vv	1241p – 1313vv		1256p – 1318vv
	1194fp – 1278vv		Room 280	1260fp – 1318vv
Room 18	1202 – 1282vv	Room 197	1241fp – 1268vv	1273p – 1318vv
1144fp – 1206vv		1183fp – 1237vv	1236fp – 1297+vv	1282p – 1318vv
1149fp – 1238vv	Room 42	1273fp – 1366vv	1238fp – 1309vv	1289p – 1318vv
1207fp – 1269vv	1196fp – 1329vv		1316 – 1373vv	1294p – 1319vv
1287fp – 1347vv	1204fp – 1330+v	Room 198		1295p – 1319vv
		1225fp – 1318vv	Room 341	1285fp – 1320vv
Room 19	Room 43		1236fp – 1303vv	1285p – 1320vv
1223p – 1252vv	1122fp – 1199vv	Room 211		1302p – 1333v
1257fp – 1301vv		1282fp – 1313vv	Room 438	
1283fp – 1311vv	Room 44		1241fp – 1274+vv	Oven 1
	1265 – 1304vv	Room 216	1251fp – 1331vv	1217p – 1277vv
Room 21	1282 – 1309vv	1281fp – 1323vv		1231 – 1278vv
1273fp – 1267vv			Great Kiva	
1250 – 1288vv	Room 114	Room 231	1138 – 1190vv	Oven 2
	1256p – 1301vv	1176fp – 1234vv	1140 – 1194vv	1179fp – 1242vv
Room 23		1248p – 1291vv	1155 – 1194vv	1197 – 1263rG
1186fp – 1247vv	Room 145	1163± – 1298+r	1155 – 1200vv	1214±p – 1274vv
1241p – 1301vv	1241fp – 1320vv	1255p – 1302vv	1146fp – 1205vv	1215 – 1279vv
1243p – 1311vv		1276fp – 1303vv	1174 – 1209vv	1237 – 1281vv
1220 – 1312vv	Room 153	1274fp – 1305vv	1171fp – 1226vv	1221±p – 1294vv
1290 – 1318vv	1257fp – 1286vv		1180fp – 1267vv	1235 – 1306+vv
1292 – 1319vv	1250fp – 1312vv	Room 246	1223p – 1272vv	1252fp – 1330vv
	1253 – 1312vv	1146p – 1228++vv	1233 – 1273vv	
Room 26	1303fp – 1326vv		1195fp – 1287vv	Plaza I, Test
1272fp – 1300v	1262fp – 1346vv	Room 269	1262fp – 1321vv	Section 502
1283 – 1302vv		1204p – 1240vv	1293p – 1336vv	1247fp – 1282vv
1249 – 1303vv	Room 164	1228fp – 1273vv	1307±p – 1347vv	
1279 – 1308vv	1273fp – 1298vv	1234fp – 1284vv		Plaza I, Test
1279fp – 1310vv		1232 – 1287+vv	Corridor	Section 514
1279fp – 1313vv	Room 183	1255fp – 1293vv	1072fp – 1090vv	1242p – 1309++vv
	1252fp – 1294vv	1273fp – 1301vv	1078fp – 1101vv	1240p – 1310vv
Room 31	1276fp – 1303vv	1248fp – 1302+vv	1079fp – 1129vv	1237p – 1311+vv
1140fp – 1280++vv	1249fp – 1305vv	1251fp – 1305vv	1155fp – 1184vv	1239fp – 1316++vv
	1273fp – 1305vv	1238fp – 1307vv	1064fp – 1190vv	1243fp – 1318++vv
Room 33	1279fp – 1309vv	1260fp – 1325vv	1209fp – 1240vv	1244fp – 1318++vv
1210fp – 1243vv	1296fp – 1319vv	1280fp – 1332vv	1228fp – 1248vv	1239p – 1319++vv
1171fp – 1305++vv	1296fp – 1319vv	1312fp – 1343vv	1230fp – 1253vv	1242p – 1320++vv
1287 – 1311vv	1226p – 1323vv		1250p – 1271vv	1266fp – 1328++vv
	1315p – 1342vv	Room 270	1174 – 1293vv	
Room 35		1160 – 1198vv	1257fp – 1304vv	Plaza II
1194fp – 1229vv	Room 187	1172fp – 1229vv	1282p – 1308vv	Square 617
1210 – 1242vv	1311fp – 1329vv		1267fp – 1311vv	1209fp – 1232vv
1208fp – 1305vv	1304p – 1330vv	Room 274		
1221 – 1305++vv	1314p – 1332vv	1199fp – 1231vv		
		1265fp – 1302vv		

Symbols used with the inside date:

year = no pith ring present.

  p = pith ring present.

 fp = the curvature of the inside ring indicates that it is far from the pith.

 ±p = pith ring present, but due to the difficult nature of the ring series near the center of the specimen, an exact date cannot be assigned to it. The date is obtained by counting back from the earliest dated ring.

  ± = the innermost ring is not the pith ring and an absolute date cannot be assigned to it. A ring count is involved.

Symbols used with the outside date:

  G = beetle galleries are present on surface of sample.

  r = less than a full section is present, but the outermost ring is continuous around available circumference.

  v = a subjective judgment that, although there is no direct evidence of the true outside on the specimen, the date is within a very few years of being a cutting date.

 vv = there is no way of estimating how far the last ring is from the true outside.

  + = one or more rings may be missing near the end of the ring series whose presence or absence cannot be determined because the specimen does not extend far enough to provide an adequate check.

 ++ = a ring count is necessary due to the fact that beyond a certain point the specimen could not be dated.

The actual analysis was under a number of restraints. First, as the number of samples varied widely from spatial unit to spatial unit, a minimum sample of five was established intuitively to avoid sampling error of the grossest kind. Second, the spatial units (rooms) could be arranged from earliest to latest only for each section of the ruin. The lack of adequate absolute dates precluded firm placement in time, and architectural evidence of wall bonds and butting could be applied only to certain sections of contiguous architecture. Thus the data base for analysis, given the minimum sample and the architectural sequence, consisted of 35 rooms or approximately one-half of all the rooms excavated from 1963 through 1971. Finally, because the number of samples from discrete architectural units varied from 5 to 80, percentages were used in the analysis rather than raw counts.

A number of assumptions underlie a study such as this. One must assume that the present proportion of species in any spatial unit is the same as the proportion that was obtained during occupancy. In other words, the problem of differential decay and of other postoccupational additions or deletions from the original wood inventory are ignored. We must also assume, lacking evidence to the contrary, that the wood remains in a spatial unit represent roofing material. Obvious associations with fireplaces or other intentional burning can be eliminated, but, with the form altered by burning or weathering, the wood contents of a unit cannot always be confidently ascribed to construction material.

Except for Room 43 with a large representation of Douglas-fir and Room 100 with an unidentified nonconifer, the study indicated that ponderosa pine and juniper were utilized almost exclusively for roofing construction. Of the remaining sample of 33 rooms, ponderosa pine dominated the assemblage in 19 rooms, whereas juniper dominated in the other 14 rooms.

Some interesting patterns were revealed when these rooms were considered in view of architectural variables such as room size and location within room blocks. The pine-dominant rooms varied considerably in size and were located in all parts of the room blocks. With two exceptions, however, each juniper-dominant room had a floor area *less* than the mean room-floor area for the east pueblo (16 square meters). In addition, the juniper-dominant rooms were located only on the periphery of room blocks. This study in refined form has been published by Sullivan (1974).

The coherence of these variables suggested cultural behavior directed toward a specific functional need. At other nearby (and somewhat related) ruins, size and location of rooms have served as criteria for function. At Broken K Pueblo, James Hill (1970a: 45) identified rooms with architectural attributes similar to those of the juniper-dominant Grasshopper rooms as storage rooms.

Unfortunately, recovery of tree-ring samples was not performed with analyses such as these in mind, so that much of the contextual observation needed to test such relationships has been lost. The tree-ring collection from Grasshopper, however, has provided tangible evidence of the value of treating such material not only as chronological and climatic tools, but also as artifacts in the traditional archaeological manner.

DENDROCLIMATIC ANALYSIS

The physiological processes that control the growth of trees are subject to the influences of various external environmental variables. Those external factors that limit the operation of these processes thereby also limit radial growth, producing a permanent record of their effects in the annual growth increment. Since climate is the primary limiting factor in the arid Southwest, the sequence of narrow and wide rings in a tree-ring chronology is a partial record of year-to-year fluctuations in climate. Research in dendroclimatology, the subdiscipline of dendrochronology concerned with the interrelationships of tree growth and climate (Fritts 1976), has produced techniques for extracting some of the contained climatic information from tree-ring series. The application of these techniques to archaeological tree-ring chronologies, such as the one available for Grasshopper Pueblo, permits the reconstruction of some aspects of the paleoclimates of the localities represented by the chronologies.

Climatic input to the growth of trees has been a major focus of attention throughout the 75-year history of dendrochronology. A postulated relationship between tree growth and the weather first stimulated the astronomer Andrew Ellicott Douglass to study the rings of trees and to develop the science of dendrochronology. Douglass and his colleague Edmund Schulman, using trees from the Southwest and other regions of western North America, demonstrated a positive correlation between tree-ring widths and the rainfall of the preceding winter (Douglass 1914; Schulman 1956: 39-51). These studies led to the formulation of a model of tree growth-environmental relationships that specified soil moisture held over from the winter into the spring growing season as the primary environmental control of tree growth. This model was widely accepted and used by archaeologists in their attempts to relate tree-ring records to prehistoric events.

In the 1960s the conjunction of three factors revolutionized the study of dendroclimatology. First, biologically-trained investigators familiar with the physiological processes of tree maintenance and growth became active in dendrochronology. Second, multivariate statistical techniques capable of controlling many variables were applied to the problems of dendroclimatology. Third, the use of high-speed electronic computers made possible the analysis of the large number of variables and the vast quantities of data involved. Recent dendroclimatic research has been focused on the interactions of the many variables that influence tree growth and has revealed the extreme complexity of the relationships involved. Two general approaches to the problem have been emphasized: (1) multivariate statistical analyses of the covariation of parameters of radial growth and of the environment (Blasing 1975; Blasing and Fritts 1975, 1976; Fritts 1966, 1971, 1974; Fritts, Blasing, Hayden, and Kutzbach 1971; Fritts, Smith, and Stokes 1965; Julian and Fritts 1968); (2)

physiological and growth studies of living arid-site trees subject to carefully measured and partly controlled environmental constraints (Brown 1968; Budelsky 1969; Fritts 1969; Fritts, Smith, Cardis, and Budelsky 1965; Fritts, Smith, and Stokes 1965). The studies of living trees elucidate the ways in which external conditions impinge on the life processes of the trees to produce the relationships indicated by the statistical analyses.

This research has produced analytical techniques for determining the quantitative effects of various factors on the radial growth of trees. Application of these techniques has shown that in general conifers growing under the limiting conditions of the lower forest border in the arid Southwest respond primarily to the precipitation and secondarily to the temperatures of the year prior to the growing season and of the growing season itself. Subordinate to this general response are climatic relationships that differ from species to species and from site to site. In effect, each species responds to conditions of different parts of the preceding year and therefore records in its growth rings climatic information slightly different from that recorded by each of the other species. Thus, in addition to the annual climatic information contained in tree-ring sequences, intra-annual (seasonal) variability in weather is preserved as well.

One result of this research has been the development of a new model of tree growth-climate relationships (Figs. 8.1, 8.2). Although far more complex than the residual soil moisture model, the new model has much greater significance for paleoclimatic reconstructions based on dendrochronological data. In this model, the link between the previous year's weather and current growth is stored food reserves rather than holdover soil moisture. Conditions during the year that favor photosynthesis over respiration result in the production of surplus food, which is stored in the cells of the tree until needed for the maintenance or growth of the tree. Much of this reserve is not used until the following spring when it is consumed to supply the energy necessary for growth. During the growing season arid-site conifers often produce no food in excess of that used in respiration, and growth is dependent entirely on stored food. If the conditions of the previous year have not been conducive to food production, the lack of stored reserves limits growth, and a narrow annual ring is formed.

The studies of the responses of tree growth to various external factors and the models derived from them are the foundation for dendroclimatic reconstructions of past environmental conditions. Several techniques have been developed for extracting environmental information from long-range tree-ring series. The simplest of these takes the departures of tree growth from the long-term mean as a measure of variability in precipitation and temperatures over the period of dendrochronological record. This method was used by Fritts (1965) to reconstruct patterns of climatic variation throughout western North America from A.D. 1500 to 1940 and by Robinson and Dean (1969; Dean and Robinson 1977) to make similar projections for the Southwest from A.D. 680 to 1970. Other techniques permit the reconstruction of atmospheric pressure-pattern anomalies (Blasing 1975;

Blasing and Fritts 1975, 1976; Fritts 1971; Fritts, Blasing, Hayden, and Kutzbach 1971) and the estimation of past surface runoff (Stockton 1975; Stockton and Fritts 1971a, 1971b). Also, an attempt has been made to use the differential seasonal climatic input into the growth of different species to identify intra-annual variations in the prehistoric climate of Mesa Verde (Kemrer, Robinson, and Dean 1971).

Two major assumptions underlie our attempt to reconstruct certain aspects of the paleoclimate of the Southwest in general and the Grasshopper area in particular. First, we take the uniformitarian position that tree growth response to climate was the same in the past as it is today. Several types of evidence support this assumption. The fact that it has been possible to construct a continuous 2200-year tree-ring chronology comprised of thousands of overlapping ring sequences representing at least five different species indicates that there has been no basic change in the growth-climate relationships of each species during the period of record. In addition, the fact that the elevational and environmental distributions of the various species involved have not changed appreciably during the last 2000 years indicates that there have been no fundamental changes in the ways in which the trees respond to climate. Finally, the statistical parameters of modern tree-ring series do not differ significantly from those of the prehistoric chronologies.

Our second major assumption is that there has been no change in the type of climate prevalent in the Southwest during the 2200-year period covered by the tree-ring chronologies. Schoenwetter (1962: 191-194) presents the case in support of this assumption, and we do not argue it here. Suffice it to say that pollen studies, geological evidence, and plant and animal distributions lend strong support to this particular position. Given this assumption, the phenomena of concern to us are relatively short-term variations within the range of a single climate-type regime.

The paleoclimate of the Grasshopper region cannot be considered in isolation from that of the rest of the Southwest. Climatic conditions in any locale are the result of related meteorological factors that encompass the whole Southwest and much of western North America; thus the climate of one area can only be understood in relation to the climate of other areas that are included in the same meteorological system. Furthermore, climatic events well beyond the limits of the Grasshopper region may have had significant repercussions for the people of the Pueblo, either directly or indirectly through their effects on neighboring populations. Therefore, we performed a paleoclimatic analysis for the period from A.D. 1250 to 1350 in order to determine how the climate of the Mogollon Rim area compared to other parts of the Southwest during the occupation of Grasshopper Pueblo.

The analysis is based on a 25-station network of archaeological tree-ring chronologies assembled by the Laboratory's Southwest Paleoclimate Project (Robinson and Dean 1969, Dean and Robinson 1977). The network represents the maximum achievable coverage of the region and ranges from the Natural Bridges area on the north to

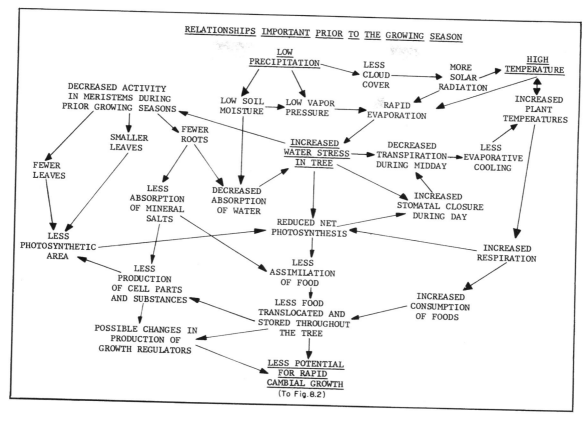

Figure 8.1. Tree growth-environment model: conditions of the period prior to the growing season that are important to tree growth in the semiarid Southwest (after Fritts 1971).

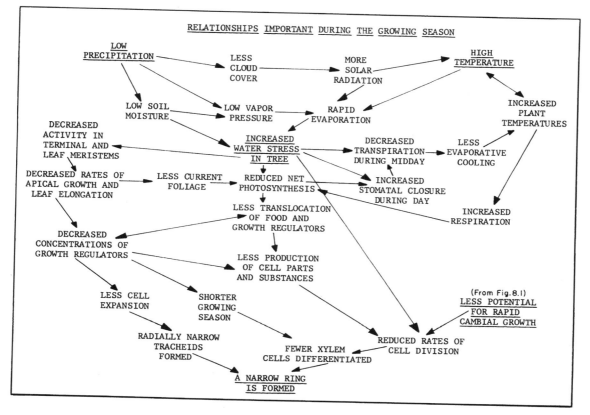

Figure 8.2. Tree growth-environment model: conditions of the growing season that are related to tree growth in the semiarid Southwest (after Fritts 1971).

the Salt River on the south and from the Coconino Plateau on the west to east of the Rio Grande. Each station chronology has been constructed so as to contain a maximum of dendroclimatic information and to represent the tree growth of a fairly restricted, environmentally homogeneous area.

The development of climatic chronologies such as these differs in many respects from the construction of dating chronologies. Individual specimen components are carefully screened to ensure that only those with a high probability of containing a large proportion of climate-related variance are included. Statistical parameters that characterize the ring series of living, climate-sensitive trees in the Southwest provide criteria for specimen selection. These parameters include the nature of the growth trend and the mean, standard deviation, mean sensitivity, and autocorrelation of the ring-width indices. This screening process eliminates specimens that, though they date, owe much of their variance to factors other than climate. Insofar as possible, only specimens with more than a hundred measured rings are used in these chronologies. Short ring series that represent young, fast growing trees contain less climatic information than do longer series, and they often present serious growth-trend problems. Furthermore, the use of short ring series in the station chronologies would limit the possibilities of detecting low frequency (long term) fluctuations in the climatic chronologies. Although we are concerned here with high frequency (annual) fluctuations, minimum specimen length is critical to other types of analysis.

Each chronology in the network has been developed for the maximum possible number of years, depending on the availability of suitable specimens from the area involved. Twelve of the chronologies have been combined with ring sequences from living trees and span nearly 2000 years continuously back from the present. Others cover only a part of this time range, and some have gaps in periods not represented by archaeological or modern tree-ring material.

In building each of these chronologies every effort was made to use specimens from sites distributed over a limited, environmentally uniform area, under the assumption that the builders of the sites did not venture any farther afield than necessary for constructional wood. Naturally, the geographic area represented varies from chronology to chronology in response to the differential spatial and temporal distributions of sites from area to area and to the availability of tree-ring samples from the sites.

Ideally, all 25 chronologies in the network should be constructed from the same species of tree; this is impossible, of course, given the geographic distributions of the various species, the selective use of species by the prehistoric peoples involved, and the vagaries of archaeological excavation and preservation. In a few cases it has been possible to build an entire station sequence from a single species, but the species involved differ from station to station. Other chronologies are comprised of ring widths from two or three different species, limiting our network analyses to statements about those aspects of climate that affect the growth of all species and prohibiting consideration of more specific information that can be derived from the analysis of a single species or of paired species.

A comprehensive review of all Southwestern archaeological tree-ring samples accumulated in the Laboratory (Robinson, Harrill, and Warren 1975: 1-2) provided quantitative data used in the construction of the climatic network chronologies. As a routine part of the review project, the ring widths of representative samples were measured to the nearest 0.01 mm. These data were analyzed by a computer program (Fritts 1976: 261-268; Fritts, Mosimann, and Bottorff 1969) that transformed them to standardized growth indices and calculated the statistical parameters of each ring series.

Standardized indices are produced by fitting a negative exponential curve to the sequentially arrayed ring-width values for each specimen and then calculating the percentage departure of each ring-width value from the value of the trend line at that point. This set of indices has a mean of 1.00 and a standard deviation unique to each series. Standardization enhances the amount of climate-related variance in each ring series by removing several variables, notably the growth trend and mean ring width, that are related to factors peculiar to the growth of individual trees rather than to external climatic conditions. The statistical parameters of the standardized data are used in the manner previously described to select specimens for inclusion in the climatic chronologies. The indices of the individual specimens chosen to represent a station are averaged to produce each of the 25 climatic sequences that constitute the network.

The network of tree-ring chronologies provides a basis for reconstructing past climatic fluctuations in the northern Southwest for any time interval represented by an array of stations that encompasses the entire region. These reconstructions are accomplished by computer programs that calculate standard normal variates from mean growth at each station, plot the values on a map of the region, and contour the array with isopleths representing equal positive and negative departures from the station means. For the Grasshopper analysis we chose the period from A.D. 1250 to 1350 and calculated departures for ten-year subintervals, each decade overlapping the previous one by five years (for example, 1250-1259, 1255-1264, 1260-1269).

The standard normal variate of one increment within a tree-ring chronology is calculated by subtracting the chronology mean from the growth index and dividing the result by the standard deviation of the chronology. Carried out for the entire length of the chronology, the operation produces a sequence of values with a mean of zero and a standard deviation of one. This procedure transforms the variability of each chronology to a common scale so that they can be compared to one another. In order to achieve an average departure from the mean for a decade, the ten standard normal variates for the decade are each multiplied by a constant ($10\sqrt{n}$, where $n=10$) and the results are summed algebraically and divided by $10n$, producing a decade departure value expressed in terms of standard deviation units. For example, a value of +2 indicates that the departure average for the decade involved is two standard deviations above the mean for that particular chronology. The ten-year departures are plotted on a map of the Southwest and contoured into zones representing standard deviation unit increments by CONTOUR, a program developed for the Southwest Paleoclimate Project by John Burns of the Division of Data Processing, Arizona State Museum (Burns 1975; Dean and Robinson 1977, 1979). The maps produced by this program give a graphic display of the spatial and temporal distributions of deviations from average growth throughout the Southwest (Dean and Robinson 1979). Variation that exceeds two standard deviation units in either direction is considered to be significant in the sense that such departures are of sufficient rarity and magnitude to have had potential adaptive consequences for plant, animal, and human populations. We are interested in those values that lie outside the range of 95 percent of the variability about the mean. On the maps (see Figs. 8.3–8.5), areas with departures greater than +2 are indicated by heavy hachure, and those with departures between +1 and +2 by lighter hatching. Areas with departures below −2 are heavily stippled, and those with values between −1 and −2 are more lightly stippled.

Before considering the results of the mapping operation, it is important that we make explicit exactly what these analyses are intended to accomplish and what their limitations are. This work and all the statements based on it are dependent on the two assumptions that were discussed above. Each local chronology represents the variation of annual tree growth around the mean growth for that station. Statistical and physiological studies show that tree growth is highly correlated with certain climatic variables, primarily precipitation and temperature. Therefore, we can consider each local chronology to be a good estimate of past fluctuations in rainfall and temperatures at that locality. The inclusion of several different species in the network chronologies limits us to statements about those climatic variables that affect the growth of all the species involved. In practice, this means that we are dealing with the combined effects of *annual* precipitation and temperatures at each station. The maps, then, represent changing spatial patterns of variations in tree growth, and therefore yearly rainfall, throughout the Southwest during the period of analysis. Positive departures indicate greater than average rainfall and lower than average temperatures; negative departures reflect lower than average precipitation and above average temperatures.

Within the limitations outlined above, the maps give a picture of relative dendroclimatic variability throughout the northern Southwest during the A.D. 1250 to 1350 study period. Except for below-normal precipitation in New Mexico and extreme eastern Arizona during the 1250s and for above-average precipitation in large areas of northern Arizona and southern Utah in the late 1250s and 1260s, the first 20 years of the study period exhibit no strong positive or negative deviations. Beginning in 1270,

the first indications of what was to become the so-called Great Drought can be seen in negative departure values in northern New Mexico and southeastern Utah. After 1275, dry conditions spread outward from the Four Corners area to encompass the entire Plateau during the 1280s (Fig. 8.3). Severe drought prevailed throughout the region until 1294; no positive decade departures are recorded for any station for the 1280 to 1294 interval.

After 1295 the situation began to ease as the regional drought was reduced to a localized pocket of aridity on the Upper San Juan with above-average precipitation prevailing along the Arizona-New Mexico border and on the upper Rio Grande (Fig. 8.4). Subsequently, conditions continued to improve, and greater-than-average precipitation persisted throughout the region until 1335, with especially high departures occurring from 1325 to 1335. Figure 8.5 illustrates the situation during the 1305 to 1314 interval when positive departures characterized most of the region and when significantly high precipitation prevailed in the Grasshopper area. After 1335 generally dry conditions spread over most of Arizona and New Mexico.

On 13 of the 20 maps that cover the study period, one or more isopleths fall between Station 6 (the Central Mountains North chronology made up of samples from the Show Low and Pinedale areas of the Colorado Plateau) and Station 7 (the Central Mountains South chronology based on samples from the lower country in the Salt River drainage south and southwest of Grasshopper). This cline (Fig. 8.4) parallels the Mogollon Rim, which passes between the two stations, and it seems likely that it is a result of the orographic effect of the escarpment on the flow of air masses across the area. Grasshopper is located between these two stations in a climatic transition zone that appears to exhibit considerable temporal persistence.

In order to get more specific information on the local climate of the Grasshopper area during the time the site was occupied, we used tree-ring specimens recovered from the ruin to build a climatic chronology for the period A.D. 1065 to 1365. The chronology is composed of 23 samples representing three species: ponderosa pine, pinyon, and juniper. Although the limitations of the Grasshopper tree-ring material made it impossible to adhere strictly to our criteria for specimen selection, the statistical parameters of the final chronology are acceptable. This chronology was used for the calculation of average departure values for ten-year intervals overlapped five years for the period from 1070 to 1365. The departure values for the period from 1150 to 1360 are plotted against time (Fig. 8.6b) to provide a graphic representation of climatic variability in the Grasshopper area.

There were only three periods when rainfall at Grasshopper deviated significantly from the mean: the 1195-1204 decade, the Great Drought from 1275 to 1295, and the postdrought maximum between 1300 and 1320. The decade departure values between 1275 and 1295 are all negative, and those for the interval between 1280 and 1295 are more than two standard deviation units below the mean. Of the 20 annual standard normal variate

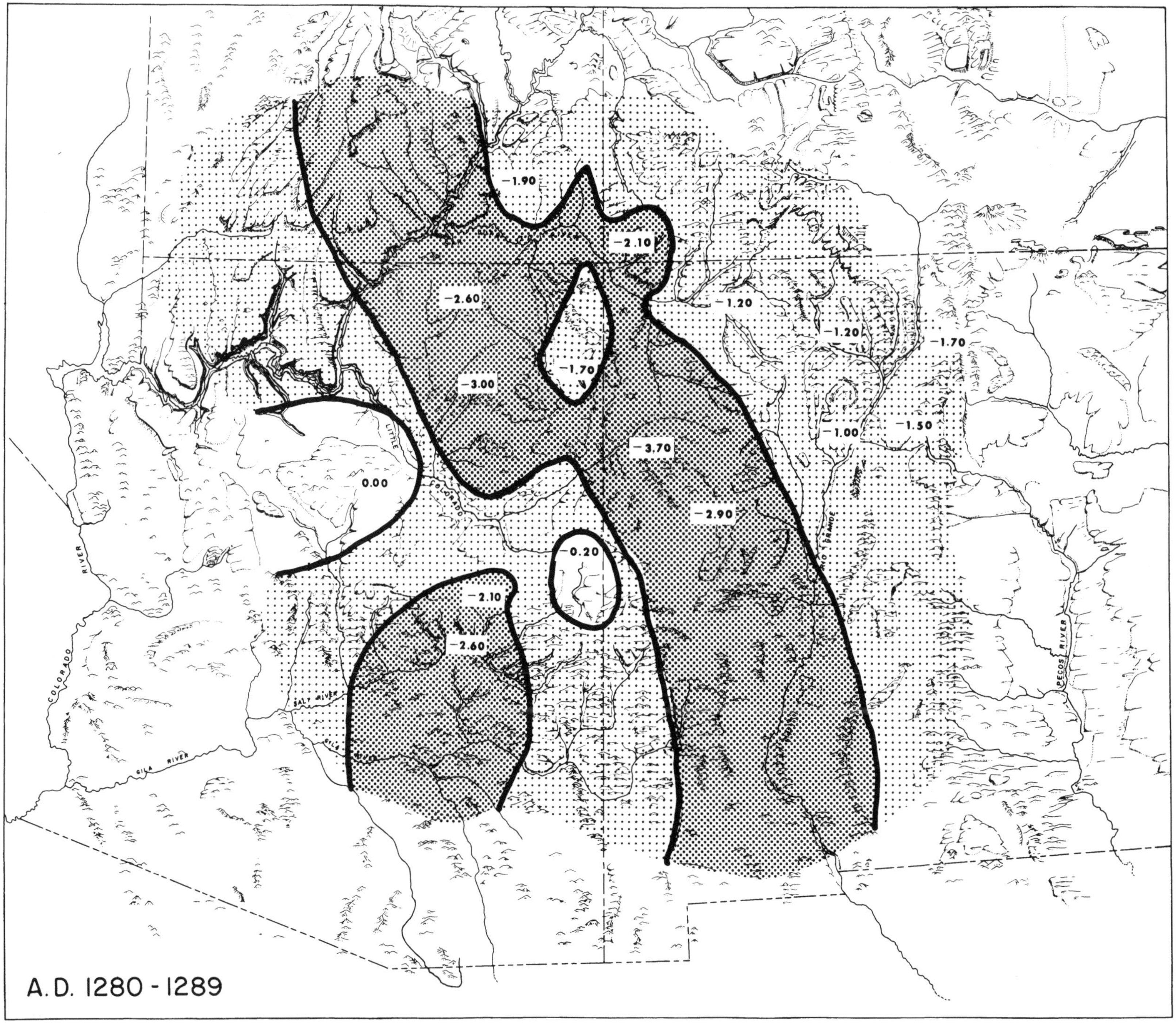

Figure 8.3. Paleoclimatic conditions in the Southwest: A.D. 1280 to 1289. Negative departures stippled; departure values indicated at station locations.

A.D. 1280 - 1289

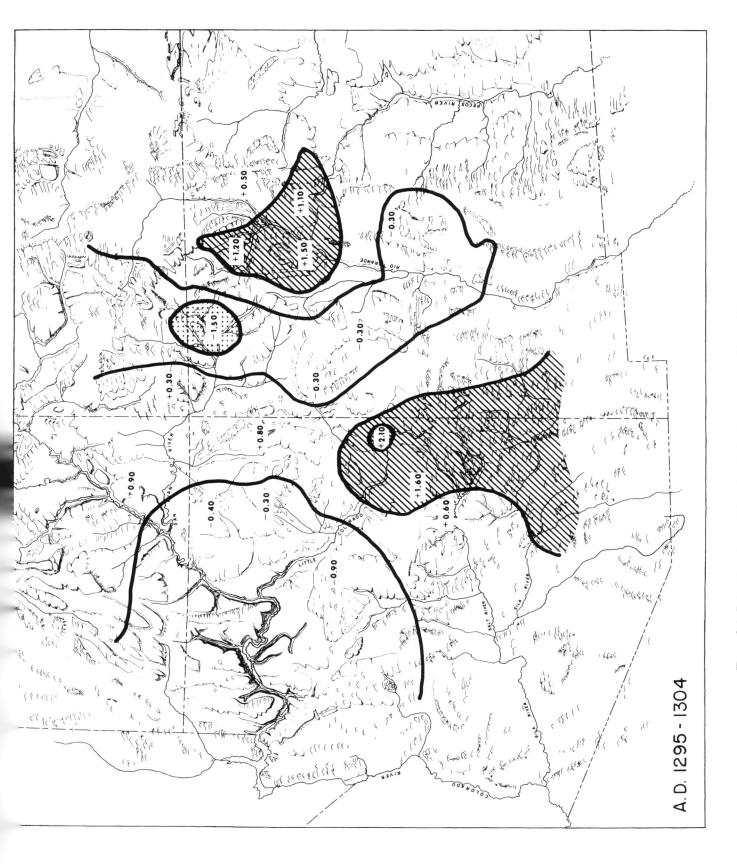

Figure 8.4. Paleoclimatic conditions in the Southwest: A.D. 1295 to 1304. Negative departures stippled, positive departures hatched; departure values indicated at station locations.

A.D. 1295 - 1304

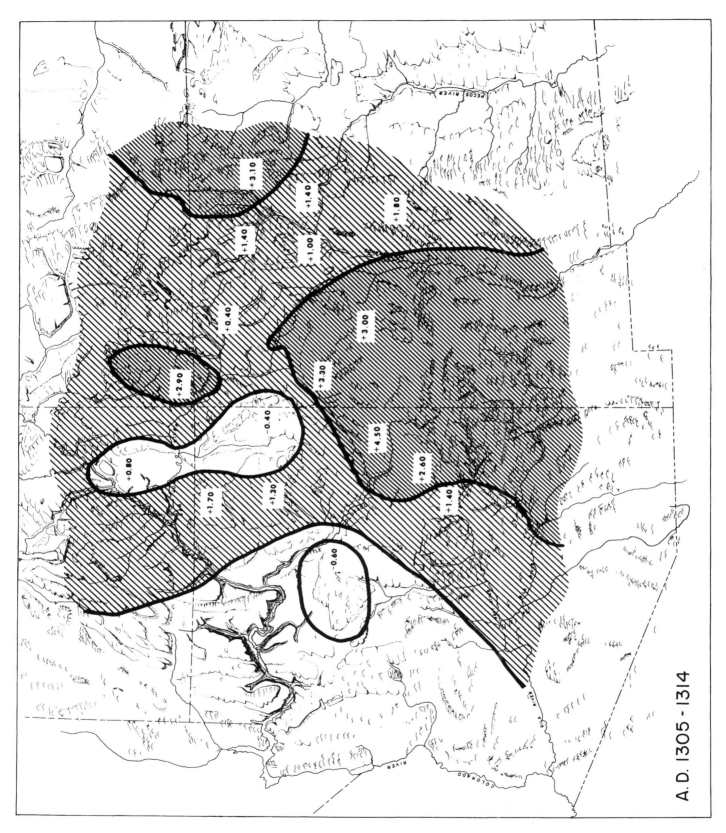

Figure 8.5. Paleoclimatic conditions in the Southwest: A.D. 1305 to 1314. Positive departure values hatched; departure values indicated at station locations.

A.D. 1305 - 1314

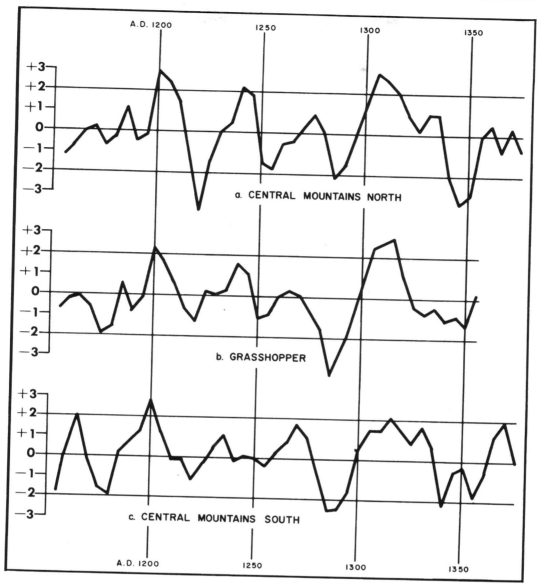

Figure 8.6. Paleoclimatic variations in the central mountains of Arizona from A.D. 1150 to 1375: *a*, central mountains north chronology; *b*, Grass-hopper chronology; *c*, central mountains south chronology.

values for the 1275 to 1295 interval, only 4 are positive; 16 of the 20 years were characterized by subnormal precipitation. Conversely, the 20 years following 1300 were characterized by rainfall significantly greater than normal, with 16 of the 20 annual deviations falling above the mean. Rainfall during the periods prior to the drought (1150 to 1275) and following the postdrought maximum (1320 to 1350) did not deviate significantly from the long-term mean for the area. Thus, the climatic history of the Grasshopper area from 1150 to 1350 conforms to that of the Southwest as a whole during the same period.

The Grasshopper departures (Fig. 8.6*b*) are plotted alongside those of the Central Mountains North chronology (Fig. 8.6*a*) and the Central Mountains South sequence (Fig. 8.6*c*) in order to get some idea of the characteristics of prehistoric rainfall along the elevational

and environmental gradients that relate the three stations. It is immediately obvious that the departure variations of the three chronologies parallel one another throughout the time period involved. In terms of significance levels, however, there are striking differences among the three sequences. There are only four periods of significant deviation from normal in the southern chronology: positive values for the 1195 to 1204 and 1310 to 1319 decades and negative departures of the Great Drought from 1280 to 1295 and of the 1335 to 1344 decade. In contrast, the northern sequence exhibits three periods of significant negative departures (1215 to 1224, 1280 to 1289, 1335 to 1354) and three intervals of significant positive departures (1195 to 1209, 1235 to 1244, 1300 to 1319). Figure 8.6 shows that periods characterized by significant positive or negative departures were not only more frequent in the north, they were also more severe and more prolonged. The Grasshopper chronology, as might be expected from its intermediate location, falls between the northern and southern sequences in terms of variability around the mean.

In order to further specify the climatic relationships among these three localities, a cross-correlation analysis was performed for the period A.D. 1150 to 1350 using six tree-ring chronologies: Grasshopper, Central Mountains North, Central Mountains South, Kinishba, Pinedale, and Showlow. The correlation coefficients show that during this period Grasshopper tree growth was more closely related to that of the northern station (r = .741) than to that of the southern station (r = .635). Temporal variations in these relationships were determined by running correlations of the six chronologies for 25-year intervals (1150 to 1175, 1175 to 1200, 1200 to 1225, and so on). This procedure in general confirmed that Grasshopper tree growth resembled that of the north more than that of the south, although there are some interesting variations through time. The intercorrelation of all six series increases during periods characterized by negative departures and decreases during wetter periods. This behavior is consistent with dendroclimatic theory in that limiting climatic conditions would be expected to produce more uniform tree growth responses than would more favorable climatic conditions, which permit other, more localized factors to exert some control on tree growth. Finally, there is a slight, although not statistically significant, tendency for Grasshopper tree growth to behave more like that of the south during dry intervals and more like that of the north during wetter periods.

The departure sequences (Fig. 8.6) and the correlation analyses indicate that between 1150 and 1350 climatic variability decreased with elevation from the summit of the Mogollon Rim south to the Salt River. As today, there undoubtedly was also a decrease in mean annual precipitation and an increase in average temperatures down the elevational gradient. The less year-to-year climatic variability in the drier, hotter south than in the wetter, cooler Rim country may have had important adaptive implications for the human inhabitants and the flora and fauna of the southern region. In an area with a low mean annual precipitation, relatively slight deviations below normal would have had more serious adaptive consequences than would greater negative deviations in a wetter area. It is possible that the lack of significant variability in the south during the study period permitted human populations to survive there while other groups were weathering fluctuations of greater magnitude in nearby, more favored areas such as the Grasshopper and Rim localities.

The archaeological significance of dendroclimatic reconstructions lies in the possible effects of the observed variations in precipitation on the behavior of the people in the area. Rainfall fluctuations could influence behavior directly through their effects on the subsistence system or indirectly through their effects on other components of the local environment. In either case, we are

dealing with adaptive responses to changes in the external environment, and we are, therefore, interested in specifying those climatic variations that might have had adaptive significance for the plant and animal (including human) populations of the Grasshopper area. The fact that Grasshopper Pueblo was occupied for several generations indicates that its inhabitants had achieved a fairly successful adaptation to the local environment, including the normal year-to-year variations in that environment. Similarly, the plants and animals that composed the local biome must have been adapted to normal variability in their operational environments. Consequently, our concern is with those variations in precipitation that fall beyond the normal range of variability, for it is these fluctuations that might be expected to have significant consequences for the adaptational systems of the area. As noted previously, we consider departure values that lie outside the range of 95 percent of the variability about the station mean to be significant in this regard. We do not argue that significant departures represent permanent systemic changes in climate, nor that they required major adaptive responses on the part of the inhabitants of Grasshopper Pueblo. Nevertheless, these deviations are rare enough and are of sufficient magnitude that observable responses within the limits of the extant adaptive system might be expected.

We are now prepared to suggest a few possible consequences, both environmental and behavioral, of the patterns of annual variability in precipitation and temperature in the Grasshopper area between A.D. 1150 and 1350. These speculative statements are based almost exclusively on the dendroclimatic evidence and are offered as hypotheses to be tested against the evidence of other disciplines involved in Grasshopper-area research.

First examined are the possible effects on the local environment of the subnormal precipitation and above average temperatures indicated for the Great Drought of 1275 to 1295. In the lower elevation forests of the semi-arid Southwest, prolonged drought reduces stand density, thereby lessening intertree competition. Less vigorous and less well-established trees, such as very old individuals and seedlings, die off leaving less dense stands composed of healthy, mature trees capable of maximum efficiency in the utilization of available resources. The reduced shading resulting from the decrease in stand density often causes a die back of underbrush. During the Great Drought, these processes may have operated in the Grasshopper area to thin out the local forest cover. This thinning could have been important in opening the Grasshopper locale to large-scale human habitation, because the forest could have become quite dense between 1150 and 1250 when there apparently were no long periods of climatic stress.

If the widespread arroyo cutting that occurred throughout the Colorado Plateau in the late thirteenth century also prevailed in the central mountains of Arizona, stream entrenchment coupled with the dry conditions of the drought would have had important effects on the local environment. Entrenchment of Salt River Draw at Grasshopper would have been accompanied by a lowering of the water table in the flats below the Pueblo. Paradoxically, this may have had positive consequences for farming in this locale. It is possible that prior to stream entrenchment the soil in the flats was saturated, even to the extent that marshy conditions existed in the bottomlands (see Chapters 7, 9, 11). If so, the soil may have been so poorly aerated that crops could not be grown on the flats, and fields would have been restricted to the valleyside slopes. The lowering of the water table that accompanied the drought and the entrenchment would have eliminated the aeration problem and opened the bottomlands to intensive agriculture.

The possible effects of the postdrought precipitation maximum on the local environment are difficult to assess. The increased rainfall undoubtedly caused a gradual increase in forest density, which could have been partially offset by the harvesting of young trees for the construction of Grasshopper Pueblo. In addition, the increased rainfall may have had a positive effect on agriculture in the bottomlands and may also have made farming possible in some areas that could not be farmed during the drought. In contrast, the lower average temperatures that accompanied the greater rainfall may have had some adverse effects on agriculture, especially in that the growing season may have been shortened.

It seems unlikely that only the rainfall itself, even during the drought, was consistently limiting to subsistence farming in the Grasshopper area, which is presently characterized by precipitation that is more than ample for the growing of corn. Temperatures may have been more directly limiting than rainfall in that the present growing season there approaches the minimum for corn, and temperatures significantly below average might have caused some crop loss. The observed variations in precipitation and temperature probably influenced agriculture chiefly through their effects on other components of the environment as described above. With this in mind, a few suggestions can be made as to the possible responses of the inhabitants of the Grasshopper area to the postulated environmental changes associated with the drought and postdrought maximum.

The thinning of the forest caused by the drought and the lowering of the alluvial water table that accompanied stream entrenchment may have created a situation more favorable to farming than that prevailing prior to 1270. Indeed, environmental changes such as these may have been at least partly responsible for the original settlement (about 1275 to 1300) of the locus that was to become Grasshopper Pueblo. Possible responses to the conditions of this period include: (1) a new focus of habitation around stream courses; (2) concentration of population in loci recently rendered suitable for intensive agriculture; and (3) expansion of population into recently opened areas within the forest.

Some possible responses to the wetter and cooler conditions of the postdrought period are: (1) amalgamation of populations into large communities at loci favorable for large-scale intensive farming; (2) movement of people into areas rendered favorable by the increased rainfall, such as the lower, drier canyon country to the southwest of Grasshopper; and (3) settlement of areas where the cooler temperatures of the period would be less limiting to crop production.

Certain population movements throughout the mountainous area of Arizona can be postulated on the basis of the dendroclimatic evidence. During the Great Drought, population movement into the Grasshopper area, if any, probably would have been from the lower, drier, hotter areas to the south and west of Grasshopper or possibly from the Little Colorado area to the north. Conversely, during optimum periods population movement might have been from the higher, cooler Rim country, where depressed temperatures threatened crop production, into lower areas rendered favorable by the increased precipitation. The occupation of the Sierra Ancha and Canyon Creek cliff dwellings may be a response to the depressed temperatures in the wetter, higher areas to the northeast. Many of these sites were first occupied during the optimum period and several appear to have been abandoned shortly after the return to average conditions (Bannister and Robinson 1971), which may have been too hot and dry for reliable crop production in the canyon environments. It seems not unreasonable to hypothesize that these canyon sites may have been "colonies" established by the inhabitants of nearby larger communities such as Grasshopper to exploit an environment that had become suitable for farming as a result of increased rainfall. Such colonies could have been permanent habitation sites or seasonal residences devoted to the production of food for consumption in the parent communities. In either case, settlement in these areas, even though relatively temporary, would broaden the agricultural base as a hedge against frost damage to crops at higher elevations or lack of water at the lower elevation sites.

SUMMARY AND CONCLUSIONS

Analysis of the more than 2000 tree-ring samples from Grasshopper Pueblo has produced three classes of information: chronological, archaeological, and environmental. Clustering within the distribution of the 164 dates indicates major pueblo construction in the early fourteenth century. Roofing of the corridor is securely dated at A.D. 1320, and the construction events that produced the Great Kiva seem to have taken place somewhat later and to have been completed by about 1350. A late noncutting date of 1373 indicates that construction or repair activities persisted into the last quarter of the fourteenth century. As yet dendrochronology has contributed little to dating the initial construction of the Pueblo, although scattered noncutting dates in the late 1200s are consistent with the estimated beginning date of about 1275 based on ceramics.

Analysis of the tree-ring samples as artifacts, although hampered by the poor preservation characteristic of the site, indicates the use of juniper and ponderosa pine in storage and habitation room contexts respectively (Sullivan 1974) and the differential use of pinyon and oak in different sets of pit ovens. Other species distributions suggest the possibility that toward the end of the Grasshopper occupation construction had depleted the available coniferous tree resources in the vicinity of the Pueblo.

Dendroclimatic analyses of a specially constructed Grasshopper climatic tree-ring chronology and of a regional grid of climatic tree-ring sequences provide data on local climatic variability during the occupation of the Pueblo and on the relationships of this variability to that of the northern Southwest. In general, Grasshopper area climatic variation paralleled that of the region, with the notorious Great Drought of 1275 to 1300 and the postdrought maximum (1300 to 1335) strongly indicated. As expected, dendroclimatic variability at Grasshopper was transitional between the high variability of the area above the Mogollon Rim to the north and the lower variability of the low-lying Salt River drainage to the southwest. The indicated local and regional dendroclimatic fluctuations and the relationships of the Grasshopper locale to adjacent areas provide a basis for inferring the effects of such changes on the local plant and animal (including human) populations of the area. The paleoen-vironmental inferences can be checked against the data of disciplines such as zooarchaeology, paleobotany, palynology, and geomorphology. Inferences made about possible population movements throughout the Grasshopper area can be checked against archaeological data.

The results of these dendrochronological analyses of tree-ring samples from Grasshopper Pueblo and of the ring sequences derived from them illustrate the contributions that dendrochronology can make to archaeological analysis when the collection of the wood and charcoal samples is fully integrated into the archaeological research program. In addition to the derivation of absolute dates to aid in the chronological placement of the site and its components, tree-ring studies provide the bases for inferences about past human subsistence behavior, population movements, and possible relationships among the inhabitants of contemporaneous communities in the area. Such inferences, restated as hypotheses, can help structure future archaeological research, a process that exemplifies the creative contribution that disciplines such as dendrochronology can make to archaeological research when the fields are properly integrated with one another from the inception of fieldwork through laboratory analysis.

9. WATER RESOURCES AND AQUATIC FAUNA AT GRASSHOPPER PUEBLO

Stanley J. Olsen

The aquatic vertebrates in the Grasshopper faunal collection have been studied in an attempt to answer some of the questions relating to water availability immediately adjacent to the Pueblo during its occupation in the fourteenth century. During the 1971 field season, the Cibecue area experienced one of its driest summers during the past fifteen years, a fortunate circumstance that facilitated comparison of the surrounding permanent and semipermanent water sources with the possible former water supply in the Grasshopper region.

To the northeast of the main ruin is a large depression, mostly filled with silt at the present time, that appears to have been the reservoir for the prehistoric community. Some 30 or 40 years ago, a local stockman built an earthen dam across the stream to the north of the older earthworks. The dam subsequently burst and a new channel was cut east of the site. Test trenches were dug with a backhoe through the drainage channel and in several localities within the pond. Contact with the ground water was made at a depth of approximately 4 or 5 m. Salt River Draw is the natural supply and drainage for the pond area, and it runs between the east and west architectural units of the Pueblo. The Draw originates about 5.6 km (3.5 miles) northeast of the ruins and makes a 152.4 m (500 foot) drop from its source to the narrows between the Pueblo units. During the trenching, a gravel bar was encountered at a depth of 5 m. It was suggested that perhaps the gravel bar was Pleistocene, but several pottery sherds contemporary with the prehistoric occupation were recovered from the interstices between the larger boulders of the bar. The gravel and small boulders varied in size from 4 or 5 mm to 18 or 20 cm in length.

Dr. Nevin Hoy, Chief of the Ground Water Branch of the U.S. Geological Survey in Florida, commented in 1971 on the nature of the prehistoric stream:

Taking into consideration the gradient of the surrounding drainage area, and the sizes of the recovered boulder samples from the old stream bed, it appears that a stream of considerable velocity and volume at flood-stage coursed past the pueblo at one time or another. It must be remembered that this stream was probably intermittent, perhaps with even several years between flood stages and would have had sufficient force to destroy a simple dam such as is suggested for containing the waters of the upper pond.

Numerous small gastropods and pelecypods were recovered from the bottom of the test trenches at the lower end of the pond. Dr. Ruth Turner, conchologist at the Museum of Comparative Zoology at Harvard University, identified the invertebrates as orbsnails, probably *Helisoma* sp. that are freshwater lake and pond dwellers, and the gastropods as *Lymnas humilis,* also a species residing in the relatively quiet waters of streams and ponds. None of these species are associated with permanent, swift-running streams, and all specimens appeared to be adult.

No vertebrates were collected from the 1971 test trenches, although sediment samples were washed, screened, and floated in our search for them. Vertebrate bones found in trash deposits within the Pueblo in rooms adjacent to the stream, however, also suggest a somewhat permanent water supply. Several vertebrae of the squawfish, *Ptychocheilus lucius,* were screened from the debris of Room 18. The largest of these vertebrae suggest a fish measuring 60 cm, or about 2 feet in length. A fish of this size would require a stream with pools of some size and depth. It is possible that this fish came from the nearby Salt River, where it was relatively common until comparatively recent times. Smaller vertebrae of the sucker (*Catostomus clarkii*) were also recovered; several individuals of this species, about 15.2 cm (6 inches) in length, were seined during July, 1971, in Canyon Creek at nearby Chediski Farms.

Several individuals of the leopard frog (*Rana pipiens*) were also found in excavations. This amphibian is a highly adaptable species occurring from the Lower Sonoran life zone to the Lower Boreal zone. It is found in either clear or muddy waters, in shallow ponds or deep ones, in springs, creeks, or rivers, and in mountain lowlands. It seems to prefer cattail swamps or marshy areas such as grassy overflows. Although cattails do not occur in the immediate vicinity of Grasshopper today, pollen analyses indicate that these plants were growing along the Salt River Draw in prehistoric times.

The only turtle fragment recovered is the right anterior portion of the plastron (bottom shell) of the Sonoran mud turtle (*Kinosternon sonoriense*). This turtle inhabits principally the Gila River drainage of central and southern Arizona and it can ascend drainages to over 1524 m (5000 feet) above sea level (Grasshopper elevation is about 1850 m ASL). It is a thoroughly aquatic species inhabiting ponds, springs, water holes in arroyos, rivers, and creeks.

The following field notations indicate water sources visited in the vicinity of Grasshopper during June and July of 1971.

Canyon Creek, Chediski Farms (1707 m ASL). The stream varied in depth from about 15 cm to 91.4 cm and averaged about 1.2 m to 1.5 m wide. Pools ranged up to 61 m long. Water trickled in a steady stream over the limestone bottoms (Paleozoic, Supai Formation). Accumulation of large boulders indicates severe flash flooding at times. The pools contained small suckers, 15 cm to 20 cm long, and small trout that had been introduced recently. No frogs were observed.

Oak Creek Canyon, Fort Apache Indian Reservation (1829 m ASL). Stained sandstone waterfall (no running water). Only collared lizards (*Crotaphytus* sp.) and spiny swifts (*Sceloporus* sp.) were collected.

Rock Springs (1524 m ASL). Stained sandstone waterfall (no running water) with eroded basins and pools located at three levels: road level, 18.3 m, and 30.5 m above road level. Pools 60 to 92 cm deep and 1.8 m in diameter. *Rana pipiens,* canyon tree frogs, and garter snakes were present, but no fish. Stagnant water.

Pumpkin Lake (2134 m ASL). Clear pond, 61 m in diameter. No runoff outlet. Fed by a spring seep. Surrounded by yellow flowering bonnets, lily pads, and cattails. Numerous *Rana pipiens.* Garter snakes were present; no fish observed.

Louse Lake (2073 m ASL). Small pond 2.4 m in diameter, mud puddle; 91.4-m flood pond area of grass surrounding it. Gray mud, produced larval salamanders and a few *Rana pipiens.*

Pryce Lake (2154 m ASL). Completely dry. No life observed.

Spring Creek (1676 m ASL). Small permanent pools fed by seeps. *Rana pipiens* were present, but no fish.

Grasshopper Spring (1829 m ASL). Stream runs over Paleozoic limestone (Supai Formation). Completely dry. Some seepage through cracks of limestone at lower end of stream channel. Stagnant pools; no fish; one *Rana pipiens* observed.

Cibecue Creek at junction with Salt River (1524 m ASL). Fine, deep supply of clear, swift running water. Trout (introduced), suckers, small minnows, and numerous harmless snakes and frogs were observed.

Cibecue Creek at the Apache town of Cibecue. Stream has a small but steady flow of water over a gravel bed. Many natural pools are present, varying from a few inches in depth to some of several feet. Damming this stream would produce a more or less permanent pond.

Considering all the comparisons made, I believe that Cibecue Creek at Cibecue is like the water supply that was present at Grasshopper Pueblo during its prehistoric occupation.

10. PREHISTORIC ENVIRONMENTAL RECONSTRUCTION BY VERTEBRATE FAUNAL ANALYSIS, GRASSHOPPER PUEBLO

John W. Olsen

During fifteen field seasons of excavation at Grasshopper Pueblo, a rich assemblage of vertebrate faunal specimens have been recovered. Although only 20 percent of the 500-room Pueblo has been excavated (Ciolek-Torrello 1978), the sample of faunal remains derived from these architectural units has been useful in interpreting prehistoric lifestyles in the Southwest (J. W. Olsen 1980).

One aspect of the zooarchaeological analysis of the Grasshopper archaeofaunal remains that has received particular attention has been the reconstruction of the paleoenvironment of the region during the period of its prehistoric occupation. Paleoenvironmental interpretation is enhanced by data derived from many divergent taxa because the collection of faunal remains from the Pueblo encompasses an extremely diverse array of vertebrates ranging in size and behavior from fish to artiodactyls.

A total of 40,246 bone fragments has been analyzed from Grasshopper. The Total Number of Identified Specimens (NISP) by class and their percentage of the entire faunal collection are: Osteichthyes, 20 (0.05 percent); Amphibia, 19 (0.05 percent); Reptilia, 57 (0.15 percent); Aves, 5243 (13.02 percent); and Mammalia, 34,907 (86.73 percent). Avian and mammalian remains constitute an overwhelming 99.75 percent, and many of the forms suggest intensive procurement activities by the prehistoric inhabitants. A significant number of the vertebrates, however, appear unrelated to the human occupation of the Grasshopper region, and as indigenous species they have been used to reconstruct the past environmental regime. Animals introduced to the archaeological record because of prehistoric activity also provide paleoenvironmental information, but the significance of animals now alien to or uncommon in the Grasshopper region must be interpreted with caution. Exotic animals were imported to the Pueblo from considerable distance, and their presence should not be construed as an indication of past environment. For example, two parrots, *Amazona albifrons* Sparrman (White-fronted Parrot) and *Ara macao* Linnaeus, were recovered from the ruin. Although the juvenile *Ara* remains may indicate this ceremonially important bird was reared at the Pueblo, it is far more likely that these animals were transported to Grasshopper through trade with communities to the south (Chapter 12; Di Peso 1974; McKusick 1974).

VERTEBRATE REMAINS FROM GRASSHOPPER PUEBLO

Vertebrate faunal remains excavated from Grasshopper Pueblo have yielded valuable data that enhance the interpretation of past environmental conditions at the site. Information derived from a broad spectrum of taxa (Chapter 11; J. W. Olsen 1980) suggests the environmental milieu characterizing east-central Arizona in the fourteenth century was considerably less montane and possibly warmer than at present. Judging from the variety of vertebrates recovered, a mosaic of niches, including Ponderosa pine forest, steppe-grassland, and well-developed riparian communities, was present.

The microfauna—fish, amphibians, and reptiles, in particular—leave no doubt about the presence of more abundant water supplies in the immediate vicinity of the Pueblo during the fourteenth century. The presence of these forms appears unrelated to human procurement activity and it is assumed these small animals represent indigenous species that constitute reliable indicators of past environmental conditions. Based on the analysis of vertebrate remains, we infer that the old channel of Salt River Draw, which separates Room Blocks 1 and 2 of the main pueblo (see Fig. 1.3), was a stream of considerable velocity and volume during much of the community's occupation (Olsen and Olsen 1970). In the archaeological faunal assemblage it is apparent that a combination of an ecologically diverse environment and climatic fluctuation resulted in the presence of taxa representing widely divergent habitats.

Both the descriptive and interpretive phases of this analysis are presented in an annotated taxonomic list to facilitate comparison of paleoenvironmental data derived from widely divergent vertebrate forms. Table 10.1 at the end of the chapter contains a complete listing of vertebrate taxa identified thus far from Grasshopper Pueblo.

Bony Fishes
Class Osteichthyes

Only 20 fish elements were recovered from Grasshopper, representing three genera (*Ptychocheïlus*, *Catostomus*, and *Pantosteus*) that are members of the order Cypriniformes. All fish remains were excavated from one early abandoned room and two late abandoned rooms that border the Great Kiva. Analysis of vertebral dimensions and provenience suggests no more than ten individuals are represented.

The number of annular rings on the anterior and posterior faces of the vertebrae indicate the Grasshopper specimens ranged in age from seven to ten years. Insufficient quantitative data exist to estimate individual weight based on vertebral dimensions using Casteel's (1976: 85-87) regression method, but a direct comparison with modern osteological material of known weight indicates that each specimen weighed about 2 kg.

The three genera of fish recovered, one minnow and two suckers, are predominantly large river fish preferring swiftly-moving channels, but the small size of the osteological elements indicate these fish may have been derived from aquatic habitats similar to that of Salt River Draw. A field survey of fish now present in the smaller watercourses of the Grasshopper vicinity (Chapter 9) suggests the fish identified in the site's archaeofauna may have come from any one of the small streams near the Pueblo, including Canyon Creek, Oak Creek, Cibecue Creek, and Salt River Draw.

Squawfish
(Family Cyprinidae)

Ptychocheilus lucius Girard may attain lengths of 2 m and weights of nearly 50 kg when taken from large bodies of water (Miller 1961; Minckley 1973: 120), and squawfish have recently occurred in the Salt River (Miller 1961; Minckley in Cowgill 1978). Certainly the aquatic resources of that river, located approximately 30 km south of Grasshopper Pueblo, were within the exploitive range of the local prehistoric population, and specimens of *Ptychocheilus* and other Osteichthyes may have been obtained there. The small size of the nine squawfish specimens recovered from Grasshopper, however, suggests that they were procured from smaller watercourses, such as Salt River Draw, in the immediate vicinity of the Pueblo.

Suckers
(Family Catostomidae)

Two suckers (*Catostomus latipinnis* Baird and Girard, and *Pantosteus* cf. *P. clarki* (Baird and Girard), have been identified; both species are generally associated with large capacity, swiftly-moving bodies of water. Minckley (1973: 157) states: "The Flannelmouth Sucker is characteristic of larger strongly-flowing streams...," and in reference to *Pantosteus clarki*, Minckley (1973: 169) concludes: "They tend to live more in rapids than in pools, or at least move to swift areas to feed and spawn as large adults, while living in flowing pools during the day." It is possible that the old channel of Salt River Draw provided suitable habitat for such forms. Hydrological analysis of aquatic resources in the Grasshopper area (Chapter 9) indicates that a stream of considerable velocity flowed down the Draw at least part of each year.

Amphibians
Class Amphibia

The scarcity of amphibian remains limits paleoecological interpretation, yet in every case a more mesic environment is indicated than that characterizing the Grasshopper region today. Many of the amphibian taxa are currently associated with Lower Sonoran habitats in the southern part of the state, suggesting a less montane climatic regime may have prevailed during the fourteenth century.

Toads
(Family Bufonidae)

At least three species of *Bufo* are present in the Grasshopper faunal assemblage: the Colorado River Toad (*Bufo alvarius* Girard), Woodhouse's Toad (*Bufo woodhousei* Girard), and the Great Plains Toad (*Bufo cognatus* Say). In addition, the diaphysis of a tibia recovered from a room can be assigned only to the generic level.

The Colorado River Toad is represented by a single complete left tibio-fibula. This large western toad is dependent on permanent water for breeding, although its preferred habitat is in arid regions in southern Arizona where it may estivate for considerable periods of time in rodent burrows (Lowe 1964: 155-156).

Only one of the two elements of Woodhouse's Toad has been definitely determined to the specific level. Like many Southwestern toads, *B. woodhousei* is: "...a riparian species occurring principally along courses of rivers and permanent and semi-permanent streams...and rarely found at any great distance from their channels or floodplains" (Lowe 1964: 156).

There are nine elements of the Great Plains Toad; two other bones possibly of this species could not be precisely classified. This toad is not dependent on permanent supplies of water for reproduction and it is currently found only in the Lower Sonoran deserts and Upper Sonoran grasslands of Arizona. Lowe (1964: 156) states: "While occasionally in low desert ranges, this species is absent from mountainous country." The presence of *B. cognatus* at Grasshopper, located in the Transition Zone at an elevation of 1829 m suggests a less montane environment may have characterized the Grasshopper region during the fourteenth century.

Tree Frogs
(Family Hylidae)

Two adult metapodials have been tentatively classified as *Hyla,* a tree frog, species undetermined. Both species of *Hyla* now known to occur in Arizona (*H. wrightorum* Taylor and *H. arenicolor* Cope) inhabit forested, well-watered areas. However, *H. wrightorum* most commonly resides in coniferous stands, while *H. arenicolor* is usually found in broadleaf deciduous associations. Both kinds of habitat were undoubtedly present prehistorically in the vicinity of the Pueblo, and the common denominator that should be noted is the association between hylids and permanent sources of water.

True Frogs
(Family Ranidae)

The Leopard Frog, *Rana pipiens* Schreber, is the only ranid yet identified at Grasshopper. Although specific classification of the remains has been possible, the species is of limited value as an environmental indicator. Stebbins (1954: 133) states: "This frog has the widest range of any North American amphibian. It is a highly adaptable species, occurring in a great variety of situations from the Lower Sonoran to Lower Boreal Life-Zone. It may be found in either clear or muddy water, in shallow ponds or deep ones, in springs, creeks, or rivers, and in the mountains or low-lands." One of the few factors limiting the distribution of Leopard Frogs is the availability of permanent supplies of water for breeding (Stebbins 1954: 133).

Reptiles
Class Reptilia

A total of 57 reptile elements were identified, representing two orders: Testudinata (turtles) and Squamata (lizards and snakes).

Mud Turtles
(Family Kinosternidae)

The 13 elements of Sonoran Mud Turtle, *Kinosternon sonoriense* Le Conte, include two partially complete carapaces from trash deposits in Rooms 183 and 269. This semiaquatic form is: "a common species in the Arizona Upland desert and in oak woodland" (Lowe 1964: 158), and is nearly always associated with permanent stands of water. It is especially common in the vicinity of the numerous spring and stream-fed ponds in the Grasshopper vicinity, and the identification of an artificially dammed pond immediately north of the Pueblo (Chapter 9) is of special importance in regard to the presence of this reptile in the site's archaeofauna.

Box Turtle
(Family Emydidae)

A single element (an adult left xiphiplastron) was identified as the Western Box Turtle (*Terrapene ornata* Agassiz). Little paleoecological interpretation can be inferred from such a small sample. However, Lowe (1964: 159) reports that at present the Western Box Turtle is common only in the southeastern corner of Arizona in Pima and Cochise counties in Upper Sonoran Grassland associations, and its occurrence at Grasshopper represents a substantial divergence from its currently known geographic range.

Lizards
(Families Iguanidae and Teiidae)

Two families of lizards (Order Squamata, Suborder Sauria) are represented by ten osteological specimens. Of the four genera represented (*Crotaphytus, Sceloporus, Phrynosoma,* and *Cnemidophorus*), only the remains of two (*Sceloporus* cf. *S. magister* Hallowell and *Cnemidophorus* cf. *C. tigris* Baird and Girard) indicate a climatic milieu significantly different from the present.

Both forms are generally associated with Sonoran life zones below 1400 m elevation (Lowe 1964: 165-166) in Arizona; their presence in the Grasshopper archaeofauna may be an indication of a less montane environment. Unfortunately, provenience information for these specimens is lacking, and in the absence of more complete osteological material that would allow a precise specific classification, interpretations based on this small sample are highly speculative.

Snakes
(Family Colubridae)

Four genera (*Thamnophis, Masticophis, Elaphe,* and *Lampropeltis*) of snakes (Suborder Serpentes or Ophidia, 29 elements) have been identified; all are nonpoisonous colubrids. As Vanzolini (1952: 453) has noted: "...many related recent species [of snakes] are indistinguishable on the basis of vertebral characters," hence the majority of these colubrid taxa have been assigned to provisional classifications.

While snakes of the genus *Thamnophis* are commonly sighted at elevations up to about 2750 m, the Coachwhip, *Masticophis flagellum* Shaw, rarely occurs higher than 1375 m elevation (Lowe 1964: 168). The Green Rat Snake (*Elaphe* cf. *E. triaspis* Cope), provisionally identified at Grasshopper on the basis of three elements, is currently found at elevations between 1200 and 1800 m, and is now restricted to Sierra Madrean ranges in southern Arizona (Lowe 1964: 168). The genus *Lampropeltis,* the most frequently identified colubrid in the archaeofauna, is not an accurate environmental indicator due to the relatively broad spectrum (1435-2775 m) of montane habitats it frequents (Lowe 1964: 170).

The colubrid remains provide some evidence of a warmer, less montane climate in the vicinity during Pueblo occupation. A number of the reptilian forms recovered are either semiaquatic or utilize riparian habitats such as may have been present along the old channel of Salt River Draw, providing corroborative evidence for locally abundant supplies of water during the fourteenth century and for the presence of fewer high-altitude environmental features than characterize the region today.

The presence of such genera as *Thamnophis* and *Lampropeltis,* however, indicates habitats that are similar to the modern environment. The fossorial activities of most of these genera, coupled with a lack of accurate provenience data in many cases, means that some of these specimens could have been derived from postoccupational intrusion.

Sample bias and taphonomic factors have undoubtedly affected the size and composition of the microfaunal collection from the Pueblo. Virtually all of the fish and herpetological remains were derived from screened and floated soil samples. The limited use of fine-mesh screens during excavation has resulted in the recovery of only a small percentage of the microfaunal remains from the site. Therefore, the relative abundance of these taxa cannot be utilized to reconstruct paleoenvironmental conditions at the site.

Birds, Class Aves

A number of conditions have resulted in the reduction of the utility of birds as environmental indicators. In addition to their high mobility, the simple presence or absence of particular bird forms in archaeological contexts may be the result of cultural influence, trading contacts, or zoogeographic fluctuation, which itself may result from climatic changes or other factors. These various possibilities are difficult to separate and the avifaunal remains from Grasshopper are of only limited value in the reconstruction of past environmental conditions. A complete taxonomic list of birds identified at Grasshopper Pueblo is presented in Chapter 12; only those that contribute to climatic interpretation are included below.

Herons
(Family Ardeidae)

The order Ciconiiformes is represented by a single genus within the family Ardeidae—?*Butorides virescens* (Linnaeus), the Green Heron. Only a single element was recovered from Room 22 and no definitive conclusions may be drawn, but the Green Heron is presently an uncommon inhabitant of stream areas south and west of the Mogollon Rim (Monson and Phillips 1964: 183). As these birds are largely dependent on aquatic fauna for subsistence, their remains corroborate data from other sources indicating the presence of increased stream habitat in the Grasshopper vicinity 650 years ago.

Ducks and Geese
(Family Anatidae)

Four genera (*Branta, Anser, Chen,* and *Anas*) within the family of swans, geese, and ducks (Order Anseriformes) have been identified. They are all reliable indicators of water such as ponds and lakes, although the ducks (genus *Anas*) are seasonal visitors in Arizona, principally in the late fall and winter (Monson and Phillips 1964: 186).

The peculiar pattern of element representation within the genus *Anas* at Grasshopper (mostly wings) may indicate these birds were important enough for ceremonial purposes that long-distance travel for their procurement was justified (Chapter 12). However, the prehistoric dammed pond north of the Pueblo would also have provided ideal habitat for these forms during the period of occupation.

Quail
(Family Phasianidae)

The presence of Gambel's Quail, *Lophortyx gambelii* Gambel, is of interest because this form is presently associated with Lower Sonoran communities in the southern half of Arizona. Gambel's Quail (Order Galliformes) is one of several southern or Mexican faunal components in the Grasshopper vertebrate assemblage, and as such it may be an indication of the extension of typically lowland habitat types into east-central Arizona during the fourteenth century.

Owls
(Family Strigidae)

Of the six positively identified species of typical owls (Order Strigiformes), only the Spotted Owl, *Strix occi-*dentalis (Xantus), is of interest in the reconstruction of past ecology.

Monson and Phillips (1964: 202) list the Spotted Owl as an: "uncommon resident of the heavily forested mountains and high mesas" in Arizona. Although the forest component in an environmental mosaic surrounding the prehistoric community might easily have supported a *Strix* population, the relative scarcity of their remains in the archaeological context (two elements) may indicate such forest habitats were not extensive during this period.

Thrashers
(Family Mimidae)

On the basis of two elements the thrasher was identified as *Toxostoma,* species undetermined. Most thrashers of the genus *Toxostoma* (Order Passeriformes) are usually associated with the lower elevations in habitats characterized by Lower to Upper Sonoran vegetation types; five species are currently found in Arizona. This bird may indicate the prevalence of less montane ecological elements.

Cardinals
(Family Fringillidae)

The cardinal, *Cardinalis* (=*Richmondena*) *cardinalis* (Linnaeus), has been identified on the basis of three elements; this bird now is usually restricted to southern Arizona. Winter records, however, place it as far north as Prescott and the Mogollon Plateau north of Grasshopper (Monson and Phillips 1964: 236). Therefore, while the presence of this bird in the archaeofauna may constitute further evidence of the extension of lowland habitat types into the Grasshopper region during the fourteenth century, the possibility also exists that these remains merely represent an occasional wanderer.

Mammals, Class Mammalia

Large mammals are generally not reliable indicators of past environmental conditions due principally to their relative mobility and ability to adapt to various ecological situations. Mammalian microfauna, however, are a valuable source of paleoenvironmental data, particularly because in most archaeological contexts the skewing effect of human procurement on the relative frequencies of different species is greatly reduced. Most microfaunal remains recovered from archaeological sites are assumed to represent indigenous taxa. Employing a combination of morphometric analyses of archaeological material and field work in the Grasshopper region with modern rodent populations, Holbrook (Chapter 11) has formulated an accurate picture of past environmental conditions in the vicinity of the Pueblo. Because Holbrook's research concentrated mainly on the rodent families Heteromyidae and Cricetidae, they are not considered in this chapter.

As with the avian species, only a few of the mammalian forms identified in the faunal assemblage are useful in the reconstruction of past climatic conditions, and only those animals are included here.

Rabbits
(Family Leporidae)

Lagomorphs (7957 specimens) of the genera *Sylvilagus* and *Lepus* constituted one of the two most important components, along with artiodactyls, of the Grasshopper Pueblo subsistence base. Complete series of cranial elements have established the presence of both *Sylvilagus floridanus* (J. A. Allen) (NISP, 452) and *S. audubonii* (Baird) (NISP, 196) in the archaeofauna.

S. audubonii now occurs in a wide range of habitats in the western United States, but it is generally found in open environments rather than closed forest associations (Nelson 1909: 222-225; Ingles 1941).

S. floridanus frequents heavily wooded zones, however, particularly riparian associations, in the western part of its range (Nelson 1909: 161). The predominance of *S. floridanus* remains over those of other species of *Sylvilagus* at Grasshopper has important paleoenvironmental implications. An analysis of the differential representation of skeletal elements of these taxa suggests many of the occurrences of cottontail rabbits within the Pueblo may be postoccupational. Clusters of adult and juvenile skeletons are apparently the remains of individuals trapped in collapsed portions of the Pueblo.

The remains of *Sylvilagus* indicate a relatively open habitat accompanied by developed riparian communities prevailed in the vicinity of the Pueblo during much of its occupation.

Two jack rabbit elements provisionally assigned to the taxon *Lepus* cf. *L. alleni* Mearns suggest the expansion of lowland climatic regimes into east-central Arizona during the fourteenth century. The Antelope Jack Rabbit is generally considered to be restricted to desert habitats in the south-central portion of the state (Cockrum 1960: 68). *Lepus* remains too large to be classified as *L. californicus* Gray were provisionally assigned to the taxon *Lepus* cf. *L. alleni* Mearns. Unfortunately, the paucity of such *Lepus* remains does not permit definitive identification or conclusions about their paleoecological significance.

Squirrels
(Family Sciuridae)

Numerous remains of Abert's Squirrel (Order Rodentia), *Sciurus aberti* Woodhouse (NISP, 243), were recovered at the Pueblo. This animal is considered to be a reliable indicator of the presence of coniferous forests (Bailey 1931: 69), so substantial stands of ponderosa pine could have existed in the vicinity in spite of forest reduction resulting from room construction and agricultural practices.

Raccoons
(Family Procyonidae)

Although the range of the raccoon (Order Carnivora), *Procyon lotor pallidus* Merriam, currently extends to within about 30 km of Grasshopper near the southwestern corner of Navajo County (Cockrum 1960: 229), relatively minor climatic differences may account for the presence of 12 elements of *Procyon* occurring in the archaeological context. This animal is almost invariably associated with developed riparian habitats (Cockrum 1964: 257), a fact that corroborates evidence gathered from other sources suggesting a more mesic prehistoric climate.

Skunks
(Family Mustelidae)

The Hooded Skunk, *Mephitis macroura* (Lichtenstein) and Hog-nosed Skunk, *Conepatus mesoleucus* Lichtenstein, are not well represented (NISP, 6). Both genera are presently restricted to the southeastern quarter of Arizona (Cockrum 1960: 240-241), and their habitats vary significantly. *M. macroura* (Lichtenstein) frequents riparian associations along rocky ledges, while *C. mesoleucus* Lichtenstein generally prefers partly wooded and brushy areas (Burt and Grossenheider 1952: 70, 73). According to a 1972 study by Thomas Mathews and Jerry Greene, the presence of these taxa in the Grasshopper sequence separated by a substantial temporal hiatus may indicate a climatological transition in the area from relatively xeric to relatively mesic throughout the span of occupation. Alternatively, an ecological mosaic of the kind suggested by other faunal remains from the site may account for the presence of these genera.

Deer
(Family Cervidae)

While the Mule Deer, *Odocoileus hemionus* (Rafinesque), occurs in relatively diverse habitats (Einarsen 1956), the Coues White-tailed Deer, *Odocoileus virginianus couesi* (Coues and Yarrow), prefers denser underbrush, and often descends from higher elevations to the pinyon-juniper forests at the onset of winter (Seton 1929: 295-312).

The proportional representation of *Odocoileus* remains at Grasshopper (*O. hemionus* NISP, 6441; *O. v. couesi* NISP, 72) suggests the predominance of open country over densely wooded terrain during occupation.

Pronghorn
(Family Antilocapridae)

The Pronghorn, *Antilocapra americana* (Ord), has been identified on the basis of 122 fragments representing at least 21 individuals, suggesting that this ungulate may have been present near the Pueblo. Primarily a steppe-grassland adapted artiodactyl, the Pronghorn is known to occasionally extend its zoogeographic range into the lower pine forests (Einarsen 1948) such as characterize much of the Grasshopper vicinity today. A steppe-grassland niche in the area of the Pueblo due to prehistoric climatic differences may account for the relative abundance of these mammals, although it is possible that a significant proportion of the animals may have been procured at some distance from the Pueblo and brought back by the community's hunters.

The sympatric occurrence of *Antilocapra* with two species of *Odocoileus* during the same time span may indicate the presence of an ecological mosaic characterized by an expanded lowland type environment in the Grasshopper region during the fourteenth century.

TABLE 10.1

Taxa of Vertebrate Remains from Grasshopper Pueblo

Scientific Name	Common Name
OSTEICHTHYES	Bony Fish
Cypriniformes	
Cyprinidae	
Ptychocheilus lucius Girard	Colorado River Squawfish
Catostomidae	
Catostomus latipinnis Baird and Girard	Flannelmouth Sucker
Catostomus species indeterminata	Sucker
Pantosteus cf. *P. clarki* (Baird and Girard)	?Gila Mountain Sucker
Genus et species indeterminata	Sucker
AMPHIBIA	Amphibians
Salientia	
Bufonidae	
Bufo alvarius Girard	Colorado River Toad
Bufo woodhousei Girard	Woodhouse's Toad
Bufo cf. *B. woodhousei* Girard	?Woodhouse's Toad
Bufo cognatus Say	Great Plains Toad
Bufo cf. *B. cognatus* Say	?Great Plains Toad
Bufo species indeterminata	Toad
Hylidae	
?*Hyla* species indeterminata	?Tree Frog
Ranidae	
Rana pipiens Schreber	Leopard Frog
REPTILIA	Reptiles
Testudinata	
Kinosternidae	
Kinosternon sonoriense Le Conte	Sonoran Mud Turtle
?*Kinosternon sonoriense* Le Conte	?Sonoran Mud Turtle
Emydidae	
Terrapene ornata Agassiz	Western Box Turtle
Emydidae/Testudinidae	
Terrapene ornata Agassiz/*Gopherus agassizi* Cooper	Western Box Turtle/Desert Tortoise
Squamata (Suborder Sauria)	
Iguanidae	
Crotaphytus collaris Say	Collared Lizard
Sceloporus cf. *S. undulatus* Latreille	Eastern Fence Lizard
Sceloporus cf. *S. magister* Hallowell	?Desert Spiny Lizard
Phrynosoma species indeterminata	Horned Lizard
Teiidae	
Cnemidophorus cf. *C. velox* Springer	?Plateau Whiptail
Cnemidophorus cf. *C. tigris* Baird and Girard	?Western Whiptail
(Suborder Serpentes or Ophidia)	
Family, genus et species indeterminata	Snake
Colubridae	
Thamnophis cf. *T. elegans* Baird and Girard	?Western Garter Snake
Masticophis flagellum Shaw	Coachwhip
Elaphe cf. *E. triaspis* Cope	?Green Rat Snake
Lampropeltis cf. *L. pyromelana* Cope	?Sonora Mountain Kingsnake
Genus et species indeterminata	Colubrid Snake
AVES	Birds
Ciconiiformes	
Ardeidae	
?*Butorides virescens* (Linnaeus)	?Green Heron
Anseriformes	
Anatidae	
Branta canadensis (Linnaeus)	Canada Goose
Anser albifrons (Scopoli)	White-fronted Goose
Chen caerulescens (Linnaeus)	Snow Goose

TABLE 10.1

(continued)

Scientific Name	Common Name
Anas platyrhynchos Linnaeus	Mallard
Anas acuta Linnaeus	Pintail
Anas species indeterminata	Duck
Falconiformes	
Cathartidae	
Cathartes aura (Linnaeus)	Turkey Vulture
Accipitridae	
Accipiter gentilis (Linnaeus)	Goshawk
Accipiter striatus Vieillot	Sharp-shinned Hawk
Accipiter cooperi (Bonaparte)	Cooper's Hawk
Buteo jamaicensis (Gmelin)	Red-tailed Hawk
Buteo cf. *B. jamaicensis* (Gmelin)	?Red-tailed Hawk
Buteo swainsoni Bonaparte	Swainson's Hawk
Buteo cf. *B. swainsoni* Bonaparte	?Swainson's Hawk
Buteo lagopus (Pontoppidan)	Rough-legged Hawk
Buteo cf. *B. lagopus* (Pontoppidan)	?Rough-legged Hawk
Buteo regalis (Gray)	Ferruginous Hawk
Buteo species indeterminata	Buteonine Hawk
Aquila chrysaetos (Linnaeus)	Golden Eagle
?*Aguila chrysaetos* (Linnaeus)	?Golden Eagle
Falconidae	
Falco mexicanus Schlegel	Prairie Falcon
Falco sparverius Linnaeus	Sparrow Hawk
Galliformes	
Odontophorinae	
Genus et species indeterminata	American Quail
Phasianidae	
Lophortyx gambelii Gambel	Gambel's Quail
Cyrtonyx montezumae (Vigors)	Harlequin Quail
Meleagrididae	
?Meleagrididae	?Turkey
Meleagris gallopavo (Linnaeus)	Turkey
?*Meleagris gallopavo* (Linnaeus)	?Turkey
Gruiformes	
Gruidae	
Grus canadensis (Linnaeus)	Sandhill Crane
Charadriiformes	
Charadriidae	
Genus et species indeterminata	Plover, Turnstone, or Surfbird
Scolopacidae	
?*Limnodromus scolopaceus* (Say)	?Long-billed Dowitcher
Columbiformes	
Columbidae	
Columba fasciata Say	Band-tailed Pigeon
Columba cf. *C. fasciata* Say	?Band-tailed Pigeon
Zenaida (=Zenaidura) macroura (Goodwin)	Mourning Dove
Genus et species indeterminata	Pigeon or Dove
Psittaciformes	
Psittacidae	
Amazona albifrons (Sparrman)	White-fronted Parrot
Ara macao (Linnaeus)	Scarlet Macaw
Ara species indeterminata	Macaw
Cuculiformes	
Cuculidae	
Geococcyx californianus (Lesson)	Roadrunner
Strigiformes	
Tytonidae	
Tyto alba (Scopoli)	Barn Owl

TABLE 10.1

(continued)

Scientific Name	Common Name
Strigidae	
Otus asio (Linnaeus)	Common Screech Owl
?*Otus flammeolus* (Kaup)	?Flammulated Owl
Bubo virginianus (Gmelin)	Great Horned Owl
Glaucidium gnoma Wagler	Mountain Pygmy Owl
Speotyto cunnicularia (Molina)	Burrowing Owl
?*Speotyto cunnicularia* (Molina)	?Burrowing Owl
Strix occidentalis (Xantus)	Spotted Owl
Asio otus (Linnaeus)	Long-eared Owl
?*Asio otus* (Linnaeus)	?Long-eared Owl
Genus et species indeterminata	Typical Owl
Piciformes	
Picidae	
Colaptes auratus (Linnaeus)	Yellow-shafted Flicker
Melanerpes formicivorus (Swainson)	Acorn Woodpecker
?*Sphyrapicus thyroideus* (Cassin)	?Williamson's Sapsucker
Passeriformes	
Corvidae	
Cyanocitta stelleri (Gmelin)	Steller's Jay
Aphelocoma coerulescens (Bosc)	Scrub Jay
?*Aphelocoma coerulescens* (Bosc)	?Scrub Jay
Pica pica (Linnaeus)	Black-billed Magpie
Corvus corax Linnaeus	Common Raven
Corvus cf. *C. corax* Linnaeus	?Common Raven
Corvus brachyrhynchos Brehm	Common Crow
Gymnorhinus cyanocephalus Wied	Pinyon Jay
Nucifraga columbiana (Wilson)	Clark's Nutcracker
Troglodytidae	
Catherpes mexicanus (Swainson)	Canyon Wren
Mimidae	
Mimus polyglottus (Linnaeus)	Mockingbird
Toxostoma species indeterminata	Thrasher
Turdidae	
Sialia mexicana Swainson	Western Bluebird
Laniidae	
Lanius ludovicianus Linnaeus	Loggerhead Shrike
Icteridae	
Sturnella species indeterminata	Meadowlark
Xanthocephalus xanthocephalus (Bonaparte)	Yellow-headed Blackbird
?*Xanthocephalus xanthocephalus* (Bonaparte)	?Yellow-headed Blackbird
Euphagus cyanocephalus (Wagler)	Brewer's Blackbird
Genus et species indeterminata	Meadowlark, Blackbird, or Oriole
Fringillidae	
Cardinalis cardinalis (Linnaeus)	Cardinal
Passerina cf. *P. amoena* (Say)	?Lazuli Bunting
Passerculus sandwichensis (Gmelin)	Savannah Sparrow
Amphispiza species indeterminata	Black-throated Sparrow
Junco species indeterminata	Junco
Genus et species indeterminata	Grosbeak, Finch, Sparrow, or Bunting
Indeterminate Birds	
Buteo spp. size; taxon indeterminata	
Corvus corax size; taxon indeterminata	
Indeterminate size; taxon indeterminata	
MAMMALIA	Mammals
Lagomorpha	
Leporidae	
Sylvilagus floridanus (J. A. Allen)	Eastern Cottontail
Sylvilagus cf. *S. floridanus* (J. A. Allen)	?Eastern Cottontail

TABLE 10.1

(continued)

Scientific Name	Common Name
Sylvilagus audubonii (Baird)	Desert Cottontail
Sylvilagus cf. *S. audubonii* (Baird)	?Desert Cottontail
Sylvilagus species indeterminata	Cottontail
Lepus californicus Gray	Black-tailed Jack Rabbit
Lepus cf. *L. californicus* Gray	?Black-tailed Jack Rabbit
Lepus cf. *L. alleni* Mearns	?Antelope Jack Rabbit
Genus et species indeterminata	Rabbit or Hare
Rodentia	
Sciuridae	
Eutamias cf. *E. dorsalis* (Baird)	?Cliff Chipmunk
Eutamias species indeterminata	Chipmunk
Spermophilus (=Citellus) variegatus (Say)	Rock Squirrel
Spermophilus (=Citellus) species indeterminata	Rock Squirrel
Cynomys species indeterminata	Prairie Dog
Sciurus aberti Woodhouse	Abert's Squirrel
Sciurus cf. *S. aberti* Woodhouse	?Abert's Squirrel
Genus et species indeterminata	Squirrel or Prairie Dog
Geomyidae	
Thomomys bottae (Eydoux and Gervais)	Valley Pocket Gopher
Thomomys species indeterminata	Smooth-toothed Pocket Gopher
Heteromyidae	
?*Dipodomys ordii* Woodhouse	?Ord's Kangaroo Rat
Dipodomys species indeterminata	Kangaroo Rat
Cricetidae	
Reithrodontomys megalotis (Baird)	Western Harvest Mouse
Reithrodontomys cf. *R. megalotis* (Baird)	?Western Harvest Mouse
Peromyscus eremicus (Baird)	Cactus Mouse
Peromyscus cf. *P. eremicus* (Baird)	?Cactus Mouse
Peromyscus maniculatus (Wagner)	Deer Mouse
Peromyscus cf. *P. maniculatus* (Wagner)	?Deer Mouse
Peromyscus leucopus (Rafinesque)	White-footed Mouse
Peromyscus cf. *P. leucopus* (Rafinesque)	?White-footed Mouse
Peromyscus boylii (Baird)	Brush Mouse
Peromyscus cf. *P. boylii* (Baird)	?Brush Mouse
Peromyscus truei (Shufeldt)	Pinyon Mouse
Peromyscus species indeterminata	White-footed Mouse
Onychomys leucogaster (Wied-Neuwied)	Northern Grasshopper Mouse
Onychomys species indeterminata	Grasshopper Mouse
Sigmodon cf. *S. minimus* Mearns	?Least Cotton Rat
Sigmodon species indeterminata	Cotton Rat
Neotoma albigula Hartley	White-throated Wood Rat
Neotoma cf. *N. albigula* Hartley	?White-throated Wood Rat
Neotoma stephensi Goldman	Stephens' Wood Rat
Neotoma mexicana Baird	Mexican Wood Rat
Neotoma species indeterminata	Wood Rat
Microtus mexicanus (Saussure)	Mexican Vole
Microtus cf. *M. mexicanus* (Saussure)	?Mexican Vole
Microtus species indeterminata	Meadow Vole
Genus et species indeterminata	Indeterminate Cricetid Rodent
Carnivora	
Canidae	
Canis familiaris (Linnaeus)	Domestic Dog
Canis cf. *C. familiaris* (Linnaeus)	?Domestic Dog
Canis lupus Frisch	Grey Wolf
Canis latrans Say	Coyote
Canis cf. *C. latrans* Say	?Coyote
Canis species indeterminata	Domestic Dog/Wolf/Coyote
?*Canis* species indeterminata	?Domestic Dog/Wolf/Coyote
Urocyon cinereoargenteus (Schreber)	Grey Fox
Ursidae	
Ursus (=Euarctos) americanus (Pallas)	Black Bear
Ursus horribilis Ord	Grizzly Bear
Ursus cf. *U. horribilis* Ord	?Grizzly Bear

TABLE 10.1

(continued)

Scientific Name	Common Name
Procyonidae	
Bassariscus astutus (Lichtenstein)	Ringtail
Procyon lotor (Linnaeus)	Raccoon
Mustelidae	
?Mustelidae	?Mustelid carnivore
Mustela frenata Lichtenstein	Long-tailed Weasel
Mustela cf. *M. frenata* Lichtenstein	?Long-tailed Weasel
Taxidea taxus (Schreber)	Badger
Spilogale gracilis Merriam	Western Spotted Skunk
Mephitis mephitis (Schreber)	Striped Skunk
Mephitis macroura (Lichtenstein)	Hooded Skunk
Mephitis cf. *M. macroura* (Lichtenstein)	?Hooded Skunk
Mephitis species indeterminata	Striped or Hooded Skunk
?*Mephitis* species indeterminata	?Striped or Hooded Skunk
Conepatus mesoleucus Lichtenstein	Hog-nosed Skunk
Felidae	
Felis cf. *F. onca* Linnaeus	?Jaguar
Felis concolor Linnaeus	Mountain Lion or Puma
Felis species indeterminata	Jaguar/Mountain Lion
Lynx rufus (Schreber)	Bobcat
Family, genus et species indeterminata	Indeterminate Carnivore
Perissodactyla	
Equidae	
Equus species indeterminata	Horse or Mule
Artiodactyla	
Cervidae	
Odocoileus (=Dama) hemionus (Rafinesque)	Mule Deer
Odocoileus cf. *O. hemionus* (Rafinesque)	?Mule Deer
Odocoileus virginianus couesi (Coues and Yarrow)	Coues' White-tailed Deer
Odocoileus cf. *O. v. couesi* (Coues and Yarrow)	?Coues' White-tailed Deer
Odocoileus species indeterminata	Mule or White-tailed Deer
Genus et species indeterminata	Cervid
Antilocapridae	
Antilocapra americana (Ord)	Pronghorn
?*Antilocapra americana* (Ord)	?Pronghorn
Bovidae	
Ovis canadensis Shaw	Bighorn or Mountain Sheep
?*Ovis canadensis* Shaw	?Bighorn or Mountain Sheep
Bos taurus (Linnaeus)	Domestic Cattle
Bovidae/Antilocapridae	
Ovis canadensis Shaw/*Antilocapra americana* (Ord)	Bighorn or Pronghorn
Family, genus et species indeterminata	Indeterminate Artiodactyl
Indeterminate Mammals	
Odocoileus size	Deer size Mammal
Canis to *Odocoileus* size	Dog to Deer size Mammal
Canis size	Dog size Mammal
Sylvilagus to *Canis* size	Cottontail to Dog size Mammal
Sylvilagus size	Cottontail size Mammal
Peromyscus to *Sylvilagus* size	Mouse to Cottontail size Mammal
Indeterminate size	Indeterminate size Mammal

11. PREHISTORIC ENVIRONMENTAL RECONSTRUCTION BY MAMMALIAN MICROFAUNAL ANALYSIS, GRASSHOPPER PUEBLO

Sally J. Holbrook

The aim of this study was to reconstruct the prehistoric environment of Grasshopper Pueblo, east-central Arizona, by analysis of mammalian microfaunal remains. Elucidation of the details of the paleoecology of the area is of particular interest because several kinds of data indicate that the climate is different now than at the time of occupation in the fourteenth century (Chapter 8; Thompson and Longacre 1966; Longacre and Reid 1974; Olsen and Olsen 1970).

Mice, because of their small size (10-40 grams) and largely nocturnal habits, were probably not an important food source for the prehistoric people of Grasshopper. Rather, these small mammals were living in and around the Pueblo, especially in storage rooms and trash heaps, during and after its occupation. At death some of them were buried and subsequently preserved by sediments filling the ruin. Because many species of mice are known to be restricted to characteristic habitats, the presence of some of these ecologically informative species in the microfaunal collections from Grasshopper enables inferences about the prehistoric habitats surrounding the site.

Once microfaunal material is identified to the species level and ecological data about the extant mouse community in the vicinity of the site are gathered, comparisons between the extant and prehistoric faunas can be made. Both the taxonomic composition of the faunas and the relative abundances of the animals in them are of potential interest. However, because of the vagaries of the processes of death, deposition, and preservation, relative abundances of fossil and extant communities are difficult to evaluate and compare directly. Therefore, this study concentrated mainly on differences in species compositions of the faunas. Because mice living in habitats in the direct vicinity of a site are included in an archaeological fauna, differences between species compositions of prehistoric and modern microfaunas may be the result of real differences in the past and present environments—and therefore the mouse communities—in the area. Other factors such as sampling effects or introduction of bone material into the Pueblo by the activities of its human occupants or of animals (carnivores, predatory birds) may also be operative. It is necessary to determine which of these are important before accurate paleoecological interpretations of archaeological microfaunas are possible. Taxa present in the extant fauna yet missing from the archaeological fauna can often be attributed to sampling errors. The animals in question may not have been recovered during the course of the excavations or they may have been present prehistorically but simply not included in or successfully preserved by the sedimentation processes at the site. Conversely, mice represented in the prehistoric fauna but seemingly absent from the present fauna may actually be living in the area but perhaps they are rare or extremely secretive, thus escaping detection by the field biologist.

Comparisons between present and prehistoric microfaunas at Grasshopper enabled reconstruction of the prehistoric environment in the area. Combined with the analysis and interpretation of other data such as the results of dendroecological, faunal, and pollen analyses, it was possible to estimate the magnitude of the temporal differences in the environment and to postulate the relative importance of climatic versus human-induced variables in the process of environmental change.

METHODS

The location of Grasshopper Pueblo (see Fig. 1.1) and the nature of the surrounding terrain and vegetation have been described in Chapters 1 and 2. The most common nocturnal rodents now living in the area are brush mouse, *Peromyscus boylii* (Allen); deer mouse, *Peromyscus maniculatus* (Merriam); and Stephen's wood rat, *Neotoma stephensi* (Goldman). These species occur commonly at higher elevations on the Colorado Plateau (Cockrum 1960). *P. maniculatus* is the most widespread, occupying many habitats including ponderosa pine and mixed coniferous forests and sagebrush (*Artemisia*)-grass associations (Bailey 1931; Findley and others 1975). *P. boylii* inhabits shrublands and pinyon-juniper woodland (Holbrook 1975; Harris 1963), and *N. stephensi* is associated with pinyon-juniper woodland (Harris 1963). Several other species are present in the vicinity of Grasshopper, including Ord's kangaroo rat, *Dipodomys ordii* (Merriam); Mexican vole, *Microtus mexicanus* (Mearns); and western harvest mouse, *Reithrodontomys megalotis* (Baird).

Identification of Archaeological Microfauna

Taxonomic efforts focused on the identification of archaeological mouse mandibles to species level because they are more abundant and often better preserved than postcranial skeletal elements. In addition, mandibles are more readily identifiable to lower taxa than most other bones. The Grasshopper microfaunal collection is dominated by species of *Peromyscus* (white-footed mice), a genus with eight species occurring in a large range of habitats in the Southwest. Thus species level identifications of these specimens were critical for paleoenvironmental reconstruction.

Subtle interspecific morphological differences preclude reliable identification to species level of isolated *Peromyscus* mandibles by comparison to reference specimens from museum collections. Archaeological specimens of *Peromyscus* present even greater taxonomic difficulties because they frequently are fragmentary and lack teeth. Even complete mandibles with relatively unworn teeth pose difficulties; Hooper (1957) showed considerable intraspecific variation and interspecific similarities in molar structure of *Peromyscus* species. Morphometric statistical analyses have been of some use in the identification of mammalian microfauna; Kennerly (1956) used univariate analyses to identify fossil *Perognathus* (pocket mice) from Florida, and Tamsitt (1957) employed them in the identification of several species of Pleistocene *Peromyscus* from Friesenhahn Cave, Texas. In addition, Martin (1968) used bivariate comparisons of mandibular measurements to identify five species of *Peromyscus* in the Friesenhahn Cave fauna. The proper use of multivariate statistical procedures, however, whereby many characters are evaluated simultaneously, greatly increases the potential information available from a morphometric analysis. These techniques provide the most potent approach to archaeological microfaunal taxonomy, and discriminant function and canonical variates analyses greatly aid reliable species-level identification of mandibles. In these analyses, a series of measurements taken on each unclassified specimen is compared to measurements taken on groups of modern specimens of known identity. The archaeological specimen is placed in the cluster (that is, the modern species) it most closely resembles statistically. These analyses assume that the mandibular morphology of each species has not changed appreciably in the past several hundred years and that the reference populations include all species that could possibly have lived prehistorically in the study area. Multivariate morphometrics have seen increasingly frequent use during the past decade and are widely reported in the literature (Blackith and Reyment 1971 and Gould and Johnston 1972 have extensive bibliographies).

Each archaeological specimen was identified to the genus level by inspection; subsequent multivariate analyses allowed species-level identifications. The reference species and sample sizes used for each genus were: *Peromyscus maniculatus* (32), *Peromyscus boylii* (37), *Peromyscus difficilis* (27), *Peromyscus truei* (24), *Peromyscus leucopus* (37), *Peromyscus crinitus* (15), *Peromyscus eremicus* (18), *Reithrodontomys megalotis* (12), *Reithrodontomys montanus* (11), *Microtus mexicanus* (12), *Microtus montanus* (9), *Microtus pennsylvanicus* (9), and *Microtus longicaudus* (13). Although many of these species do not currently occupy east-central Arizona, the possibility that some of these might have occurred in the Grasshopper area in the past was considered. The

reference specimens were adult animals trapped in various locations in New Mexico and Arizona and were from the collections of the Museum of Vertebrate Zoology (University of California, Berkeley), the Museum of Southwestern Biology (University of New Mexico), and the Department of Ecology and Evolutionary Biology (University of Arizona). The reference clusters presumably incorporated a reasonable amount of morphological variation, because adults of various ages and from a variety of local habitats composed the samples.

Up to 17 measurements (Holbrook 1975) were made on each mandible with an EPOI Measuring Shopscope. Each measurement was made to the thousandths of a millimeter and rounded off to hundredths of a millimeter for the statistical analyses. Broken mandibles had missing measurements. Missing data routines were not employed in the computer analyses; only those measurements actually taken on each archaeological specimen were used. Most mandibles with 9 to 17 measurements were readily identifiable.

Ecological Studies

The study of the extant nocturnal rodent fauna in the vicinity of Grasshopper entailed documenting what species occur there currently and what local habitats each occupies. This information was necessary to any interpretations of the significance of species in the prehistoric (archaeological) rodent fauna. The ecological investigation consisted of two approaches. First, during 1975 and 1978 a series of rodents were collected from various habitats in the area, including ponderosa pine forest, manzanita-oak shrubland, juniper-oak shrubland, pinyon-juniper woodland, and grassland. Elevation of the sampling sites ranged from 1575 m to 1880 m. The skin and skeleton of each trapped animal were saved; these enabled positive identification of each specimen. The collecting effort probably produced evidence of the occurrence of most if not all of the small rodent species that actually inhabit the Grasshopper area at the present time. There is some chance that certain rare species escaped detection.

Second, three local habitats within 2 km of the Grasshopper ruin underwent detailed ecological study. In each of these habitats, two 1.5 ha study sites were established. Live trapping (mark and recapture) studies of the rodents on each site revealed the details of vegetational use by the resident species. Each area had 100 trap stations arranged in a 10-by-10 m grid with 12 m intervals. Sherman live traps baited with rolled oats and set in the evening were used to capture rodents. The animals were examined, marked with a numbered stainless steel ear tag, and released the following morning. During the summers of 1975, 1976, and 1977 each grid was trapped two or three consecutive nights each week. The vegetation on each grid was mapped in detail, including the estimated size and diameter of each woody plant. Thus, rodent captures could be examined with respect to the frequency of occurrence of certain plant species and also the total density and three dimensional structure of the vegetation. In addition, on each grid 40 "arboreal" trap stations were established by permanently affixing a horizontal wooden platform on a log or in a bush or tree. At these stations, the trap was always set in the above-ground position; no trap was set on the ground. The other 60 stations on each grid were "ground" stations. Arboreal stations were distributed randomly over each grid; more heavily vegetated portions of the grids did not necessarily contain more arboreal trap stations. Captures of rodents at the arboreal trap stations enabled a delineation of the amount and nature (if any) of arboreal activity of each rodent species. For each grid, the total season captures for each individual animal and each species were analyzed in conjunction with vegetation use, arboreal activity, and spatial distribution with respect to other individuals and other species.

During the 1976 and 1977 field seasons, several ecological experiments helped to reveal the existence of possible competitive interactions and habitat selection among the three most common nocturnal species in the area— *Peromyscus maniculatus, Peromyscus boylii*, and *Neotoma stephensi*. These experiments included the removal (by live trapping) of one or two resident species on a grid and documentation of any changes in spatial occurrence, population density, or habitat use by the species remaining on the plot. Presumably, if a competing species were removed from an area, the remaining species might compensate by expanding or altering their patterns of resource utilization. Since the relationship between vegetation and rodent species was of primary concern in this study, these aspects were monitored during the removal experiments. Several different removals provided data about competitive interactions and how these influence rodent species use of the vegetational resources in several local habitat types. In a pinyon-juniper woodland and manzanita-oak shrubland, *N. stephensi* was removed and the effects on *P. boylii* monitored. In a juniper-oak shrubland and grassland, *P. boylii* was removed; *P. maniculatus* and *N. stephensi* remained. Subsequently both *P. boylii* and *N. stephensi* were removed and the effects on *P. maniculatus* documented. For each experiment, one grid was experimental and the other member of the grid pair (in the same vegetation type) was left as an undisturbed control. Both grids were trapped on the same nights. In addition, the experimental grids had all been trapped during the 1975 field season, prior to the beginning of any population manipulations.

The second ecological experiment involved the delineation of habitat selection by the three rodent species. The habitat on one half of a study plot in manzanita-oak shrubland was altered midway during the 1976 field season, and the rodent species response monitored. During a one-week period, the crowns of all woody plants on the treatment plot were cut at ground level and removed from the area. The root systems of the plants remained intact; there was a minimum of disturbance to the substrate. A second grid in manzanita-oak shrubland served as a control. It was expected that *P. boylii* and *N. stephensi*, species that always occur in shrubland and woodland habitats with a high amount of three-dimensional habitat structure and that never occur in open (grassland) habitats, would react to the newly opened area by avoiding it. By contrast, *P. maniculatus*, a common inhabitant of open habitats, might prefer the opened patch. Trapping of the cleared area during the second half of the 1976 field season documented the response of individual marked animals to the opened space. Continued trapping of the grid during 1977 delineated the longer term response of the rodent populations to the cleared area. In some ways the reaction of the rodent species to this habitat disturbance might be comparable to their response to the prehistoric clearing of plots for agriculture.

RESULTS

Ecological Relationships of the Extant Rodents near Grasshopper

Both the snap trapping and live trapping revealed that four species of mice and two species of rats occur at present in the vicinity of Grasshopper, including *Peromyscus maniculatus, P. boylii, Reithrodontomys megalotis, Microtus mexicanus, Neotoma stephensi*, and *Dipodomys ordii*. There were 247 snap trapped animals: *P. boylii*, 165; *P. maniculatus*, 59; *R. megalotis*, 11; *D. ordii*, 1; and *N. stephensi*, 11. Total captures of these species during 1975 to 1977 on the live-trapping grids were: *P. maniculatus*, 236; *P. boylii*, 1467; *R. megalotis*, 58; *M. mexicanus*, 5; *N. stephensi*, 468; and *D. ordii*, 176. During the past three years, *P. boylii* has been by far the most common mouse in the vicinity of Grasshopper. It occurs in a wide variety of woodland and shrub habitats, including pinyon-juniper woodland, manzanita, oak, and juniper shrublands, and ponderosa pine forests. Grass-covered valley bottoms are the only local habitats in which *P. boylii* does not occur. Throughout most of its range in the Southwest, *P. boylii* is usually closely associated with oak or chaparral habitats. Perhaps the absence at Grasshopper of *Peromyscus truei*, a common inhabitant of Southwestern pinyon and juniper woodlands, enables *P. boylii* to occur in those vegetation types near Grasshopper as well. *P. maniculatus* is ubiquitous throughout most of the Southwest. Near Grasshopper, it is most abundant in grassland and sparse shrubland habitats; it is less common in the more thickly vegetated habitats. It has been considered to be competitively excluded from woodland and shrubland habitats by other *Peromyscus* species, being left to exploit the more sparsely vegetated, less preferred local habitats (Findley and others 1975). Both *M. mexicanus* and *R. megalotis* were captured less frequently than the two *Peromyscus* species. Typically, *M. mexicanus* occupies grassy areas in ponderosa pine forest, although it occasionally occurs in pinyon-juniper woodlands. The few captures of this species in the vicinity of Grasshopper occurred in grass areas in manzanita-oak shrubland. Since *Microtus* construct runways in grass, it is usually easy to tell if they are present in an area. I never found runways near Grasshopper, even in apparently suitable habitat, but at higher elevations (2120 m) about 9 km away, there was abundant evidence of *Microtus* near small ponds and other sources of permanent moisture. The species thus seems to be an uncommon member of the extant mouse fauna near Grasshopper.

TABLE 11.1

Vegetational Affinities of Three Rodent Species in Different Habitat Types of the Grasshopper Region
(M = manzanita; O = oak; J = juniper; P = pinyon)

	Most common vegetation	Rodent species		
		P. boylii	*P. maniculatus*	*N. stephensi*
Grid 1	M; MO; manzanita with other taxa	M; manzanita with other taxa	absent	PJ
Grid 2	M; MO; manzanita with other taxa	M	absent	PJ
Grid 3	M; MO; oak with other taxa	M; MO	M; O (-)	M; O (-)
Grid 3c	MO; oak with other taxa	M	O (-)	M; juniper with other taxa; O (-)
Grid 4	J; JO	JO; O	J; O (-)	P; juniper with other taxa; O; J (-)
Grid 4c	J; JO	O	J; G; O (-)	P; J; O

Note: (-) indicates negative association of species and vegetational type; all others are positive associations.

TABLE 11.2

General Characteristics of Above-ground Activity of Three Rodent Species in the Grasshopper Region

	Rodent species (weight)		
Characteristics	*P. boylii* (20 grams)	*P. maniculatus* (20 grams)	*N. stephensi* (200 grams)
Proportion of time spent on above-ground resources	high	low	high
Plant taxa climbed in—preference	none	none (?)	none
Shape of objects climbed	variety of shapes	logs, small shrubs	logs most important, uses spreading shrubs
Platform height above ground	uses a range of platform heights	no preference (?)	tends to use low and medium platforms
Height of object climbed	variety of heights, varies from habitat to habitat	preference for low objects (?)	some preference for low and medium objects
Is amount of arboreal activity related to habitat type?	no	?	no

R. megalotis occurred in shrubland habitats, especially those dominated by manzanita and oak. I never trapped it in pinyon-juniper woodland or ponderosa pine forest. This species might actually be more abundant near Grasshopper than its relatively few trapping records indicate. Its small size and apparently secretive habits make it a difficult animal to catch.

As is typical of the species, *N. stephensi* was caught in pinyon-juniper woodlands or stands of young juniper and oak. It did not occur in open habitats such as grassland, or in ponderosa pine forest. *Dipodomys ordii* lived only in areas of loose soil sparsely vegetated with either grass or shrubs.

Live trapping revealed the details of vegetational use, particularly arboreal activity, by *P. maniculatus, P. boylii,* and *N. stephensi.* Tables 11.1 and 11.2 summarize vegetational utilization and arboreality, which are fully described in Holbrook (1979a, b). *P. boylii* and *N. stephensi* spend about half their time climbing in foliage and on logs. By contrast, *P. maniculatus* is almost exclusively terrestrial. Removal of *P. boylii* from a habitat in which the three species were sympatric (juniper-oak shrubland and grassland) resulted in a slight increase in the population density of *P. maniculatus,* an increase in its activity on the plot, and an expansion in the range of vegetational resources it used, including some previously utilized by *P. boylii.* This increased activity and expansion in resource use occurred within the area of the grid that had been exclusively occupied by *P. boylii* and *N. stephensi. N. stephensi* also responded to the removal of *P. boylii.* It

TABLE 11.3

Stratigraphic Occurrence of Mammalian Microfauna from Grasshopper Pueblo

Species	Floors	Fill between first story floors	Roofs	Fill	Subfloors	Pre-room occupation surfaces	Unknown	Total
Peromyscus eremicus	26	19	2	43	14	0	5	109
Peromyscus maniculatus	32	33	0	29	9	3	10	116
Peromyscus truei	12	3	0	5	0	0	0	20
Peromyscus boylii	3	2	0	4	0	0	0	9
Peromyscus leucopus	22	18	1	13	2	1	3	60
Reithrodontomys megalotis	4	2	0	7	1	0	0	14
Microtus mexicanus	0	0	0	1	1	1	0	3
Onychomys leucogaster	0	0	0	2	0	0	0	2
Peromyscus sp.	4	5	0	12	1	0	0	22
Total	103	82	3	116	28	5	18	355

was caught in vegetation previously used by *P. boylii,* and it climbed in the highest vegetational strata that *P. boylii* had previously monopolized. When both *P. boylii* and *N. stephensi* were removed from the plot, *P. maniculatus* increased the range of its resource use even further, and it displayed increased arboreal activity. By contrast, in a pinyon-juniper woodland and manzanita-oak shrubland where only *P. boylii* and *N. stephensi* occurred, the removal of *N. stephensi* had almost no effect on the population density, spatial occurrence, arboreal activity, or vegetational utilization of *P. boylii.*

These experiments suggest that the three species have evolved preferences for certain habitat types. Competitive interactions temper these preferences and help account for the observed patterns of habitat use. The results of the habitat alteration experiment further support this idea; *P. boylii* and *N. stephensi* would not occupy the opened habitat, just as they will not use naturally-occurring open habitats such as grassland. Even in the absence of potentially competing species, each of the three species selects only certain gross kinds of habitats to occupy. Competitive interactions then help to determine the details of vegetational use within each habitat.

Archaeological Microfauna

Taxonomic efforts were mainly concerned with the smallest rodents (mice). Larger species, such as wood rats (*Neotoma*) and kangaroo rats (*Dipodomys*), although potentially good environmental indicators, are not included in the analyses. Rats might have been a food source for the prehistoric human occupants of Grasshopper and the rat remains in the archaeological fauna could result from human predation rather than reflect local paleoenvironmental conditions. Of the 355 mandibles identified, 333 were classified to the species level. Eight species

occurred in the prehistoric fauna: three were common—*P. maniculatus* (116), *P. eremicus* (109), and *P. leucopus,* (60)—and five were rare—*P. boylii* (9), *P. truei* (20), *Reithrodontomys megalotis* (14), *Onychomys leucogaster* (2), and *Microtus mexicanus* (3). Most of the microfauna was recovered from room occupation levels, primarily floors (103), subfloors (28), roofs (3), fill between first story floors (82), fill between roof and floor (116), pre-room-occupation surfaces (50), and unknown proveniences within rooms (18). The frequencies of occurrence of each rodent species in depositional units are given in Table 11.3. The five rodent species that have sample sizes greater than nine did not have significantly different occurrences in the strata ($X^2 = 23.82$, NS), suggesting that similar processes affect the deposition of the different rodent species. A few specimens were recovered from room overburden near the present ground surface; these may reflect postoccupational burrowing and are not considered here. Specimens obtained from occupation levels are assumed to be roughly contemporaneous with the period of prehistoric room use by humans.

Microfaunal Species Diversity

The microfaunal collections from the rooms in the Pueblo contained one to seven species, and I considered the microfauna from each room separately to see what factors might influence the number of species occurring in a room. A multiple regression analysis ("Stepwise" of Barr and others 1976) of the number of species in each room sample (dependent variable) on the total number of specimens in the room, the room construction phase (1-8), the room abandonment phase (1-4), the size of the room (square meters), and the number of occupation floors (independent variables) revealed that together the number of specimens in the collection and the abandonment phase of the room account for 59

TABLE 11.4

Frequencies of Rodent Species in Each Room Abandonment Class at Grasshopper Pueblo

Species	Room abandonment classes			
	Floors of early abandoned rooms (Rooms 41, 47, 146, 16, 23, 164, 270, 274)	Trash above floors of early abandoned rooms; floors of probably early abandoned rooms (Rooms 18, 24, 40, 41, 195, 187)	Floors of probably late abandoned rooms (Rooms 22, 35, 69)	Late abandoned rooms, fill and floors (Rooms 279, 31, 70, 280, 269, 21, 183, 210, 246, 62, 68, 19, 215, Great Kiva)
Peromyscus maniculatus	6	6	5	99
Peromyscus eremicus	9	14	7	79
Peromyscus leucopus	5	5	3	47
Peromyscus truei	1	3	3	13
Peromyscus boylii	0	3	0	6
Peromyscus sp.	0	3	0	19
Reithrodontomys megalotis	0	1	1	12
Onychomys leucogaster	0	0	0	2
Microtus mexicanus	3	0	0	0

percent of the variance in the number of species occurring in each room. Each of these variables is positively associated with the number of species occurring in each room. That room collections with larger sample sizes tend to contain more species than those with smaller sample sizes is not surprising; it is an artifact of the sampling process. Late abandoned rooms have more species in their faunas than early abandoned rooms, but sample sizes are also smaller for early abandoned rooms. Construction phase, room size, and the number of occupation floors did not contribute significantly to the explained variance in the regression model. I also tried to delineate other relationships between the architecture of the room and the number of species in the samples. There was no apparent influence of room block on the total number of species. Six species occurred in the rooms of Room Block 1 (n = 30); Room Blocks 2 and 3 had 7 species (n = 106 and n = 209 respectively; 10 specimens came from other room blocks).

Four of the eight mouse species identified in the prehistoric fauna occur at present at Grasshopper. No room collection contained all eight species; only two rooms had six or more. Of the 30 room faunas, 20 had 3 or fewer species.

Microfaunal Species Composition

Table 11.4 shows the species composition for rooms (and strata) in four abandonment classes: floors of early abandoned rooms; trash above floors of early abandoned rooms and floors of probably early abandoned rooms; floors of probably late abandoned rooms; and floors and fill of late abandoned rooms. The room abandonment classes are from Reid (1973) and are based on the frequency of potsherds in the fill. Three species predominate in the prehistoric fauna from Grasshopper: *Peromyscus maniculatus, P. eremicus,* and *P. leucopus.* Even though relative abundances in fossil faunas do not necessarily reflect actual prehistoric species abundances,

the large numbers of these three species indicate that prehistorically they were probably not rare near Grasshopper. *Microtus mexicanus, P. truei, O. leucogaster,* and *R. megalotis* are uncommon in the fauna and are rare or absent in the vicinity at present, yet *P. boylii,* also rare in the archaeological fauna, is now the most abundant small rodent species near Grasshopper. Also, the relative frequencies of the species do not change significantly across the abandonment classes. If deposition of rodents occurred during and immediately following the occupation of a room, then the species composition of faunas from a temporal sequence of rooms might reveal possible changes in species composition of the rodent community near Grasshopper during the occupation span of the Pueblo. The presence of some of the species, *P. maniculatus, P. eremicus, P. leucopus,* and *R. megalotis,* in both early and late abandoned rooms indicates that they may have been present throughout the entire occupation span. *Microtus mexicanus* apparently occurred only in the early part and *O. leucogaster* and *P. boylii* in the later portion of the occupation. Thus there is a suggestion of faunal turnover during the period of occupation, but the sample sizes of fauna from early abandoned rooms are relatively low so that conclusive evidence for temporal species replacement is lacking. Evidence for faunal turnover can also be obtained by documenting changing faunal composition of successive deposition strata within a room. Table 11.5 shows the fauna from different occupation levels of Room 21, Room 246, Room 279, and Room 280, all late abandoned rooms with at least two defined occupation surfaces (not counting second stories). There are no apparent within- or between-room temporal trends in occurrence of various species from the earliest to the latest times of room use.

In summary, the Grasshopper microfauna has several interesting characteristics. First, the modern small rodent fauna in the vicinity is only half as diverse as the prehistoric fauna (four versus eight species), and all of the

TABLE 11.5

Stratigraphic Sequences of Microfaunas from Rooms 246, 21, 279, and 280 at Grasshopper Pueblo

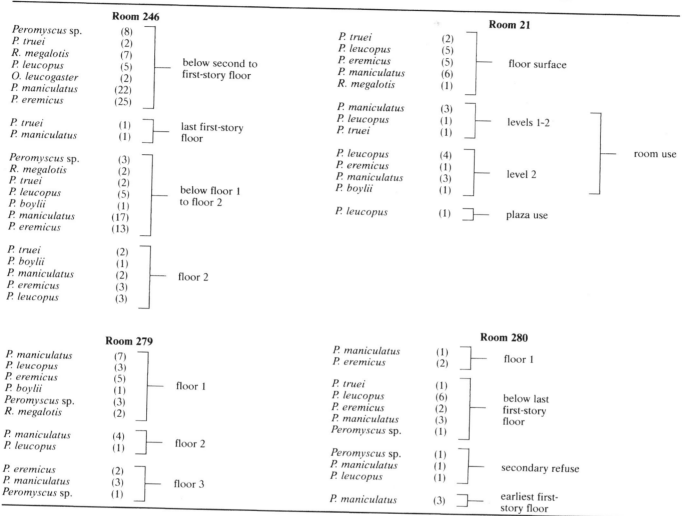

present-day species occur in the prehistoric fauna. Second, two of the numerically most abundant species in the fossil fauna, *P. leucopus* and *P. eremicus*, do not live in the immediate vicinity of Grasshopper today. Third, although the present and prehistoric faunas are quite different in species composition and diversity, there are no conclusive indications of faunal turnover during the occupation span of the Pueblo.

DISCUSSION

The Cibecue area is of inherent biogeographic interest because of its proximity to the Mogollon Rim, a zone of rapid topographic and ecological transition that bisects east-central Arizona (see Fig. 1.1.). The rim itself is forested; open grasslands and pinyon-juniper woodlands predominate to the north. South of the Mogollon Rim are forested mountain areas as well as chaparral and shrub associations at lower elevations. The marked habitat changes in this part of Arizona, particularly the 335-km-long forested rim, present a barrier to the distri-

bution of many rodent species. Some species reach the southern limits of their distribution at the Mogollon Rim; others only extend as far north as the Salt River. Grasshopper is located in an area where the ranges of many rodent species abut. Fairly small alterations in climatic regimes, resulting in vegetational changes in this area, could potentially result in range extension or reduction for a variety of rodent species, leading to new combinations of sympatric species.

Unfortunately, the details of rodent species distributions within southern Navajo County, especially the White Mountain Apache Reservation, have not been thoroughly investigated. Some species now might have somewhat different geographic ranges in this region than have been actually documented. The fact that species distributions in this critical transitional area within a radius of about 60 km of Grasshopper are not well known makes the interpretation of the paleoecological significance of the prehistoric fauna from Grasshopper difficult. The ecological characteristics of the species in the prehistoric

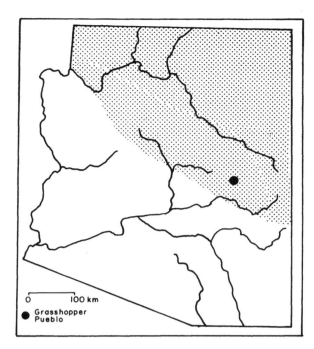

Figure 11.1. Current Arizona range of *Peromyscus truei*, indicated by stippling (after Cockrum 1960).

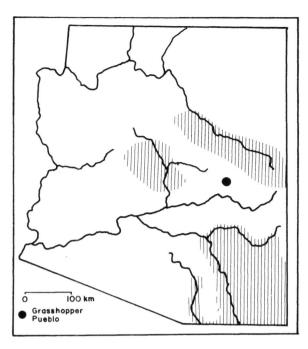

Figure 11.2. Current Arizona range of *Peromyscus leucopus*, indicated by hatching (after Cockrum 1960).

fauna can be inferred by examining their current distributions, but the sorts of habitats nearest Grasshopper the species now occupy are not known in all cases. Sometimes species utilize a variety of habitats in different parts of their range; a species at the margins of its distribution or in other areas where it is comparatively rare might not occur in its "optimal" or "typical" habitat. However, without more detailed information about the ecological characteristics of these species in such areas, paleoecological reconstruction must be based on whatever is currently known or can be inferred about their habitat associations.

As indicated, of the eight small rodent species occurring in the prehistoric fauna, four currently live in the immediate vicinity of Grasshopper: *P. maniculatus, P. boylii, R. megalotis,* and *M. mexicanus* (see Table 11.6 at the end of this chapter). Populations of *P. truei* occur about 20 km south of Grasshopper, at an elevation of 1870 m, in a pinyon-juniper-oak vegetational association. Cockrum (1960) includes southern Navajo County in the Arizona range of *P. truei,* and specimens have also been collected about 50 km north of Grasshopper in the vicinity of both Snowflake and Shumway (Fig. 11.1). Throughout most of its geographic range in the Southwest, *P. truei* is associated with pinyon and juniper, but the species is occasionally found in riparian vegetation, or in stands of oak, pine, and fir. *P. truei* is usually most abundant in pinyon-juniper woodland. Although apparently suitable habitat (pinyon-juniper woodland) for this species occurs at Grasshopper, the species seems not to occupy the local area at present.

The current geographic ranges of the other three species in the prehistoric fauna—*P. leucopus, P. eremicus,*

and *O. leucogaster*—do not include the Grasshopper area. Presumably, they could be excluded from the area now by either adverse climatic conditions, lack of suitable habitat (vegetation or soil types), or biotic factors such as competition from other rodent species. Unfortunately, only detailed studies can reveal which of many such factors determine the range of distribution of a given rodent species, and these kinds of studies are rarely attempted. The most practical approach is to make inferences about prehistoric conditions based only on the physical (climatic) conditions and vegetation types that would have been necessary to support populations of the species.

Populations of *P. leucopus* reach their western limit in Arizona; currently they almost surround Grasshopper (Fig. 11.2). The species has been trapped about 60 km west of Grasshopper, near Payson, and about 60 km east of Grasshopper in the vicinity of McNary. Populations are also known to occur on the Little Colorado River near Winslow, St. John's, and Springerville. The species is abundant on the Verde River near Camp Verde. In the Southwest, *P. leucopus* is often associated with fairly well-developed riparian vegetation or with river bottom brush and grass communities (see Table 11.6). It has been trapped in marshes, in cottonwood and willow groves, in mesquite thickets, and in grasslands. *P. leucopus* is definitely not a woodland or forest dwelling species. The factors limiting its distribution in Arizona are unstudied, but at present it tends to occur principally along the major river drainages in the Southwest. Since the species often occupies relatively mesic habitats along streams or arroyo bottoms, it could conceivably occur along Cibecue Creek, Canyon Creek, or Carrizo Creek, all within a few

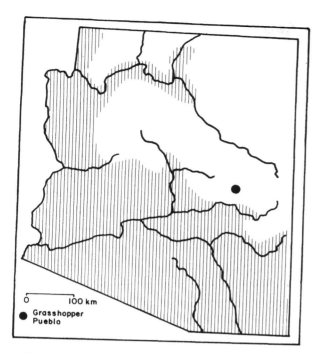

Figure 11.3. Current Arizona range
of *Peromyscus eremicus*, indicated by hatching
(after Cockrum 1960).

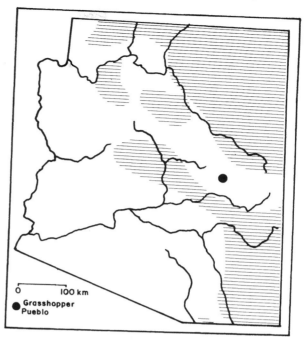

Figure 11.4. Current Arizona range
of *Onychomys leucogaster*, indicated by hatching
(after Cockrum 1960).

miles of Grasshopper. Prehistorically, conditions of somewhat increased moisture resulting in enhanced stream flow in the general vicinity of Grasshopper might have enabled *P. leucopus* populations to move into the area. If the upper portion of Salt River Draw contained a perennial stream, appropriate habitats for this species would seemingly have been available adjacent to Grasshopper Pueblo.

Populations of *P. eremicus* now inhabit areas to the south and west of Grasshopper (Fig. 11.3). Specimens have been obtained on the Salt River, about 30 km south of Grasshopper, and near Roosevelt Lake about 50 km to the southwest. The species is primarily associated with dry, rocky grasslands and brushlands, but it is also found in pinyon-juniper woodland as well as in well-developed riparian vegetation (see Table 11.6). It occurs in valley bottoms, in arroyos and riverbeds, and in foothills; like *P. leucopus,* it is not a montane species.

Gennaro (1968) studied populations of *P. eremicus* in New Mexico and hypothesized that the northern limit to the range of this species in New Mexico was determined in part by the absence of mesquite and in part by temperature. He noted that the average annual maximum temperature is 71 degrees F (21.7 degrees C) at the northernmost occurrence of New Mexico populations of *P. eremicus,* and suggested that temperatures lower than this might be unfavorable for the species. The distribution of *P. eremicus* in Arizona occurs only in areas where the average January temperature is 35 degrees F (1.4 degrees C) or higher; the average July temperature in these areas is above 75 degrees F (Sellers and Hill 1974, Cockrum 1960). The average January temperature near Cibecue is between 35 and 40 degrees F, but the average

July temperature is a few degrees less than 75 (Sellers and Hill 1974). Thus climatic conditions, summer temperatures that are too low, might partially account for the absence of *P. eremicus* in the Grasshopper area at present. Additionally, the current abundance of *P. boylii* in chaparral and shrub habitats near Cibecue might result in the competitive exclusion of *P. eremicus.* When they are sympatric, *P. boylii* is much more abundant in shrub habitats than *P. eremicus.* Throughout their ranges in the Southwest, *P. boylii* often occurs in shrublands and woodland zones while *P. eremicus* occurs at somewhat lower elevations in grasslands and transitional woodlands. The two species often are locally sympatric in ecotonal areas (Findley and others 1975; Cockrum 1960; Bailey 1931; Blair 1940). The extent to which competitive interactions between the two species might be responsible for these patterns is not known. *P. eremicus* is much more abundant in the Grasshopper Pueblo microfauna than *P. boylii* (87 versus 6 specimens). If these frequencies are accurate reflections of the species abundances during the 1300s, it would suggest that ecological conditions then favored *P. eremicus.* Now the situation is apparently reversed and *P. boylii* is the most common mouse in the vicinity of Grasshopper today.

The Grasshopper microfauna includes two specimens of *Onychomys leucogaster.* The range of this species apparently does not include the Grasshopper area at present, but like *P. leucopus,* populations of *O. leucogaster* occur in several directions within about 50 to 60 km (Fig. 11.4). The species is mainly an occupant of grassland, mesquite thickets, and other relatively open habitats (see Table 11.6). Populations may possibly occur near Cibecue where there is seemingly appropriate habitat in the area. However, *O. leucogaster* is sometimes much more difficult to capture than other rodents because of its insectivorous habits; this factor, combined with the paucity of rodent trapping on the Fort Apache Reservation, results in uncertainty about the exact distributions of its populations.

Paleoecological inferences based on the species composition of the mammalian microfauna suggest that environmental conditions during the prehistoric occupation of Grasshopper were somewhat different than at present. Perhaps due to somewhat increased precipitation, Salt River Draw may have been permanently flowing, with well-developed riparian vegetation. Also, summer temperatures may have been a few degrees higher than at present, resulting in a longer growing season for agriculture. Some of the rodent species that must have been living adjacent to the Pueblo (for example, *P. boylii* and *P. eremicus*) indicate that relatively open shrublands and woodlands probably predominated instead of the current ponderosa pine forest.

These interpretations generally coincide with other available evidence about the Grasshopper paleoenvironment. Stratigraphic trenching operations revealed that a stream flowed prehistorically in Salt River Draw, and that at one time a dam impounded water to form a small pond. Olsen and Olsen (1970) analyzed the fish and amphibian faunas from Grasshopper. The presence in the fauna of two toad species (*Bufo alvarius* and *Bufo cognatus*), a frog (*Rana pipiens*), and the Sonoran Mud Turtle, each dependent on a water supply during all or part (the breeding season) of the year, suggests the Salt River Draw probably contained a permanent stream. In addition, the Sonoran Mud Turtle (*Kinosternon sonoriense*) now lives only below 1530 m elevation in Arizona. If the specimen was indigenous perhaps the Grasshopper climate was somewhat less montane.

Analyses of tree-ring specimens by Dean and Robinson (Chapter 8) revealed that the late A.D. 1200s were characterized by increased aridity at Grasshopper, corresponding to the Great Drought in other portions of the Southwest, followed by a period of increased effective moisture during the early 1300s. Additionally, Dean and Robinson postulated that the drier conditions of the late thirteenth century might have resulted in a thinning of the forest near Grasshopper, yielding increased availability of land suitable for agriculture.

There is also evidence that environmental conditions were different during the 1300s in Arizona. For instance, Minckley and Alger (1968) analyzed fish remains from a Pueblo IV site near Perkinsville, Yavapai County, and suggested that the Verde River had a much higher water level during the 1300s. Woodbury (1961) argued that the modern distribution of trees at Point of Pines extends to lower elevations than in prehistoric times. He based this idea on the observed distribution of occupation and agricultural sites with respect to the current distribution of trees. Similarly, Stein (1963) identified the heteromyid rodent *Perognathus* in fauna from the Canyon Creek Phase (A.D. 1325-1400) of Point of Pines. Species of this genus occupy fairly warm, arid habitats, and apparently the genus does not occur now at Point of Pines. Several species of *Perognathus* reach the limits of their distribution within less than 80 km of the site: *P. flavus, P. baileyi, P. penicillatus, P. intermedius,* and *P. amplus.* Perhaps increased warmth or aridity would result in the spread of one or more of these species to Point of Pines.

Hevly (1964) reconstructed the prehistoric environment of the Upper Little Colorado River by pollen analyses and use of dendroclimatological data. From about A.D. 1100 to 1300, conditions of decreased effective moisture with heavy summer rainfall prevailed in the area. After A.D. 1300, however, increased effective moisture and a biseasonal pattern of precipitation developed, which may have led to perennial stream flow of previously ephemeral rivers. A variety of evidence indicates that during the 1300s more streams in east-central Arizona were flowing year-round. In addition, at least during the late 1200s, somewhat warmer conditions than at present prevailed.

Could habitat disturbance by the human occupants of Grasshopper Pueblo rather than climatic change possibly account for the prehistoric occurrence of the four additional species nearby? There is evidence that prehistoric human impact on the vegetation near Grasshopper was probably significant. Kelso (Chapter 14) suggests that the drop in frequency of pine pollen and the concomitant rise in frequency of Cheno-Am and Compositae types in pollen profiles resulted from the local clearing of pine trees and subsequent invasion of plants favoring disturbed conditions. An increase in pine and other arboreal pollen accompanied by a decrease in Cheno-Ams and Compositae apparently coincides with the time of abandonment of Grasshopper. Presumably, plant succession on the abandoned fields accounts for this pattern. Additionally, the occurrence of a few *Zea mays* pollen grains during the period of pine pollen increase suggests that the trees may have started reforestation while Grasshopper was still occupied, thus implying that abandonment of the Pueblo was gradual. From her analysis of pollen samples and plant macrofossils from occupation levels in the Pueblo, Bohrer (Chapter 13) documents an increased incidence of plants that occur in disturbed habitats.

It is possible to estimate the amount of land utilized for farming by the prehistoric inhabitants of Grasshopper. Longacre (1975) estimated the peak population to be about a thousand people during the mid-A.D. 1300s. Estimates of planted acreage needed for per capita support by Southwestern agriculturalists vary, but ethnographic studies suggest figures from 0.2 to 1.2 ha per person (Woodbury 1961; Cook 1972). From 200 to 1200 hectares may have been in production near Grasshopper by A.D. 1350. Whether this land was forested and had to be cleared or whether it was mostly relatively open habitat originally is unclear. Dean and Robinson (Chapter 8) argue that the conditions of increased warmth and decreased moisture in the late 1200s would have resulted in a thinning of the local forest cover, making the area

TABLE 11.6
Modern Habitat Preferences of Rodent Species Occurring Prehistorically in the Grasshopper Area

Species	Habitat type	Geographic locality	Author
Peromyscus eremicus (Baird)			
	Rocky foothills; mesquite flats; plains, bajadas	New Mexico	Findley and others 1975
	Blackbrush/greasebush/prickly pear association	Northeastern Arizona	Hoffmeister 1971
	Short grass/mesquite association, mesquite/cholla association, grama/bluestem association	Southwestern Texas	Blair 1940
	Malpais lava community (mesquite); sotol/ocotillo community; rocky arroyos	Southern New Mexico	Dice 1930
	Creosote bush commuity; riparian of desert springs and along large washes	Southern Nevada	Bradley and Mauer 1973
	Pinyon-juniper woodland	Charleston Mts., Southern Nevada	Deacon and others 1964
	Mesquite groves; floodplains adjacent to Rio Puerco and Rio Grande	Central New Mexico	Gennaro 1968
	Foothills of desert ranges; rocky arroyos, canyons; in cactus, mesquite, sumac	New Mexico	Bailey 1931
	Mesquite, agave, yucca associations	Huachuca Mts., Arizona	Hoffmeister and Goodpaster 1954
	Lower Sonoran, ocotillo, mesquite, *Opuntia*	Chiricahua Mts., Arizona	Calahane 1939
	Flats and alluvial fans below woodland	Graham Mts., Southeastern Arizona	Hoffmeister 1956
	Along Santa Cruz River (riparian)	Southern Arizona	Burt 1933
Peromyscus truei (Schufeldt)			
	Pinyon-juniper woodland	New Mexico	Findley and others 1975
	Pinyon-juniper woodland; riparian; cultivated lands (near pinyon-juniper woodland); rocky hillsides; flats; sand dunes	San Juan Basin, New Mexico	Harris 1963; Harris and others 1967
	Pinyon-juniper woodland; Gambel oak and white fir stands; rocky brushy gullies on alluvial slopes	Bernalillo Co., New Mexico	Ivey 1957
	Upper Sonoran; pinyon-juniper woodland; rocks, cliffs; and brushy canyon bottoms	New Mexico	Bailey 1931
	Pinyon-juniper woodland	Southern Colorado	Armstrong 1972
	Pinyon-juniper woodland; rocky areas and woodpiles	Sandia Mts., New Mexico	Wilson 1968
	Rocky areas with pinyon trees	Northeastern Arizona	Hoffmeister 1971
	Pinyon-juniper woodland; pine-oak woodlands	Rio Arriba Co., New Mexico	Holbrook 1978
Peromyscus leucopus (Rafinesque)			
	Arroyos; grasslands below woodland; mesquite; cottonwood groves along creeks	New Mexico	Findley and others 1975
	Arroyo sides in saltbush	Sandia Mts., New Mexico	Wilson 1968
	Short grass/mesquite association; mesquite/cholla association; cottonwood association; riparian/oak association; catclaw association	Southwestern Texas	Blair 1940

TABLE 11.6

(continued)

Species	Habitat type	Geographic locality	Author
	Riparian woodlands; brush communities	Southeastern Colorado	Armstrong 1972
	Open country; valleys; field edges and along irrigation ditches; thickets of cottonwoods, willow, *Baccharis;* canyon and river bottoms	New Mexico	Bailey 1931
	River bottom communities; tamarisk/ saltbush flats; Russian olive thickets; margins of lagoons; cattail marshes; cottonwood forests	Bernalillo Co., New Mexico	Ivey 1957
	Oak, walnut, maple, Douglas fir forest near springs	Huachuca Mts., Southeastern Arizona	Hoffmeister and Goodpaster 1954
	San Simon Valley in grasses, sedges, cattails; near standing water	Chiricahua Mts., Arizona	Calahane 1939
	Cactus, mesquite, sparse grass	Graham Mts., Southeastern Arizona	Hoffmeister 1956
	Along Santa Cruz River (riparian)	Southern Arizona	Burt 1933
Peromyscus boylii (Baird)			
	Oak and shrub associations	New Mexico	Findley and others 1975
	Arid, rocky, brushy slopes	Bernalillo Co., New Mexico	Ivey 1957
	Upper Sonoran-Transition Zone, dense brushy areas	Sandia Mts., New Mexico	Wilson 1968
	Pinyon-juniper flats; cottonwood/willow association; brushy/weedy associations	Northeastern Arizona	Hoffmeister 1971
	Upper Sonoran; pinyon-juniper and oak communities; riparian	New Mexico	Bailey 1931
	Pinyon-juniper and shrub associations; rough, rocky plateaus, mesas, and canyons	Southern Colorado	Armstrong 1972
	Rocky areas; heavy plant cover; riparian; pinyon-juniper woodlands; lower parts of ponderosa pine/Douglas fir forest	San Juan Basin, New Mexico	Harris 1963
	Pinyon-juniper-oak association	Rio Arriba Co., New Mexico	Holbrook 1978
	Oak/juniper, pinyon/juniper, catclaw, yellow pine/juniper, grama/bluestem communities	Southwestern Texas	Blair 1940
	Juniper association, red cedar association, yellow pine/scrub oak association	Northeastern New Mexico	Hill 1942
	Oak woodland; pine and fir forests	Huachuca Mts., Southeastern Arizona	Hoffmeister and Goodpaster 1954
	River bottom brush piles; rocky situations high in mountains	Southern Arizona	Burt 1933
	Oak belt, 5300–8900 feet	Graham Mts., Southeastern Arizona	Hoffmeister 1956
	Pinyon; rocky areas in ponderosa pine and Douglas fir, 5000–9000 feet	Chiricahua Mts., Arizona	Calahane 1939
Reithrodontomys megalotis (Baird)			
	Large variety of habitats	New Mexico	Findley and others 1975

much more suitable for agriculture. Even if local habitats were vegetated more sparsely than they are at present, much land in the general vicinity of the Pueblo had to be opened for farming; felled trees undoubtedly were used for building and firewood. As certain fields fell into disuse and other plots were cleared for farming, a mosaic of habitats representing different stages of plant succession probably was formed. The area would have contained patches of agricultural land, untouched habitats such as shrubland and woodlands, and a variety of plots with mixtures of grasses and herbaceous and shrub species typical of early and middle stages of succession.

TABLE 11.6

(continued)

Species	Habitat type	Geographic locality	Author
	Croplands; marshes; wash edges; pinyon-juniper; canyon walls	San Juan Basin, New Mexico	Harris 1963; Harris and others 1967
	Weedy drainage ditches; sagebrush/rabbit brush association	Northeastern New Mexico	Hill 1942
	Upper Sonoran; tamarisk/saltbush flats; pinyon-juniper; white fir forest; rabbit brush communities	Bernalillo Co., New Mexico	Ivey 1957
	Short grass; short grass/yucca; riparian; riparian/oak; pinyon/juniper; grama/bluestem associations	Southwestern Texas	Blair 1940
	Grasslands, thickets; sagebrush flats; boreal forests	Northeastern Arizona	Hoffmeister 1971
	Lower and Upper Sonoran	New Mexico	Bailey 1931
	Floodplain vegetation; disturbed areas	Colorado	Armstrong 1972
	Under logs and brush near creeks; mesquite	Chiricahua Mts., Arizona	Calahane 1939
	Grass at 9000 feet; grass, mesquite and yucca at less than 4700 feet	Graham Mts., Arizona	Hoffmeister 1956
	Thick grass along fence rows; grass near ponds; Douglas fir, white fir, aspen	Huachuca Mts., Arizona	Hoffmeister and Goodpaster 1954
Onychomys leucogaster (Wied-Neuwied)			
	Sagebrush flats	Northern Arizona	Hoffmeister 1971
	Sandy grasslands; mesquite stands	New Mexico	Findley and others 1975
	Sandy ridges and banks; grassland; Upper Sonoran range, hills, and bottomlands	Bernalillo Co., New Mexico	Ivey 1957
	Sagebrush; grasslands; sparse pinyon-juniper	San Juan Basin, New Mexico	Harris 1963
	Grasslands; shrub-grasslands; pinyon-juniper	Chuska Mts., New Mexico	Harris and others 1967
	Shrub-grasslands	New Mexico	Gennaro 1968
	Lower Sonoran; desert grassland	Huachuca Mts., Southeastern Arizona	Hoffmeister and Goodpaster 1954
	Yucca and mesquite flats	Graham Mts., Arizona	Hoffmeister 1956
	Grasslands	Arizona	Cockrum 1960
Microtus mexicanus (Saussure)			
	Montane grasslands in ponderosa and mixed conifer forest; pinyon-juniper woodland	New Mexico	Findley and others 1975
	Grassy areas in woodlands of ponderosa pine	Mesa Verde National Park, Colorado	Armstrong 1972; Anderson 1961; Rodeck 1956
	Transition Zone; open areas in ponderosa pine forest	New Mexico	Bailey 1931
	Ponderosa pine, pinyon-juniper woodlands	New Mexico	Findley and Jones 1962

This spatial mosaic was in a continual state of change, as new plots were opened and old ones abandoned. In addition, the dam on Salt River Draw that created a small reservoir near the Pueblo added to the human impact on the local environment. Such spatial and temporal diversity of local habitats within a few miles of the Pueblo could probably have supported a diverse range of rodent species.

Habitat disturbance and recovery may account for the high diversity of rodent species, representing a range of local habitat types, in the archaeological collection. Following a habitat disturbance like clearing (by logging or fire), rodent populations quickly recover their total density (Tevis 1956a, 1956b; Cook 1959; Hooven and Black 1976; Turkowski and Watkins 1976; Turkowski and Reynolds 1970), but the species composition of the disturbed plot may remain basically the same or it may change in response to the vegetation change (Tevis 1956a, 1956b; Beck and Vogl 1972; Krefting and Ahlgren 1974; Sims and Buckner 1973; Turkowski and Reynolds 1970; Lillywhite 1977; Cook 1959; LoBue and Darnell 1959). Usually, previously forested plots during early succession tend to support populations of species that prefer open habitats with little three dimensional structural diversity. Later in succession, these species may be replaced by woodland- and forest-dwelling rodents. Some rodent species with flexible habitat preferences may persist on the plot during the entire succession. However, the particular species present in the disturbed area as it recovers (that is, undergoes plant succession) depends entirely on the species locally available to colonize the plot. It is unlikely that species living further away than a mile or two (1.6 to 3.2 km) would have much opportunity to colonize a disturbed area.

Human impact on the land in the vicinity of Grasshopper, which must have been substantial, probably resulted in an array of local habitat types, each inhabited by different rodent species. Continual habitat disturbance, in the form of clearing new plots for fields and letting others revegetate via succession, might have maintained the total rodent species diversity at a relatively high level (Connell and Slatyer 1977, Connell 1978), and any of these species might have become incorporated in the Grasshopper microfauna. This possibility helps explain the fact that species characteristic of different local habitats compose the fauna of the Pueblo. However, it does not adequately explain the occurrence of species such as *P. leucopus, P. eremicus,* and *O. leucogaster* in the Grasshopper fauna because such populations do not now occur in the vicinity. Even if a habitat disturbance comparable to the prehistoric one occurred today, the local species diversity would probably not be increased because source populations of additional species are too distant. Thus, prehistoric environmental conditions must have been different over a wider range than that dis-

turbed by humans for agriculture to enable populations of these three species to enter the study area. The period of drying and increased warmth in the late 1200s probably enabled *O. leucogaster* and *P. eremicus* to spread into the Grasshopper area; the enhanced stream flow in Salt River Draw during at least part of the occupation might indicate the availability of perennial streams and riparian vegetation that would have provided habitat for *P. leucopus.* In sum, several lines of evidence support the idea that the prehistoric species diversity at the Pueblo is the result of both areal climatic change and local human impact.

One interesting characteristic of the Grasshopper microfauna is that it contains twice the number of species as the extant small rodent fauna. Furthermore, five species of *Peromyscus* occur in the paleofauna and only two species in the genus are known to occupy the area at present. The factors that enhance rodent species diversity in communities are not well understood; many variables probably determine the number of species that coexist in a particular area at a certain time (Connell 1978; Holbrook 1977; Rosenzweig and Winakur 1969; Brown and Lieberman 1973). An abundance and diversity of critical resources could heighten rodent diversity, but biotic interactions (such as predation) and abiotic factors (for example, climate) can also have a profound effect on the number of coexisting species. It is not possible to suggest a simple difference between the prehistoric and modern communities that may account for the observed differences in species diversity. One observation that can be made is that the prehistoric small rodent fauna was not especially diverse; many areas in the Southwest support about eight species of mice (Rosenzweig and Winakur 1959; Holbrook 1975; Findley and others 1975), and four or five species of *Peromyscus* can be sympatric in Upper Sonoran, Transitional, and Woodland habitats. At present, the five species of *Peromyscus* characterizing the Grasshopper fauna are locally sympatric in central Arizona near Montezuma's Well (Cockrum 1964). The extant fauna at Grasshopper is somewhat depauperate; given the current range of habitat diversity in the vicinity, I would expect more mouse species to coexist there.

12. AVIFAUNA FROM GRASSHOPPER PUEBLO

Charmion R. McKusick

By investigating patterns of procurement and utilization, analyses of prehistoric avifauna assemblages provide valuable data to archaeologists. The study of avian material at Grasshopper Pueblo identified several ways in which birds were introduced to the community, including exchange, domestication, hunting, and live capture. Different use expectations affected procurement practices, the deposition of individual birds, and the subsequent recovery of different parts of birds from the archaeological record.

Over 5,000 bird bone elements have been recovered from Grasshopper. Based on the sample of those elements collected as of 1972, 645 birds were identified in the asemblage, representing over 40 species. In addition, 35 elements were unidentified; 16 bone fragments represented large birds (probably turkeys or hawks), 12 were Passeriformes (the order including ravens and jays), and 7 were Fringillidae (the family including sparrows and juncos). Many of these bones were from immature specimens that could not be precisely classified.

To aid identification, modern comparative collections of birds were made in the Grasshopper area by the National Park Service. An annotated list of bird species, comments on their prehistoric distribution, and a minimum faunal count are presented at the end of the chapter. Data on archaeological occurrences of bird species are from the National Park Service Avian Crossfile.

PATTERNS OF PROCUREMENT

The taxonomic lists of avian species from many widely distributed southwestern sites representing various time spans document the importance of birds to prehistoric human populations, and suggest that avian resouces were not utilized solely on the basis of availability, abundance, or practicality. Instead, avian exploitation was affected by economic, social, and possibly ritual components of the cultural system. As a result, the occurrence of particular bird species at prehistoric sites does not necessarily provide unambiguous information about the climatic regime or environmental conditions surrounding the community during occupation. John Olsen (Chapter 10) discusses the possible environmental significance of selected bird species.

Phillips noted (1968: 129) that as early as 1933 Lyndon L. Hargrave suggested that prehistoric occurrences of bird species should not be viewed uncritically in terms of their recent distribution. Of 203 species of native diurnal land birds that breed in Arizona, 34 have changed their range within the past 50 to 100 years (Phillips 1968: 129-162). Pollen and other studies indicate that the reasons for these changes are not all cimatic; human impact on the environment is probably also involved.

The occurrence of birds at Grasshopper may be traced to three procurement strategies (assuming that postoccupational intrusion is not significant): (1) exchange from communities both within and outside the region, (2) raised within the community as domesticated species or as captured individuals, and (3) hunted or snared from the surrounding area. Birds were occasionally brought to the community alive through exchange and capture, although the preponderance of bird wing and leg elements indicates that most birds procured were killed and dismembered shortly thereafter (Table 12.1).

Given the wide geographic range of many Southwestern bird species, it is difficult to document possible exchange practices, but the occurrence of the White-fronted Parrot and the macaw (*Ara macao*) certainly can be attributed to trade (see Chapter 10). It is also possible that hawks and eagles, or their wing fans, may occasionally have been exchanged.

Of the 13 macaws recovered from Grasshopper as of 1972 (two more have since been excavated, see Olsen and Olsen 1974), all but one were of immature or older age. Eight of the 12 specimens were assigned to one of seven age categories (Table 12.2); two of these individuals represent adult birds. An aged macaw was recovered at Pueblo Bonito; one breeding-age macaw was found at Wupatki, and two at Point of Pines (Hargrave 1970b). The Grasshopper faunal collection thus includes a third of all adult macaws found in the Southwest.

The juvenile macaw from Grasshopper is the first such specimen known north of the Mexican border and is too young to have been imported from the humid tropical lowlands of Mexico where wild populations of this species occur. Although it may have hatched at Grasshopper, a more likely source is Casas Grandes, Chihuahua, where macaws were raised in limited numbers (Di Peso 1974; McKusick 1974).

There has been considerable discussion about the possible source of macaws found in the Southwest. Hargrave felt (1970b: 30) that the immature macaws from Room 30 at Pueblo Bonito were perhaps different from the other immature specimens examined. Comparison

TABLE 12.1

Body Part Count of Unworked Bird Bone from Grasshopper Pueblo

Species	Head	Body	Wings	Legs	Relatively Complete
Butorides virescens (heron)			1		
Branta canadensis (goose)	1	2	4	1	
Anser albifrons (goose)		1			
Chen hyperborea (goose)			1	2	
Anas platyrhynchos (duck)			2		
Anas acuta (duck)			1	1	
Cathartes aura (vulture)		1	1		
Accipitridae sp. (hawk)		1			
Accipiter gentilis (hawk)				1	
Accipiter striatus (hawk)			2	1	
Accipiter cooperii (hawk)		2	4	7	1 (juvenile)
Buteo sp. (hawk)		6	13	3	
Buteo jamaicensis (hawk)	7	10	31	29	5
Buteo swainsoni (hawk)		2	11	7	
Buteo regalis (hawk)			2		
Aquila chrysaetos (eagle)		2		2	2
Falco mexicanus (falcon)			1		
Falco sparvarius (falcon)		2	21	8	
Odontophorinae sp. (quail)		1		1	
Lophortyx gambelii (quail)			2		
Cyrtonyx montezumae (quail)		2	2	3	
Meleagris gallopavo merriami (turkey)					
Domestic	8	53	47	71	3
Wild	2	31	51	24	
Grus canadensis tabida (crane)			1		
Limnodromus scolopaceus (sandpiper)		1			
Columba fasciata (pigeon)			3	1	
Zenaidura macroura (dove)		1	2	3	
Ara sp. (macaw)	1		3		
Ara macao (macaw)	2		2	1	7
Geococcyx californianus (roadrunner)			3	2	
Otus asio (owl)	1		5	5	
Bubo virginianus (owl)		3	3	4	1
Glaucidium gnoma (owl)	1				
Speotyto cunicularia (owl)				1	
Strix occidentalis (owl)				1	
Asio otus (owl)		1	1	4	
Colaptes auratus collaris (flicker)	2	1	3	2	
Melanerpes formicivorus (woodpecker)			4	2	
Sphyrapicus thyroideus (sapsucker)			1		
Cyanocitta stelleri (jay)			6	2	
Aphelocoma coerulescens (jay)			1		
Corvus corax (raven)	2	15	47	26	1
Corvus brachyrhynchos (crow)			8	6	
Gymnorhinus cyanocephalus (jay)	1		2	1	1
Nucifraga columbiana (nutcracker)				1	
Sialia mexicana (bluebird)			3		
Sturnella sp. (meadowlark)			2		
Xanthocephalus xanthocephalus (blackbird)			1		
Euphagus cyanocephalus (blackbird)	1	1	11	5	2
Junco sp. (junco)	1		2	1	

of sample means of macaw bone measurements, from five sites in the Southwest with large samples, reveals no significant differences in bone size or proportion (Table 12.3). Specimens from Pueblo Bonito and Turkey Creek Pueblo seem on average to be a little older than those in the other samples. The mean depth of the cranium of macaws from Pueblo Bonito is only 0.04 mm greater than the value for the Casas Grandes sample. Macaws were present at Casas Grandes from A.D. 1060 to 1340, and there is no reason to believe there was more than one

TABLE 12.2

**Age Distribution of Scarlet Macaws
from Grasshopper Pueblo**

Group	Number of Individuals
Aged	1
Breeding (4 or more years)	1
Adolescent (13 months-3 years)	0
Newfledged (11-12 months)	4
Immature (4-11 months)	1
Juvenile (7 weeks-4 months)	1
Nestling (hatching-7 weeks)	0

source of macaws for the Southwest during this period. There is evidence to suggest, however, that the demand for macaws changed through time as a result of changes in the distribution and density of prehistoric human populations in the Southwest. Between A.D. 1000 and 1100 Pueblo Bonito and other Chacoan communities received the greatest number of macaws, but this pattern shifted after A.D. 1100 as large pueblo communities in the mountainous zone of Arizona were established. At first the Flagstaff area around Wupatki was the center of trade. By A.D. 1300, however, communities to the south such as Grasshopper and Point of Pines that experienced rapid population increase were the focus of exchange activity for macaws from Casas Grandes (Hargrave 1970b, Fig. 16).

TABLE 12.3

**Sample Means of Scarlet Macaw Bone Measurements From the Southwest
(From Hargrave 1970b and McKusick 1974)**

Measure Number	Bone	Description	Pueblo Bonito[1] (n = 8)	Wupatki (n = 13)	Turkey Creek (n = 7)	Point of Pines Ruin (n = 15)	Casas Grandes (n = 10)
1	Premaxilla	maximum width hinge line	31.14	31.76	—	31.47	31.30
2	Cranium	maximum axial length of crown	58.56	59.07	60.58	57.95	57.30
3	Cranium	minimum interorbital width of crown	42.63	43.49	46.86	44.36	42.40
4	Cranium	minimum width suborbital bridge	3.65	3.73	4.06	3.53	4.03
5	Cranium	maximum width eye socket	19.98	19.83	19.85	19.44	19.40
6	Cranium	maximum depth eye socket	19.36	18.86	19.00	18.83	19.20
7	Cranium	maximum depth at anterior point of basitemporal plate	31.64	31.81	32.50	31.67	31.60
8	Scapula	maximum length	56.06	56.05	57.30[2]	55.93	54.80
9	Scapula	maximum width coracoidal head	13.32	13.71	13.90[2]	14.00	13.80
10	Coracoid	maximum axial length	53.38	53.38	56.10[2]	53.53	53.70
11	Coracoid	maximum width sternal attachment	15.07	15.00	15.00[2]	15.78	14.80
12	Furcula	maximum length	35.00	36.10[2]	—	—	—
13	Furcula	maximum width	23.25	27.80[2]	—	—	—
14	Pelvis	maximum width across antitrochanters	39.15	39.90[2]	—	—	—
15	Humerus	maximum length	82.97	82.79	86.25	81.39	81.60
16	Humerus	maximum width proximal head	22.08	22.32	22.55	21.51	21.60
17	Humerus	maximum width distal head	17.12	17.09	17.52	16.76	16.80
18	Ulna	maximum length	103.87	103.37	106.00	103.27	103.00
19	Ulna	maximum width, proximal head, palmar view across condyles	12.29	12.37	12.60	12.17	12.30
20	Ulna	maximum width distal end internal view	10.53	10.68	10.53	10.44	10.10
21	Ulna	maximum width distal end anconal view	11.41	11.70	11.70	11.50	11.30
22	Radius	maximum length	95.17	94.76	99.15	95.03	94.80
23	Radius	maximum width distal end	8.15	8.26	8.30	8.06	7.90

1. Specimens from Room 30   2. Single measurement only

(table continued next page)

TABLE 12.3

(continued)

Measure Number	Bone	Description	Pueblo Bonito[1] (n = 8)	Wupatki (n = 13)	Turkey Creek (n = 7)	Point of Pines Ruin (n = 15)	Casas Grande (n = 10)
24	Carpometacarpus	maximum length	63.06	63.38	—	62.65	62.10
25	Carpometacarpus	maximum width proximal end interview width	15.77	15.87	—	15.67	15.30
26	Carpometacarpus	maximum width distal end	9.69	9.80	—	9.83	9.50
27	Femur	maximum axial length	59.78	60.51	57.10	59.81	58.60
28	Femur	maximum width distal end	12.90	13.09	12.50	12.77	12.60
29	Femur	maximum width proximal end posterior view	13.65	13.78	12.75	13.32	13.30
30	Femur	maximum depth distal end posterior view	9.98	9.34	9.15	9.55	9.80
31	Tibiotarsus	maximum length	83.10	88.70	84.80[2]	83.70	82.60
32	Tibiotarsus	maximum width proximal end posterior view	13.98	14.92	14.80[2]	13.98	13.90
33	Tibiotarsus	maximum width distal end anterior view	11.83	11.30	10.80[2]	11.16	11.10
34	Tarsometatarsus	maximum axial length	30.84	31.56	—	30.75	30.20
35	Tarsometatarsus	maximum width distal end, anterior view, axial position	14.92	15.34	—	14.91	14.60
36	Tarsometatarsus	minimum width shaft, anterior view, through metatarsal facet	6.30	6.33	—	6.10	6.00

1. Specimens from Room 30
2. Single measurement only

Of the domesticated birds or those captured and kept alive at Grasshopper (including macaws and possibly eagles and hawks), the Large Indian Domestic Turkey was numerically most important. This domestic progenitor of Merriam's Wild Turkey can be segregated from prehistoric and modern wild turkeys by smaller size, gracility, and a greater range of variability. The Large Indian Domestic can be separated also from the Small Indian Domestic, which is even smaller, much more gracile, and exhibits character differences. The presence of turkey egg shells, and the age and sex distribution of the Large Indian Domestics from Grasshopper (Tables 12.4, 12.5) are comparable to the large collections of domestic turkeys from excavations at other sites. Individuals of all age classes are present and the sexes are approximately evenly represented in the sample of remains. Furthermore, the distribution of age and sex in the domestic variety of turkey diverges from the larger specimens at Grasshopper.

Females are almost three times as numerous as males, and no juveniles or young adults are represented in the sample of wild turkeys (Tables 12.4 and 12.5). There are only two immature individuals in the sample suggesting that wild turkeys were most often hunted during winter or spring prior to the breeding season. Merriam's Wild Turkey inhabits forested mountains from 6,000 to 12,000 feet (1829 to 3658 m) elevation (Ligon 1964: 1), and Grasshopper would have been on the lower edge of their

TABLE 12.4
Percentage Distribution by Age of Turkeys from Grasshopper Pueblo

Age	Large Indian Domestic Turkey (n = 155) %	Wild Turkey (n = 93) %
Old Adult	2	3
Adult	74	95
Immature	11	2
Juvenile	13	0

Note: $X^2 = 22.07$, 3 d.f., $p < .01$

TABLE 12.5
Sex Distribution of Turkeys from Grasshopper Pueblo

Sex	Large Indian Domestic Turkey	Wild Turkey	Total
Male	72	26	98
Female	63	67	130
Total	135*	93	228

*Sample excludes juvenile specimens that could not be sexed.
Note: $X^2 = 14.46$, 1 d.f., $p < .01$

winter range. The mating bond is established on the winter range or before the nesting grounds are reached. Although harem size averages about five females for every male of the eastern subspecies (Schorger 1966: 255), the group size among western wild turkeys is two to three hens to each gobbler (Ligon 1964: 10), a ratio similar to the wild turkey male-female specimens recovered from Grasshopper Pueblo. The data suggest that hens and full-grown gobblers were hunted between January and March, just prior to the mating season when body fat is at a maximum (Hewitt 1967: 85). At that time turkeys would have been moving out of their winter range from the north to lower elevations around Grasshopper. Merriam's Wild Turkey is still present in the Grasshopper area today.

Intact and complete skeletons of golden eagle, raven, owl, and red-tailed hawk may mean that other species, although not tamed, were captured alive and brought to the Pueblo. Ethnohistorical evidence indicates that such practices were common among all Puebloan groups, especially with hawks and eagles (Schroeder 1968). It is possible that at Grasshopper some complete owl skeletons may represent postoccupation deposition in collapsing rooms.

EXPLOITATION OF BIRDS

Intact bird skeletons are relatively rare at Grasshopper; they occur primarily as burials. Portions of the body are even more rare when compared to the large number of wing and leg elements found at the site (the difference is still striking when the number of leg and wing elements is halved). Perhaps different functional considerations were employed in the introduction of various portions of the body to the prehistoric pueblo, or those parts were subsequently affected by different processes or were differentially incorporated into the archaeological record (Binford 1979).

Intact bodies (that is, with wings, legs, and body articulated) seem to have been procured as a source of feathers or occasionally for food. Of all the bird species, only the Canada Goose and wild turkey (and to a much lesser extent the domestic turkey) may have been eaten. A small sample of bone from these species exhibits butchering marks, but they may be the result of bone preparation for working. The best evidence that wild turkey may have been eaten comes from the distribution and condition of bone elements within the site, plus the timing of hunting. Wild turkey elements occurred only as random bones that were often broken or gnawed (probably by carnivores or rodents). Three wild turkey bones were burned, although stewing was the most probable method of cooking. However, by hunting turkeys just prior to the mating season when body weight is at a maximum (Hewitt 1967: 85) a substantial quantity of meat (high in protein and fat) would have been obtained. By hunting turkeys in March about two pounds of fat would have been available from the breast sponge alone (Hewitt 1967: 85), an important consideration to a population dependent on agricultural products.

The Canada Goose is the only other species of bird for which there is evidence of human consumption. It, along with the other waterfowl recovered from Grasshopper (White-fronted Goose, Snow Goose, Pintail, and Mallard), would have been attracted to the reservoir just north of the village (see Chapter 9) during the fall migration.

By far the greatest proportion of birds at Grasshopper were not eaten; butchering marks are rare and body portions do not represent the parts with the greatest amount of meat. Some of these specimens may have been hunted as pests raiding gardens or cultivated fields, but most were probably brought to the village for other purposes.

The birds introduced to the community intact but not eaten served several functions. Those kept alive may have provided a replenishable source of feathers. Domestic turkeys, although perhaps occasionally eaten, were probably raised for feathers that were twined into blankets or robes. Ethnohistorical evidence indicates that this was the purpose of turkey raising after A.D. 1500 in nearly all pueblo communities that the Spanish visited (Schroeder 1968: 96-101). Grasshopper was situated in a fairly temperate climatic zone in which cotton cloth or fiber probably had to be imported (Chapter 13), thus its prehistoric occupants may have used turkey feathers in their textiles.

Captive birds such as macaws, eagles, and hawks may have supplied renewable feathers for nonutilitarian purposes, including fetishes, shrines, and decoration. Similarly, wing fans from hunted birds may have been selected, in part, as a source of feathers. Tail feathers were probably also plucked and used, a practice that would not have resulted in the deposition of any skeletal remains. Feathers are now used by all puebloan groups in a wide range of ritual and ceremonial activities. Feathers also play an important role in agriculturally-related ritual activities among the pueblos (Bloom 1933-1938). They are thought to ensure adequate rainfall and good crops, and consequently are buried in fields. Given the preponderance of skeletal parts associated with colorful feathers in the Grasshopper collection, an analogous pattern of feather use is postulated.

The presence of captive birds of different species and their burial distribution at Grasshopper provides information on features of social organization. As late as 1880 captive birds of particular species (such as macaw and turkey) were generally present at pueblos only when clans or moieties of the same name as the bird species lived at the village (see Schroeder 1968). This pattern is not surprising because clan names appear to have a totemic function in some pueblo societies (see Eggan 1950; Kroeber 1917; Titiev 1944), particularly among the Hopi and Zuni. At Grasshopper, burials of Red-tailed Hawk, Golden Eagle, and macaw are concentrated in the Great Kiva located in Room Block 2 on the west side of the old Salt River Draw channel. Two macaws and one eagle were buried in or adjacent to two small kivas in the western two room blocks. Furthermore, remains of sparrow hawks, blue-feathered birds (jays and bluebirds) and black-feathered birds (ravens, crows, and blackbirds) are clustered in the vicinity of the Great Kiva. If we assume that these bird species are totemic representations of named clans or moieties (following the Hopi and Zuni tribes in which named bird clans figure prominently), then their clustering in the Great Kiva area may mean that the kiva indeed functioned as a pan-community integrative mechanism.

There is additional evidence suggesting that, if particular species of birds were associated with named social units, there were significant residential clusters. All three turkey burials are located in Room Block 1, *east* of the old Salt River Draw channel. Most of the remaining glossy dark-feathered birds (like ravens and crows) occur by Room Block 1. These bird species occurrences in the room blocks located on either side of Salt River Draw is paralleled by differences in human skeletal material (Chapter 6), in architecture, and in burials (as indicated by J. Reid). Possibly some sort of dual community organization existed, perhaps similar to the Summer or Macaw Moiety and the Winter or Raven Moiety at Zuni (Cushing 1896: 384-386). F. Plog (1978) has argued that moiety community organization may be a successful way to incorporate diverse social groups. Given the rapid population increase at Grasshopper and substantial immigration into the community (Chapter 3; Longacre 1975, 1976; Reid 1973), this kind of dual organization may have emerged for the reasons Plog describes.

The emphasis on wing and especially leg procurement of hunted birds as well as of captive or domesticated species was also affected by decisions regarding bone working. Every worked piece of bird bone, with one or two exceptions, was manufactured from bone of the wing or leg. Over 50 percent of the sample of worked bird bone was from turkey. This is not surprising, since turkey was abundant and the bones were large enough to be suitable for modification. The production of whistles, tubular beads, and tube stock at Grasshopper (Sandra Olsen 1979) emphasized wing and leg bones in different proportions (Table 12.6). Leg bones were used more often to make whistles, and wing bones to make tube stock. The proportion of wing and leg bones used to make tubular beads was nearly evenly divided.

TABLE 12.6

Distribution of Bird Body Parts by Class of Worked Bone at Grasshopper Pueblo*

| Worked Class | Body Part | | |
	Wing	Leg	Total
Whistle	8	13	21
Tubular bead	27	25	52
Tube stock	20	8	28
Total	55	46	101

*Data are from Sandra Olsen 1979, Tables 2, 3, and 4.
Note: $X^2 = 6.65$, 2 d.f., p < .05

SUMMARY AND COMPARISONS

The occurrence of the major bird species at Grasshopper is similar to the sample of avifauna from the pueblos at Turkey Creek and Point of Pines (Table 12.7).

Hawks, eagles, falcons, and turkeys make up the large proportion of birds recovered from each prehistoric si The large number of ducks and geese from Point Pines may be attributed to heavier procurement fro the reservoir associated with that pueblo and others the region (Wheat 1952). The proportion of ravens a crows at Grasshopper, however, is probably not the res of their availability in the area and may reflect delibera selection for feathers. Furthermore, the presence of rav bone refuse, apparently the by-product of the manufa ture of a "scratcher" (see Gilpin 1968: 235), sugge these birds may have been selected for ritual or cere nial bone working.

TABLE 12.7

Percentage Distribution of Bird Species at Turkey Creek Pueblo, Grasshopper Pueblo, and Point of Pines Pueblo

Species	Turkey Creek (n = 243) %	Grasshopper (n = 645) %	Poin of Pin (n = 8 %
Ducks and Geese	4	2	12
Hawks, Eagles, Falcons	34	26	23
Turkeys	47	39	43
Macaws	6	2	3
Owls and Woodpeckers	1	6	4
Ravens and Crows	5	15	9
Other	3	10	6

The variety of bird species recovered from Grassho per is unsurpassed at other archaeological sites in t Southwest. This variety reflects, in part, the excavatic procedures employed at Grasshopper, but to a lar extent the number of bird species procured by t prehistoric population attests to the importance of tl resource to the community. Given the number of sp cies present, their diverse environmental and seasor occurrences, and the range of ages represented, it clear that for some time Grasshopper was occupi throughout the year. Although birds were not an impo tant food resource (with the exception of wild turke they do reflect important characteristics of the adap tion of the prehistoric population.

The Grasshopper avifaunal assemblage adds suppc to the general proposition made by Binford (1979: 486-48 that residential locations reflect the accumulated deb of multifaceted adaptation composed of numerous stra egies. The occurrences of different proportions of bi species and parts of their bodies have documented tl exchange of captive birds, exploitation for feathers us symbolically or ritually, domestication of turkeys f feathers for robes or blankets, and possibly the impo tance assigned to particular species as totemic represe tatives of certain social groups.

It has been possible only to document rather coar patterns of bird procurement and utilization at Gra hopper. As the temporal and social context of the preh toric community is refined, more fine-grained analys may be undertaken to determine, for example, changing patterns of species utilization. The results from this study, however, show that different prehistoric procurement and utilization strategies affected the proportion of different parts of birds in the assemblage at Grasshopper.

Except for wild turkeys, not much time was invested in hunting birds for food. Although much bird hunting was probably opportunistic, hunters shared a set of dismemberment behaviors that focused on the procurement of wings and legs. Domestic and captive birds received much different treatment and as a result they are recovered more frequently as whole or intact skeletons. These patterns confirm expectations by Binford (1977: 482) that particular arrays of bone are produced by structured sets of procurement, utilization, and depositional behavior.

ANNOTATED TAXA OF BIRD REMAINS FROM GRASSHOPPER PUEBLO

This listing of identified bird remains, and the Minimal Faunal Count and percentage, include only those specimens recovered before 1972. Although subsequent excavations have increased sample size, it is unlikely that the proportions of Minimal Faunal Count (MNI) have changed appreciably. The MNI is based on analyses by Thomas Mathews in which age, sex, and size differences were used to estimate minimum numbers.

Herons

Butorides virescens (MNI, 1; less than one percent of the collection). The Little Green Heron is represented by a fragmentary right ulna. This species has been identified from the Swallet Cave Site at Montezuma Well, which dates between A.D. 1100 and 1300.

Geese and Ducks

Waterfowl represent 2.02 percent of the collection. The three species of geese recovered from Grasshopper occur in proportion to their present availability. The Canada Goose is by far the most common, followed by the Snow Goose and the White-fronted Goose. Mallards and Pintails are extremely common in Arizona, and might have been obtained at almost any time of the year.

Branta canadensis (MNI, 7; 1.09 percent). Canada Goose specimens range from a young adult to one with indications of age; one element has butchering marks. Bones included a head, breast, right leg, left wing, and four right wings. The Canada Goose is frequently recovered from southwestern sites dating after A.D. 500.

Anser albifrons (MNI, 1; less than one percent). White-fronted Goose is represented by an intact left coracoid. Archaeological occurrences range from as early as A.D. 1 at Snaketown to later sites at Houck, Swallet Cave, and the Point of Pines area in Arizona; Casas Grandes, Chihuahua; and Puaray and Gran Quivira in New Mexico.

Chen hyperborea (MNI, 3; less than one percent). Snow Goose elements include a left tibiotarsus, a right femur, and a right carpometacarpus. This species is found as early as 300 B.C. at Snaketown, later at Swallet

Cave and the Point of Pines area, Arizona; Casas Grandes, Chihuahua; and Pueblo Largo and Gran Quivira, New Mexico.

Anas platyrhynchos (MNI, 1; less than one percent). Mallard was identified from an intact right radius and ulna.

Anas acuta (MNI, 1; less than one percent). A fragmentary right tibiotarsus was identified as Pintail. Both Mallards and Pintails are frequently found in southwestern archaeological sites from as early as 100 B.C.

Vultures

Cathartes aura (MNI, 2; less than one percent). Turkey Vulture bones include a left humerus and a right scapula from an immature and an adult. They are common throughout the Southwest during the summer and occur in limited numbers at many sites.

Hawks and Eagles

Hawks and eagles, with the family, falcons, constitute 25.89 percent of the unworked bird bone; Buteonine hawks total 18.29 percent and Accipiters 2.79 percent. Eagles are rare at Grasshopper. The Goshawk and Sharp-shinned hawks, which generally inhabit mountains and forests, are present but not in as large numbers as the common Cooper's hawk, a bird usually found in more open country than now occurs in the Grasshopper area. Among the buteos, the Red-tailed Hawk is the most numerous, while Swainson's and Ferruginous hawks are less common. Both prefer to hunt in open country. The quantity of Swainson's hawks and Cooper's hawks in the sample suggests that in prehistoric times permanent meadows existed between stands of pine, just as they do today.

Accipitridae (MNI, 1; less than one percent). Two cervical vertebrae are from an unidentified hawk.

Accipiter gentilis (MNI, 1; less than one percent). The Goshawk, represented by a right tarsometatarsus and pedal phalanx, has been recovered from the Serrano Site, Colorado, dating from A.D. 800 to 900, and from later sites in the Point of Pines area and in northern and northwestern New Mexico.

Accipiter striatus (MNI, 3; less than one percent). Sharp-shinned Hawk was identified from right and left ulnae and a left tibiotarsus. It has been identified from a site dated before A.D. 1100 at Corduroy Creek south of Showlow, Arizona, in addition to occurrences in the Largo-Gallina and Galisteo Basin areas of New Mexico that are contemporary with the occupation of Grasshopper.

Accipiter cooperii (MNI, 13; 2.02 percent). Cooper's Hawk specimens include three juveniles and two immature individuals. Elements represent three right and three left legs, three right and one left wings. Cooper's Hawks occur with increasing frequency after A.D. 700 in sites in Arizona, New Mexico, and Colorado.

Buteo sp. (MNI, 26; 4.03 percent). Buteonine Hawk specimens of undetermined species are mostly fragments of the shafts of wing and leg bones.

Buteo jamaicensis (MNI, 72; 11.16 percent). Red-tailed Hawk is represented by elements from 19 right wings, 16 left wings, 16 right and 16 left legs, and by the head or body of 13 individuals. This hawk is reported from Basketmaker II levels at Sand Dune Cave, Utah (Hargrave 1970a: 14), and from after A.D. 600 at Long House, Mesa Verde. Red-tailed Hawks are common in southwestern sites, particularly from A.D. 1200 to 1400.

Buteo swainsoni (MNI, 18; 2.79 percent). Swainson's Hawk remains are from six right and five left wings, six left and one right leg, and two axial skeletons. Swainson's Hawk may occur as early as 100 B.C. at Snaketown. Although widely distributed in southwestern sites, they are not as numerous as Red-tailed Hawks.

Buteo regalis (MNI, 2; less than one percent). Ferruginous Hawk was identified from a right ulna and a left radius, ulna, cuneiform, carpometacarpus, and manual phalanx. The species is usually limited to sites in eastern Arizona, Colorado, New Mexico, and Chihuahua. These specimens may represent rare local birds, or the remains of wing fans of feathers brought from areas to the east.

Aquila chrysaetos (MNI, 6; less than one percent). Golden Eagle specimens are extremely rare at the site, consisting of two bird burials, two pedal phalanges, and two fragments of pelves. Starting in Basketmaker II times, golden eagles are widely distributed in southwestern sites.

Falcons

Prairie Falcons are now scarce, but formerly they were more common (Phillips, Marshall, and Monson 1964: 26). Sparrow Hawks still hunt insects in the meadow below Grasshopper.

Falco mexicanus (MNI, 1; less than one percent). Prairie Falcon is represented by a right ulna. Archaeologically it occurs in small numbers throughout eastern Arizona and New Mexico.

Falco sparvarius (MNI, 24; 3.72 percent). Sparrow Hawk elements are derived from 13 left wings, 6 right wings, 6 right legs, and 3 left legs. Like the Prairie Falcon, the Sparrow Hawk is found in many southwestern sites, but usually in considerably greater numbers. Occurrences may date as early as 300 B.C. at Snaketown.

Quail

Quail constitute 1.40 percent of the collection.

Odontophorinae (MNI, 2; less than one percent). Quail of undetermined genus and species are represented by a fragmentary tarsometatarsus and pelvis.

Lophortyx gambelii (MNI, 2; less than one percent). A right humerus and left radius were identified as Gambel Quail. They are known from Snaketown as early as 300 B.C., from Swallet Cave and Tuzigoot in the Verde Valley, Tonto Cliff Dwellings, the Point of Pines area, and the University Indian Ruin in Arizona, and from Wet Legget Pueblo and Pottery Mound in New Mexico.

Cyrtonyx montezumae (MNI, 5; less than one percent). Harlequin Quail specimens include bones of the wings, legs, and axial skeleton. Other sites where they are found are Corduroy Creek, AZ W:10:50 at Point of Pines, Arizona; and Pottery Mound, Las Madres Pueblo, Pueblo Largo, Gran Quivera, and Gila Cliff Dwellings in New Mexico.

Turkeys

Turkeys represent the largest group, totaling 39.38 percent of the unworked bird bone. Both the Large Indian Domestic Turkey, the dominant breed in the Southwest after A.D. 600, and Merriam's Wild Turkey are present.

Meleagris gallopavo (MNI, 161; 24.96 percent). There is no evidence that the Large Indian Domestic breed was regularly eaten at Grasshopper. Only two specimens showed any sign of pathology. The tarsometatarsus of a large adult male had accretions on the bone and abnormal spur core; the right ulna of another was warped and the proximal head was greatly enlarged. Only three turkey burials were recovered. Major elements except the feet of a female, Bird Burial 12, were recovered from Room 108. The bones were badly broken and no tarsal splints were recovered, indicating that the flesh was removed before the bones were deposited. An old female was buried with an egg in the subfloor near the hearth of Room 121. The third burial was a large young adult male associated with Burial 337. The other sample of eggshell was found in Room 143 on the west side of the Great Kiva. Domestic turkeys from Grasshopper are morphologically quite similar to specimens from Canyon de Chelley and Point of Pines, Arizona, and Casas Grandes, Chihuahua.

Meleagris gallopavo merriami (MNI, 93; 14.42 percent). The minimal faunal count for wild turkeys may be low, because fragmentary specimens could not be separated from the main body of turkey remains. Wild turkey specimens occurred only as random bones; nine of them have butchering marks. Archaeological occurrences of Merriam's Wild Turkey follow the Mogollon Rim from southeast to northwest and include the Gila Cliff Dwellings; Tularosa Cave; AZ W:10:15, AZ W:10:50, and AZ W:10:51 at Point of Pines; AZ P:16:1; Bear Ruin; and Swallet Cave. The time range extends from before A.D. 600 through A.D. 1450.

Cranes

Greatern Sandhill Cranes are listed as former summer residents at Mormon Lake and in the White Mountains. The immature specimen recovered from Grasshopper is young enough to suggest that it was hatched in the area.

Grus canadensis tabida (MNI, 1; less than one percent). Greater Sandhill Crane is represented by the fragmentary right radius of an immature bird. Unworked bone of the subspecies has also been recovered from Mesa Verde in Colorado, Gran Quivera in New Mexico, and the Point of Pines area, Arizona.

Sandpipers

Limnodromus scolopaceus (MNI, 1; less than one percent). The Long-billed Dowitcher was identified from a right scapula. The bird would have been available as a fairly common spring or fall migrant (Phillips, Marshall, and Monson 1964: 36). This species occurred during the A.D. 1300s at Las Madres Pueblo, New Mexico.

Doves

Both species of doves recovered from the excavation are summer residents in the Grasshopper area today. Only bones of the wings were recovered.

Columba fasciata (MNI, 3; less than one percent). Band-tailed Pigeon is known from Corduroy Creek and Point of Pines in Arizona, Casas Grandes in Chihuahua, and the Largo-Gallina district of New Mexico.

Zenaidura macroura (MNI, 3; less than one percent). Mourning dove is widely distributed in southwestern sites, starting at 300 B.C. at Snaketown.

Macaws

Thirteen macaws, 2.02 percent of the unworked bird bone collection, were recovered from Grasshopper as of 1972. The temporal distribution of macaws in the southwestern United States (Hargrave 1970b: 54) follows fluctuations of occurrence at Casas Grandes fairly closely, but may vary by 50 years in some cases.

Ara sp. (MNI, 4; less than one percent). These four macaws are represented by fragmentary and random elements. The radius of one measures beyond the range of prehistoric Military Macaws, so it is probably a Scarlet Macaw. Military Macaws were not a standard item of trade in the prehistoric Southwest, and there is no reason to suspect that any macaw from Grasshopper would be of this species.

Ara macao (MNI, 9; 1.40 percent). Three Scarlet Macaws occurred as single bird burials, and a pair as a double bird burial. One peculiar specimen was spread-wing on the chest of a buried child and was made up of spare parts from more than one individual. The head, wings, and sternum are those of a large aged bird, while the pelvis and legs appear to be from a small immature about 11 months old. Burial disturbance prior to excavation is indicated because part of the premaxilla, some manual, and pedal phalanges of the macaw and three fragments of human bone were found near but not in the burial pit. Five of the macaws manifested the roughened ulnae common among captives of this species. One 11-month-old individual had the right ulna fused to the humerus in a flexed position, and pathological deformity of the second manual phalanx of both second digits. Hargrave (1970b: 53) reports that 47 percent of 145 macaws from north of the Mexican border were pathological; 40 percent of those from Grasshopper had the same types of pathology.

Ground Cuckoos

Geococcyx californianus (MNI, 5; less than one percent). Roadrunner was identified from two left tibiotarsi, two left ulnae, and a left humerus. The elevation of Grasshopper is high for roadrunners but rocky canyons with more suitable habitat at a lower elevation occur nearby. Roadrunners are found as early as A.D. 100 at Snaketown. Later occurrences include Wupatki, Tonto Cliff Dwellings, and the University Indian Ruin in Arizona; Casas Grande in Chihuahua; and Gran Quivera, Las Madres Pueblo, Pueblo Largo, and Gila Cliff Dwelling in New Mexico.

Owls

Owls total 4.34 percent of the unworked bird bone collection. Of the six species of owls found at Grasshopper, probably four were local residents and two were from lower elevations. If prehistoric distributions were similar to present ones, the Great Horned Owl would have been a fairly common resident, the Pygmy and Spotted owls less common, and the Long-eared Owl rare. The number of Long-eared owls in Grasshopper excavations suggests deliberate selection by man.

Otus asio (MNI, 11; 1.71 percent). Screech Owl is represented by bones of three right and three left wings and two right and two left legs, a fragmentary mandible, and three unguals. It has been recovered from Long House at Mesa Verde, Colorado; Sand Dune Cave, Utah; Nalakihu and Point of Pines, Arizona; Chaco Canyon, Las Madres Pueblo, Pueblo Largo, Tijeras Canyon, and Atsinna Pueblo in New Mexico.

Bubo virginianus (MNI, 8; 1.24 percent). One Great Horned Owl skeleton was complete except for the head, distal left wing, and some pedal phalanges. It may have been discarded after desired parts were removed, or it may be a bird burial. Other samples include bones of one right and two left wings, one left and two right legs, a left coracoid, and a pelvis. Great Horned Owl is common in southwestern sites as early as the Basketmaker II period.

Glaucidium gnoma (MNI, 1; less than one percent). Pygmy Owl was identified from a cranium minus the premaxilla. Pygmy Owls are not known from other sites.

Speotyto cunicularia (MNI, 1; less than one percent). The left tibiotarsus of a juvenile was identified as Burrowing Owl. The species is known from Point of Pines, Wupatki, and Nalakihu in Arizona; Casas Grandes in Chihuahua; and Pindi Pueblo, Las Madres Pueblo, Pueblo Largo, Pottery Mound, Pueblo Pardo, and Gran Quivira in New Mexico.

Strix occidentalis (MNI, 1; less than one percent). A fragmentary right tibiotarsus of the Spotted Owl accompanied Bird Burial 2, a Red-tailed Hawk. Other occurrences include Casas Grandes in Chihuahua and Step House at Mesa Verde, Colorado.

Asio otus (MNI, 6; less than one percent). Bones of Long-eared Owls were from two left and two right legs and two left wings. Small numbers of Long-eared Owls are known from Swallet Cave, Nalakihu, and Houck in Arizona; and the Largo-Gallina district, Chaco Canyon, Gran Quivira, and Pratt Cave in New Mexico.

Woodpeckers

At present the Red-shafted Flicker and Acorn Woodpecker are common summer residents near Grasshopper. Williamson's Sapsucker would have been available as a winter resident. Woodpeckers represent 1.71 percent of the collection.

Colaptes auratus collaris (MNI, 8; 1.24 per cent). A cranium with the left quadrate but no mandible was found in a bowl with Burial 92. Other samples include another cranium, a sternum, and bones from three left wings and two right legs. Red-shafted Flicker is known from Long House at Mesa Verde, Colorado; several sites at Chaco Canyon, the Largo-Gallina district, the Galisteo Basin, and Pratt Cave, New Mexico; and Point of Pines in Arizona. The earliest occurrence is in Basketmaker II levels at Sand Dune Cave, Utah.

Melanerpes formicivorous (MNI, 2; less than one percent). Acorn Woodpecker specimens include bones from two right and two left wings and a right and left leg. Other occurrences of this woodpecker are at Pueblo Largo, New Mexico; Point of Pines area, Arizona; and Casas Grandes, Chihuahua.

Sphyrapicus thyroideus (MNI, 1; less than one percent). Williamson's Sapsucker, identified from a right ulna, was also found at Pratt Cave, New Mexico.

Corvids

Corvids, 16.90 percent of the collection, form the third most numerous group. Those represented could all have been obtained close to Grasshopper, including Clark's Nutcracker that sometimes visits chaparral habitats not far from the site. With the exception of some of the raven bones, the corvid remains represent wings and legs.

Cyanocitta stelleri (MNI, 8; 1.24 percent). Stellar Jay elements are derived from three left and three right wings and two left legs. They occur in sites in the Largo-Gallina district and in the Galisteo Basin of New Mexico.

Aphelocoma coerulescens (MNI, 1; less than one percent). Scrub Jay is represented by a right ulna. It is known between A.D. 300 and 700 from Sand Dune Cave, Utah, and Snaketown, Arizona. Later occurrences include Point of Pines and Swallet Cave, Arizona; Mesa Verde, Colorado; the Galisteo Basin, Wet Leggett Pueblo, and Pratt Cave, New Mexico.

Corvus corax (MNI, 80; 12.40 percent). Presence of major elements of a very small juvenile Common Raven and a few fragments of the axial skeleton indicate that some ravens were brought to the pueblo intact. However, the majority of bones are from limbs; there are 22 left and 31 right wings, and 17 left and 12 right legs. Raven remains are widely distributed in the Southwest, beginning at 100 B.C. at Snaketown.

Corvus brachyrhynchos (MNI, 14; 2.17 percent). Common Crow is represented by bones from two left and four right wings, and three left and four right legs. Crow, much less commmon than raven, is known from sites at Mesa Verde, Colorado; the Largo-Gallina district, the Galisteo Basin, and Gran Quivira, New Mexico; and Point of Pines, Arizona. The earliest occurrence is in Basketmaker II levels at Sand Dune Cave, Utah.

Gymnorhinus cyanocephalus (MNI, 5; less than one percent). Pinyon Jay is represented by a nearly complete skeleton, bones of the head, two left wings, and a right leg. This species was recovered from Basketmaker II levels at Sand Dune Cave, Utah. Later occurrences include Mesa Verde, Colorado; Chaco Canyon, the Galisteo Basin, and Gran Quivira, New Mexico; and Point of Pines, Arizona.

Nucifraga columbiana (MNI, 1; less than one percent). A left tarsometatarsus is identified as Clark's Nutcracker. The species has been recovered from sites in the Galisteo Basin, New Mexico.

Bluebirds

Sialia mexicana (MNI, 2; less than one percent). Western Bluebird, common summer residents at Grasshopper, were identified from a right ulna and left humerus and carpometacarpus. The Western Bluebird occurred at Antelope House in Canyon de Chelley.

Icterids

The meadows in the vicinity of Grasshopper are ideal habitat for all three of the Icterid species represented at the site.

Sturnella sp. (MNI, 2; less than one percent). Meadowlark is represented by a right and left humerus. Meadowlarks are known from Snaketown as early as 300 B.C. and from later sites in central and north-central New Mexico.

Xanthocephalus xanthocephalus (MNI, 1; less than one percent). The left humerus of a Yellow-headed Blackbird is in the size range of the more colorful male. The earliest occurrence of this species is at Snaketown from 300 B.C. Later recoveries are from Point of Pines, Arizona, and the Largo-Gallina district and the Galisteo Basin in New Mexico.

Euphagus cyanocephalus (MNI, 18; 2.79 percent). Brewer's Blackbird specimens include major elements of two, a cranium, a sternum, and bones from seven left and three right wings and three left and two right legs. Thirteen of the bones were within the size range of the more glossy black-feathered males. Brewer's blackbirds have been recovered from contemporaneous sites at Pueblo Largo in New Mexico, Point of Pines in Arizona, and Casas Grandes in Chihuahua.

Junco sp. (MNI, 2; less than one percent). Junco specimens include a premaxilla, a left humerus, a right ulna, and a right tarsometatarsus. Juncos were found at Snaketown, Arizona, from sites dating after A.D. 1200 in the Galisteo Basin, and from elsewhere in New Mexico.

13. PLANT REMAINS FROM ROOMS AT GRASSHOPPER PUEBLO

Vorsila L. Bohrer

The vegetation near Grasshopper Pueblo forms a mosaic of juniper (*Juniperus deppeana* and other species), ponderosa pine (*Pinus ponderosa*), and oak, both evergreen (*Quercus grisea*) and deciduous (*Q. gambellii*). Manzanita (*Arctostaphylos pungens* and *A. pringlei*) and pinyon pine (*Pinus edulis*) grow in rockier and sunnier habitats such as mesa edges and canyons (see Chapter 2). Part of the research program at Grasshopper has been a consideration of how the vegetation in the vicinity of the Pueblo may have affected its prehistoric occupants, and an exploration of the problem of change in the plant-man relationship during the century of occupation (A.D. 1300 to 1400). Pollen and seeds recovered from archaeological excavations represent samples of the former vegetation, often selected by the prehistoric inhabitants. Past vegetation was influenced by many environmental components, including soil, fire, and biotic factors, as well as climate. Man, a biotic factor, seems to have influenced the former vegetation more than small climatic shifts.

METHODS OF RECOVERING AND TREATING PLANT MATERIAL

Sediment from different features in the ruin were sampled by flotation in search of high densities of seeds. Until mid-1970, the excavated sediment sample was scattered on the surface of a bucket of water. The heavier soil, stone chips, and potsherds sank to the bottom, while plant debris, small bone, and snail shell floated. A sieve was used to scoop up the floated debris. It was then dried, sorted, bagged, and tagged. After mid-1970, a nonreagent grade of sodium silicate called *egg keep* was added to the water to increase the specific gravity. The sediment sample was poured into the water along with sodium carbonate (washing soda), which was used to break up the clumps of soil. Slight stirring of the mixture allowed the lighter material to rise to the surface where it was skimmed off with a sieve.

Pollen samples were collected from pottery vessel interiors, metates, portions of the room floor, room fill, burials, and test trench stratigraphic levels. Pollen extraction methods follow Mehringer (1967: 136-137) and the typology of pollen follows that of Hevly, Mehringer, and Yokum (1965: 128), with the exception of the Compositae. New Compositae categories include the *Senecio* type (Kapp 1969: 156) and low sharp-spine Compositae as opposed to the short round-spine type. The two short-spine categories seem to provide a better distinction between Ambrosiae (Ragweed) and the other Compositae that have spines less than 1.5 to 2 microns long (for example, *Gutierrezia*). Pollen was mounted in 200 centistoke silicon oil, and a count of 200 grains per spectrum was secured. Gerald Kelso kindly supplied the pollen data for Room 22.

PLANT REMAINS

Cultivated Plants

Maize, generally in the form of carbonized cob segments or cupules, floated more frequently than any other plant residue and it came from a greater variety of locations (room fill, floor, hearth, oven, and mortuary bowl). Indications of other cultivated plants were infrequent. The remains of *Phaseolus vulgaris* (common bean) from Room Block 1 and fragmentary remains from Room Block 2 (Table 13.1) presumably indicate regular cultivation, as beans are seldom recovered in abundance at any archaeological site. The *Cucurbita* (squash) pollen from Room 22 (see Table 13.4) probably represents a cultigen; I know of no wild species growing in the area. The single lot of nine seeds of *Gossypium hirsutum* (cotton) may represent a local cultivated crop rather than a trade item. Although Grasshopper lacks modern weather records, Arizona climatic maps provide estimates for the area of 120 to 140 days without killing frosts (U.S. Department of Agriculture 1941: 770). Lewton (1912: 7) stated that Hopi cotton ripens bolls within 84 days after sowing of the seed. Prehistorically, if favorable habitats were selected to encourage early maturation, cultivation probably was at least plausible. The inhabitants of Point of Pines (Arizona W:10:50) at an elevation of 6000 feet (1829 m) may have raised cotton, for carbonized seed and textiles are common in burned rooms (Bohrer 1973).

Cultivated sunflower (*Helianthus annuus*) or amaranth remains were not recovered. The Hopi raised a sunflower with blue-black achenes for a basketry, textile, and ceremonial dye, as well as for the edible kernel (Whiting 1939: 97). It is not known how late the cultivated sunflower was acquired or even if it enters the prehistoric record. Sunflower seeds from historic Hawaikuh are evidently wild (Smith and others 1966: 229). The small seeds from Grasshopper suggest similarity to present weedy, roadside sunflowers. The lack of preservation or recovery of small *Amaranthus* seed may reflect a bias; taxonomically its identity may be contained in the Cheno-am pollen category.

TABLE 13.1
Seed Distribution in Room Blocks at Grasshopper Pueblo

Rooms listed in sequence of construction	Maize	Juniperus	Arctostaphylos	Opuntia	Juglans	Other
Room Block 1						
Room 47 fill	X[1]	1				*Phaseolus vulgaris*
Room 40 feature 1[2]		1	2	1	X	*Gossypium hirsutum*
features 9, 13	X	8	3	2	X	
Room 41 fill		6				
Room 43 floor		5				
Room 39 features 6, 7, 8	X	1	1	2		
Room 116						*Vitis* (1)
Room Block 2						
Room 164	X	7	1			
Room 146 features	X	3	4	Cf		*Phaseolus, Vitis* (1)
Room 153 hearth	X					
Room 197 feature	X	2			X	*Vitis* (1), unknown (2)
Room 197-143 feature 1-2	X	1			X	*Rhus trilobata* type (2)
Room 143 feature 5	X					
Room Block 3						
Room 270 fill	X	2			X	
Room 218 feature 20	X	16	3			
Room 215	X	3				
Room 206	X	3				*Rhus trilobata* type (1) unknown (1)
Room 210	X	8	2		X	
Room 205 floor	X	1				*Chenopodium,* Gramineae, Compositae (?), unknowns

1. X = present.
2. Rooms indented in the listing were constructed at the same time (see Chapter 3).

The *Salvia reflexa* type seed (botanically a nutlet) merits mention, although it is not certain that the plant was cultivated. The whitish nutlet measured 2 mm in breadth, 2.5 mm in length, and resembled a low isosceles triangle in cross-section. Ten nutlets of *Salvia reflexa* supplied by the University of Arizona herbarium average 0.1 and 0.2 mm smaller than the prehistoric seed. The greatest difference between the prehistoric and modern *Salvia reflexa* seems to be in the width of the nutlet—modern ones range from 1.25 to 1.75 mm and the prehistoric type measures 2 mm in width.

Several explanations may account for the larger *Salvia* nutlet: (1) the parent plant grew in an especially favorable environment; (2) the nutlet benefited from a food supply normally shared with three others; (3) the nutlet derived from another species of *Salvia,* as yet uncollected, which has similar but larger seeds; (4) the nutlet came from a cultivated plant. The Huichol, Tarahumara (Beals 1932: 62), and other people in central and northern Mexico cultivated a species of *Salvia* and made a beverage from the seeds (Havard 1896: 44, Bukasov 1930: 532). The Pima of southern Arizona similarly used wild

Salvia columbaria (Russell 1908: 77). Archaeological evidence here or southward may eventually support the historic tradition of cultivation.

Wild Plants

Wild fruits used included *Arctostaphylos* (manzanita), *Helianthus* (sunflower), *Rhus trilobata* (squawbush), *Juglans* (walnut), *Juniperus* (juniper), *Opuntia* (prickly pear or cholla) and *Vitis* (grape). Both *Arctostaphylos* and *Juniperus* were recovered more frequently than any other wild species.

Plant remains in oven fill (Table 13.2) probably resulted from (1) the initial use of the oven and (2) later deposition of trash. The dual nature of the fill made it difficult to recognize what was actually prepared in the oven. Certainly maize could have been roasted there. Small, thin-coated seeds like *Cleome,* or pulpy fruits like *Vitis* or even *Rhus,* seem questionable. Degradation promoted by standing water in the oven probably explains the lack of seeds in the lower level.

TABLE 13.2
Distribution of Seeds in Ovens at Grasshopper Pueblo

| | | | | | | Seeds |
Provenience	Maize	*Juniperus*	*Arctostaphylos*	*Opuntia*	*Juglans*	Other
Test Trench 7D-9B						
Feature 2, Oven 1	X	1	1			*Helianthus* type
Room 205, Oven 1						
Level 1		4		1		
Level 2	X	10	4		X	Cf. acorn
Level 3	X	8	1	1	X	*Cleome, Vitis, Rhus*
Level 4	X	1				Compositae receptacle?
Level 5	X	1				unknown
Room 205, Oven 2			(no seeds)			
Room 205, Oven 3						
Level 2	X					
Level 4						*Rhus* type

Seed remains associated with burials provide further evidence of the importance of certain plants. Because seed remains may have been inadvertently deposited with a burial as part of the trash fill, only the contents of bowls that were included with two burials in Room Block 1 (B-400 and B-391) were considered. Presumably the bowls of food furnished nourishment for the spirit (Parsons 1939: 302). Two burials each had bowls containing a single carbonized cupule of maize. Both bowls associated with Burial 391 held a sunflower achene (*Helianthus* type). The two apparently uncarbonized whitish achenes, measuring 2 mm by 5 mm, are comparable in size to wild roadside species. The achenes might have swelled slightly when parched. One of the bowls retained the carbonized remains of a juniper seed and the other contained a seed morphologically similar to an annual species of *Salvia* (cf. *S. reflexa*) that grows in the area today.

Modern accounts suggest how the prehistoric plants may have been used. Mature juniper berries could be pounded into a meal cake, as the Zuni did historically (Standley 1912: 458). Walnut meats must have been eaten throughout the area where trees were accessible; walnut shells come from Cordova Cave (Kaplan 1963: 345) and Cameron Creek Village in New Mexico (Bradfield 1931: 11), Canyon Creek Pueblo (Haury 1934: 59), Point of Pines Pueblo (Bohrer 1973), and Tonto National Monument in Arizona (Bohrer 1962). *Helianthus* (sunflower) seeds were parched and eaten, and the oil was used by the Hopi to grease the piki stone (Harrington 1967: 314). Remains of wild *Helianthus* seeds accompanying burials have been reported from Mesa House Ruin, southeastern Nevada (Schellbach 1930: 101) and from Hawaikuh near Zuni, New Mexico (Smith and others 1966: 229).

Opuntia fruits were eaten in many parts of the southwestern United States (Bohrer 1962: 97), and the seeds were apparently used as a famine food by the Hohokam (Bohrer 1970). *Rhus trilobata* fruits (squawberries), whether ripe or immature, could be pounded and the water infusion drunk (Nequatewa 1943: 20). The berries could also be dried for food (Palmer 1878: 597) and were sometimes roasted (Havard 1896). Another local species, *Rhus glabra,* may have been similarly used. *Vitis arizonica* fruits (wild grape) were eaten fresh, but the pits could be saved and ground fine. Dried grapes were sometimes ground and cooked (Palmer 1878: 599). Ground *Cleome* seeds could be added to other meal and *Cleome* greens might be used as a vegetable or as a carbon paint (Harrington 1967: 72).

Arctostaphylos (manzanita) fruits were dried, pounded, and the pulp mixed with water to make a fermented drink in California. The dried pulp might also be mixed with flour and water and baked as a flat cake. The seeds could be ground fine and made into a mush as well (Palmer 1878: 599). The people from San Juan Pueblo, New Mexico, gather the berries of *Arctostaphylos pungens* for food (Ford 1968: 273), but most Pueblo Indians dwell some distance from the species. *Arctostaphylos* pits are rarely recovered from archaeological sites in Arizona.

Pollen

The smallest unit of a conventional pollen diagram, the pollen spectrum, represents the different frequencies of each pollen type in a single sediment sample. Various pollen spectra in a room document spatial differences in frequency. Each spectrum can be compared with its neighbor, but none subordinates the other in time of deposition, as in a conventional pollen diagram.

TABLE 13.3
Pollen Spectra from Four Samples in Room 39, Grasshopper Pueblo
(n = 200)

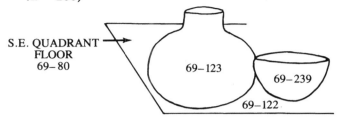

S.E. QUADRANT
FLOOR
69–80

Pollen Type	Provenience (sample number)			
	Floor (69-80) %	Floor (69-122) %	Jar interior (69-123) %	Bowl interior (69-239) %
Pinus	6.0	2.5	4.5	4.5
Juniperus	1.5	1.0	2.0	.5
Quercus	1.5	2.0		2.5
Cheno-am	35.0	42.0	35.0	33.5
Compositae				
Short sharp spine	8.5	11.0	5.0	14.5
Short round spine	21.0	27.0	*45.5*	25.5
*Long spine	5.5	6.5	2.5	2.5
Artemisia type	1.0		.5	.5
Senecio type	3.5			
*Liguliflorae	3.0	1.5	.5	.5
Gramineae	3.5	2.5	1.0	6.0
Zea mays	3.0	1.5		1.0
Alnus			.5	
*Cruciferae	.5	.5		
Cyperaceae	.5			
Ephedra torreyana type	.5			
*Eriogonum	.5			
*Liliaceae	1.0			
*Malvaceae	.5			
Plantago type	.5			1.0
Sarcobatus				.5
Typha	1.5			
Unknowns	1.5	2.0	3.0	7.0

*Insect pollinated categories
Note: Frequency in italics shows pollen spectral distortion; see text.

However, when spectra from different rooms are compared, it is quite possible some rooms predate others.

Several methods have been used to recognize sequences of room construction or occupation. Reid and Shimada (Chapter 3) analyzed wall abutments at Grasshopper. Hill and Hevly (1968) found that results of analyses of percentage of arboreal pollen were in essential agreement with results of archaeological methods in indicating the sequence of room construction at Broken K Pueblo. Both the order of construction and the length of room occupation must be closely correlated to allow pollen spectral distinctions. At Grasshopper the arboreal pollen percentages remained so low, even in the earliest rooms (two to six percent), that the small fluctuations seemed without significance. Thus, instead of making inferences concerning time of room occupation, investigation focused on recognizing and interpreting unusual concentrations of pollen from house floors.

Pollen spectra from prehistoric house floors are similar to pollen spectra derived from sediments free of human influence. Both kinds of spectra contain a predominance of wind-pollinated plants like *Ambrosia* (ragweed), *Chenopodium* (goosefoot) and *Pinus* (pine). These plants bear abundant pollen on inconspicuous catkins or other inflorescences on the terminal portions of the plant. Relatively few pollen grains from insect-pollinated plants become part of the spectrum, due to the much lower pollen production, and the heavier, enlarged grains. Human occupants could increase the frequency of any wind-pollinated category (1) by direct introduction of the floral parts, or (2) by introduction of mature seed that is well dusted with pollen (Bohrer 1972: 26). Similarly, the frequency of insect-pollinated types on occupation surfaces could be increased by deliberate use of floral parts for flavoring, food, or medicine. The repeated preparation of a plant on a grinding stone or the custom-

TABLE 13.4

Pollen Spectra from Room 22, Grasshopper Pueblo[1]

Pollen type	Provenience (sample number)							
	NE Quad., Floor 1 (60) %	SW Quad., Floor 1 (73) %	Vessel (95) %	SE Quad., Vessel (104) %	NW Quad., Vessel (98) %	Miniature Vessel[2] (208) %	Metate[2] (220) %	Metate (226) %
Pinus	6.0	4.0	0.5	6.5	1.5	3.0	4.5	4.0
Juniperus	2.0		0.5	2.0	1.0	0.5	4.5	3.5
Quercus	1.0	0.5		0.5				
Cheno-am	26.0	24.5	*50.0*	33.0	22.0	27.5	*52.5*	18.0
Compositae								
Short spine	20.0	18.5	17.0	19.0	31.0	8.5	21.0	39.0
*Long spine	11.0	19.0	15.0	20.0	12.0	19.5	10.0	11.0
Artemisia type	1.0	1.5	0.5	0.5			0.5	
*Ligulifloreae	1.0	1.0	2.0	0.5				
Ephedra torreyana type	1.0		0.5	0.5				
Ephedra nevadensis type			0.5	0.5				
Gramineae, except	10.0	11.0	2.0	4.0	*22.0*	13.5	2.0	16.0
Zea mays	11.0	9.5		1.0		18.0	0.5	
*Cleome				0.5		1.0	0.5	
*Cruciferae							0.5	
Cucurbita		1.5		0.5		1.0		
Cyperaceae	3.0	2.5	2.0	3.5		1.0		1.0
*cf. *Eriogonum*	2.0	2.0	3.0	3.0				
Euphorbia					2.5		1.0	1.5
*Malvaceae								
*Nyctaginaceae			0.5	0.5				
*Onagraceae			0.5				0.5	0.5
Opuntia	1.0	0.5						
Typha		1.0						0.5
Umbelliferae				1.5		1.5		1.0
Unknown	4.0	3.0	5.5	2.5	8.0	5.0	2.0	4.5

1. All pollen samples were obtained in 1965; n = 200 except for vessel 98, where n = 100.
2. Probably associated with Floor 2.
*Insect pollinated categories.
Note: Frequencies in italics show pollen spectral distortion; see text.

ary storage of a plant in a pottery vessel may leave a concentration of pollen (pollen spectral distortion) that provides some suggestion as to the former use of the utensil.

The recognition of pollen spectral distortion may be subjective. The rarity of some insect-pollinated categories in surface samples makes their presence on a former house floor noteworthy, especially if modern Pueblo Indians have uses for the plant. A number of insect-pollinated plants in the southeast quadrant of Room 39 (Sample number 69-80, Table 13.3) might have been used in that room. Because of the plant family designations characterizing pollen, one can only speculate within a family which particular taxa might have been used. Tansy-mustard (*Descurainia*) seeds were formerly a widespread and popular food in the Cruciferae. *Eriogonum* had numerous medicinal uses. *Yucca* and *Nolina* (beargrass) bear edible flowers and useful leaves (*Liliaceae*). Another local member of the lily family, *Tradescantia pinetorum,* may have been eaten (Whiting 1939).

The *Cleome* (cf. Rocky Mountain beeweed) pollen from Room 22 probably indicates use of the plant as either a vegetable or pigment (Table 13.4). The *Cucurbita* (squash) pollen from the same room provides the only evidence for the presence of cultivated squash; no wild species have been observed. The Hopi (Whiting 1939: 93) and Zuni (Stevenson 1915: 46) had special uses for squash flowers in ceremonies, medicine, and food. The *Opuntia* cactus pollen may represent the use of buds, pads, or canes as a vegetable; the pollen clings to any of the roughened surfaces (that is, spiny areolas) of the plant (Bohrer 1972: 26).

Room 22 apparently was built during a phase of rapid construction during the postdrought maximum in precipitation (Chapter 8). Cyperaceae (sedge) pollen came from floors, the interior of three vessels, and a metate surface (Table 13.4). *Typha* (cattail) pollen was present on the floor and on a metate. It is impossible to determine whether the widespread, low frequencies of this pollen were associated with the former living surface or with the fill. Regardless, it seems reasonable to suggest that *Typha* grew in marshy areas created by man or promoted by nature. *Typha* does not now grow in the immediate area. Because of the former presence of *Typha*, I believe species of Cyperaceae adapted to wet habitats were also formerly present. The typical habitat for the common modern sedge (*Cyperus fendlerianus*) is beneath the ponderosa pine canopy scattered among grass. Historically *Typha* and Cyperaceae (*Scirpus*) leaves were woven into mats; the growing shoots, pollen, and seed were esteemed for food (Harrington 1967).

Recognition of pollen spectral distortion in wind pollinated categories is less subjective if confidence intervals of the binomial distribution are used. As previously indicated (Bohrer 1972: 24), an interpretation of pollen spectral distortion seemed justified when a prehistoric frequency was so high that it failed to come within the limits of the 95 percent confidence interval (binomial distribution) of the highest probability of occurrence in a known normal spectrum. It would be ideal if the same criterion for pollen spectral distortion could be applied to Grasshopper, but problems arise when we evaluate a *normal* spectrum. The changes in density of ponderosa pine and grass since occupation by modern settlers (Cooper 1960) seem of sufficient magnitude to make comparison of the local prehistoric spectra with the modern pollen spectra of dubious value. Instead, recognition of pollen spectral distortion based on comparisons with different subsamples of house floors or other sediments of similar age seem more trustworthy. On applying these new criteria to pollen frequencies from the Hay Hollow site, I reached virtually the same general conclusions in regard to pollen spectral distortion as I did originally. The largest specific difference was in Pit House 32, which was particularly rich in Cheno-am pollen. By using contextual comparison, fewer samples were identified as showing Cheno-am spectral distortion, but it remained apparent that Cheno-am pollen was a culturally introduced factor in the pit house. Seeking associated, circumstantial evidence apparently provides a more conservative recognition of pollen spectral distortion, although the method risks overlooking much culturally introduced pollen.

In the southwest quadrant of Room 39, two adjacent vessels provided spectra that differed in frequency. Because all the pollen samples were taken on the same day (July 29, 1969), except for the bowl interior (Sample number 69-239) that was washed later (August 3), there should have been no more chance introduction of low-spine Compositae into one vessel than another, nor onto the floor surface. Differential preservation due to depositional conditions seems unlikely. In a sample of 200 grains, the mean number round-spine Compositae in the vessel and from the floor beneath the vessel show little overlap (Table 13.5); the two samples are probably different. The low-spine Compositae placed in the bowl when in use doubtless increased the pollen frequency. The low-spined Compositae category includes the ragweeds (*Ambrosia* spp.), sumpweeds (*Iva* spp.) and cocklebur (*Xanthium*). Because we have no remains of seeds or floral parts, genus and use can only be a matter of speculation. Medicinal uses for *Iva* or *Ambrosia* have been reported for the Navajo (Vestal 1952: 52), the Shoshone (Train, Henricks and Andrew 1941: 91), and Laguna and Acoma (Swank 1932: 26). *Iva annua* seeds were consumed prehistorically in the eastern United States (Watson and Yarnell 1966: 844).

Other examples of pollen spectral distortion come from samples from Room 22 with high Cheno-am frequencies from a vessel interior (50 percent) and a metate (53 percent; see Table 13.5). The pollen frequency from the vessel interior contrasted sharply with the frequency of pollen from the floor on which it rested (26 percent NE quadrant, 24.5 percent SW quadrant). Examination of the 95 percent confidence interval (Table 13.5) suggests that these differences are significant. Either a pot full of seeds dusted with pollen from the indeterminate infloresence or greens collected in the floral stage could explain the unusually high frequencies. We do not have a pollen sample from the presumed second story floor, with which the metate may have been associated. However, the 37 percent Cheno-am frequency maximum derived from sediments near the Pueblo during occupation provides some comparison (Table 13.5). Considering the general trend of the Cheno-am frequencies, it is tempting to infer that Cheno-am seeds (*Chenopodium* or *Amaranthus*) were ground on that metate.

Vessel 98 from Room 22 has an unusually high concentration of grass pollen compared with the frequencies of pollen found on the floor (Tables 13.4, 13.5). Like the Cheno-am infloresence, grass seed can become dusted with the pollen of flowers blooming above. Storage of grass seed in a vessel may explain the high count.

COMMENTS

Disturbed Habitats

An inspection of Table 13.6 reveals that at least six of the twelve genera utilized by prehistoric man proliferate in disturbed habitats. Modern annuals like *Chenopodium, Cleome serrulata,* and *Helianthus* thrive within and near the edges of cultivated fields. Fires in the past might have increased the vigor of individual plants of *Juniperus deppeana* (alligator juniper) and *Arctostaphylos* (manzanita), if not their actual abundance. The fire scars on the upper limbs and trunks of widely-spaced, old alligator junipers not only testify to the former presence of fire, but also of the resistance of the bark to fire injury. In addition, young *J. deppeana* resembles oak and manzanita in its ability to stump sprout (Little 1950: 22); the species also sends up shoots from lateral roots (Cotner 1963: 3). Reforestation need not await the growth of seedlings, for initial vigorous growth begins from large healthy root systems of *J. deppeana* already present. Fire also scarifies the pits of *Arctostaphylos* (Emery 1964: 84) and some species of *Rhus* (Daubenmeyer 1959: 320) to facilitate germination.

TABLE 13.5
**Frequency and 95 Percent Confidence Intervals* of Selected Pollen
Types from Grasshopper Pueblo**

Pollen	Frequency	Lower Limit	Upper Limit
Short, round-spine Compositae in vessel (69-123), Room 39	*45.5*	40	53
Short, round-spine Compositae on floor beneath vessel (69-122), Room 39	27	21	34
Cheno-ams in vessel interior (65-95), Room 22	*50*	43	57
Cheno-ams in NE quadrant of floor 1 (65-60), Room 22	26	20	33
Cheno-ams on SW quadrant of floor 1 (65-73), Room 22	24.5	19	32
Cheno-ams on metate (65-220), Room 22	*52.5*	46	59
Cheno-ams from test trench north of site (70-74-B), Column B	37	31	44
Gramineae in Vessel 98, Floor 1, NW quadrant, Room 22	*22*	17	29
Gramineae in NE quadrant, Floor 1, Room 22	10	6	15
Gramineae in SW quadrant, Floor 1, Room 22	11	7	17

*Derived from tables for n = 200 (Fryer 1966)
Note: Frequencies in italics show pollen spectral distortion; see text.

TABLE 13.6
Modern Habitats of Native Plants Recovered from Grasshopper Pueblo

Scientific Name	Common Name	Habitat
1. *Arctostaphylos*	manzanita	Sunny slopes of hills or escarpments, especially after fires
2. *Chenopodium* sp.	goosefoot	Disturbed ground
3. *Cleome serrulata*	Rocky Mt. beeweed	Disturbed ground
4. *Helianthus* sp.	sunflower	Disturbed ground
5. *Juglans major*	walnut	Canyon bottoms or areas of high water table
6. *Juniperus* sp.	juniper	Various, including forested land recovering from fire
7. *Opuntia* spp.	prickly-pear and cholla	Canyon margins, sunny slopes, grassland
8. *Rhus trilobata* type	squawberry	Various
9. *Vitis arizonica*	wild grape	Canyon bottoms
10. *Salvia reflexa* type		Meadows, swales
11. *Ambrosia, Iva,* or *Xanthium*	ragweed, sumpweed, or cocklebur	Disturbed, often damp, places
12. *Typha*	cattail	Marsh

Increasing amounts of disturbance by forest clearing and by cultivation would tend to increase the numbers of many economic plants. Since the full size of Grasshopper Pueblo was attained gradually during its span of occupation, the disturbance created by the first inhabitants might be regarded as a positive feedback mechanism that increased the human carrying capacity of the land and permitted further growth of the Pueblo. The below average moisture condition in the Grasshopper area prior to occupation (A.D. 1275 to 1295) as revealed by tree-ring studies (Chapter 8) might have enhanced the availability of disturbed habitats. Not only would timber density be reduced through moisture stress alone, but fires caused by lightning or human carelessness could

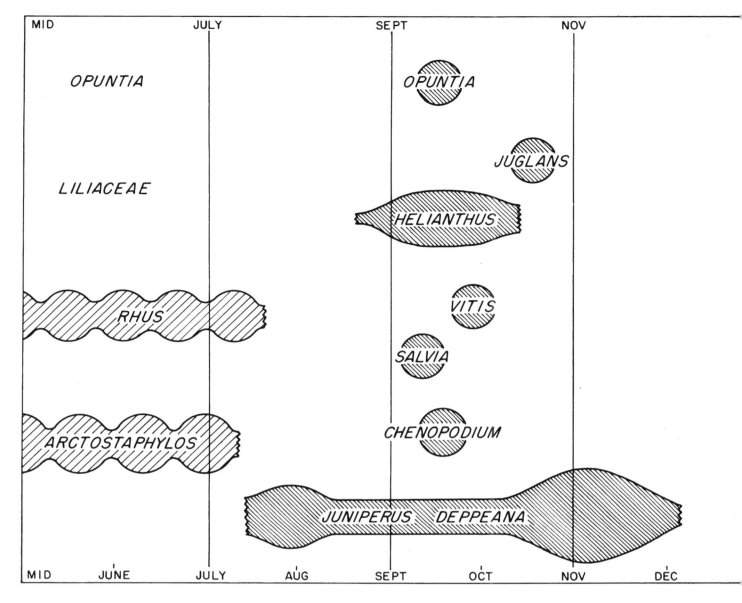

Figure 13.1. Botanical maturity and season of harvest of wild plants, Grass-hopper region. Length of bar suggests duration of harvest, width of bar indicates intensity of harvest. Hatched bars represent genera that probably vary in date of maturation from year to year.

spread quickly through the parched grass understory and severely prune new growth (Cooper 1960). Prior to government fire control efforts in Arizona, fire scars on stumps of trees reveal that the average interval between fires ranged from 4.8 to 11.9 years. If destruction by fire is added to the 10,000 to 12,000 trees estimated by Dean and Robinson (Chapter 8) to have been felled for the construction of the Pueblo and to the timber used for heating or cooking on a daily basis, the area clearly was undergoing substantial human disturbance.

Seasonality

Many types of fruit and seeds abound in September and October compared to other times of the year (Fig. 13.1). The least frequently recovered wild seeds (Tables 13.1, 13.2) mature in autumn together with many others, domesticated and wild. The first priority of harvest effort evidently went toward maize, and the remaining labor was diffused over a variety of wild plant products.

At other times of the year, there should be large harvests of *Juniperus* or *Arctostaphylos*. Although *Juniperus deppeana* fruit matures in August, the actual harvest could either precede or follow the September-October crop harvest period, for the berries remain on the tree for about a year after maturity (U.S. Department of Agriculture 1948: 206). *Arctostaphylos* (manzanita) pits were less numerous in the collection than *Juniperus* seeds. While the low numbers may simply mean less use, they may also indicate greater utilization of manzanita pits for gruel as Palmer (1878) observed.

Reliability

A subsistence farmer first experiences economic stress when his cultivated crops fail, but the situation grows serious when wild crops fail also. If we are to understand the relationship between plants and man, we must know more about the year-to-year reliability of the wild fruit harvests in a given locality. Wild fruits provide direct sustenance and indirect subsistence through their linkage to the food chain of game animals. For example, the abundance of wildlife in the mid-west can be predicted by the size of the acorn harvest (Sharp 1958: 1). Although the year-to-year reliability of the taxa in Table 13.6 has not been rigorously investigated, it is possible to make some general comments.

If the summer rains start late, the roadsides of New Mexico and Arizona lack their borders of wild *Helianthus* (sunflowers). The Hopi say that when sunflowers are numerous, the crop harvest will be plentiful (Heiser 1945: 166). While erratic production of *Juniperus deppeana* fruits could occur in pinyon-juniper communities (Vestal 1952: 12), productivity might be expected to be more regular at Grasshopper where ponderosa pine also grow (U.S. Department of Agriculture 1948: 206). Nonetheless, all *J. deppeana* only bore token amounts of fruit in August, 1971. Local residents claimed the preceding winter was one of intense cold and the spring one of severe drought. One or both of these conditions may have affected the juniper and other shrubs. Few *Arctostaphylos* bore healthy leaves and many branches of the shrubs had died; no signs of earlier flowers or fruit were evident. *Ceanothus,* another shrub whose foliage was affected, possessed a few flowering branches in August. *Opuntia,* the prickly-pear and cholla cactus genus, would be the least likely to suffer from drought. Both seeds and pollen were recovered at Grasshopper, although the plant is not abundant in the area today.

14. TWO POLLEN PROFILES FROM GRASSHOPPER PUEBLO

Gerald K. Kelso

Stratigraphic pollen data from Grasshopper are drawn from two profiles collected in Test Trench 70-2 just north of the site during the 1970 field season. The analysis of these profiles was conducted at the Laboratory of Paleoenvironmental Studies, University of Arizona, and pollen extraction procedures followed Mehringer (1967: 137). Terminology also follows Mehringer (1967), except that the pollen of the Compositae are referred to as "Ambrosia-type" and "other Compositae," rather than "low-spine" and "high-spine."

Profile B (Figure 14.1) was taken from clays deposited by Salt River Draw; Profile A (Fig. 14.2) was situated a few meters east of the arroyo channel. The slightly lower and consequently more moist location of pollen Column B is reflected in the higher representation of sedge pollen and the presence of occasional *Typha* monads in this profile. The single peak of 14 Cyperaceae pollen recorded at the 35 to 40 cm depth in Profile B coincides with a clay band thought to mark a pond created behind an early twentieth century dam (see Chapter 1). Both the Compositae and plants producing Cheno-am-type pollen tend to be found in disturbed soils. The larger Compositae contribution to Profile A and the greater amount of Cheno-am pollen in the lower portions of Profile B probably reflect the better drained condition of deposits at the location of the former pollen column. Within the Compositae group, the factor responsible for the extreme variation of the counts of the higher-spined, presumably zoophilous (Martin 1963: 49) "other Compositae" is not obvious. Fluctuations of this type of pollen are also prominent in the lower part of the fill, where they strongly influence pine representation. In the middle portion of each column other Compositae appears to co-vary with Ambrosia pollen. Extreme local mechanisms might have been involved, and smaller interval sampling might have revealed that large, very rapid fluctuations in the Compositae population were characteristic of this particular spot.

The most notable aspect of both Grasshopper pollen profiles is the marked drop in the frequency of pine pollen and the concomitant rise in Compositae, especially Ambrosia-type, and Cheno-am percentages between 1.2 m and 2.2 m from the base of pollen Column A. Similar fluctuations in the ratio between tree and herb pollen are apparent in pollen diagrams from other southwestern archaeological sites. Martin (1963: 48) noted that the most significant feature of the pollen counts from the Reserve Phase Dry Prong Reservoir at Point of Pines,

Arizona, was a postoccupational decrease in *Ephedra* and a concomitant rise in pine pollen frequence. Martin (1963: 48) suggested these fluctuations represented cultural rather than climatic factors, because he did not detect increases in pine pollen representation from desert alluvium deposits contemporary with the reservoir.

A similar increase in the representation of pine pollen occurred in postabandonment deposits at Wetherill Mesa (Martin and Byers 1965: 125). Reforestation of habitats from which trees had been cleared, the replacement of plants favoring disturbed soils by climax species, or a combination of these processes, may account for the resurgence of pine pollen representation rather than climatic change.

Pollen data from the fill of Reservoir Two at Casas Grandes, Chihuahua, seem to reflect circumstances analogous to those at Wetherill Mesa and Point of Pines. Here, in desert grassland, the beginnings of a downward trend in the frequency of Cheno-am pollen and an upward trend in pine pollen representation coincide at a depth of 110 cm with the disappearance of maize pollen from the fill. According to Charles Di Peso, a corresponding shift in the color of the sediments may indicate abandonment of the community. Apparently marked fluctuations in the representation of pine pollen may be expected in the pollen sequence of any large southwestern archaeological ruin.

These depressed pine pollen values, which invariably rise in frequency after abandonment of the community, are a function of cultural rather than climatic mechanisms. At Grasshopper, the segment of pollen Column A between roughly 1.2 m and 2.2 m from the base most likely represents the period of occupation. This interpretation is not corroborated by any archaeological data for Profile A, but the upper portion of a similar curve may be seen in Profile B, where pine pollen frequencies seem to indicate that abandonment occurred when ground level was at 115 cm to 130 cm below datum, and sherd material, fairly common in the deeper deposit, was not indicated above 125 cm to 130 cm in the stratigraphic drawing of the Profile B sediments.

Both prior to and following abandonment of the Pueblo, pine pollen percentage approximated 50 percent of the samples, a figure that Hevly's (1968, Fig. 5) data suggest is reasonable for the vicinity today. Data concerning the effect of disturbed site plant pollen production on pine pollen frequencies at this elevation are not presently available, but certainly it was a significant

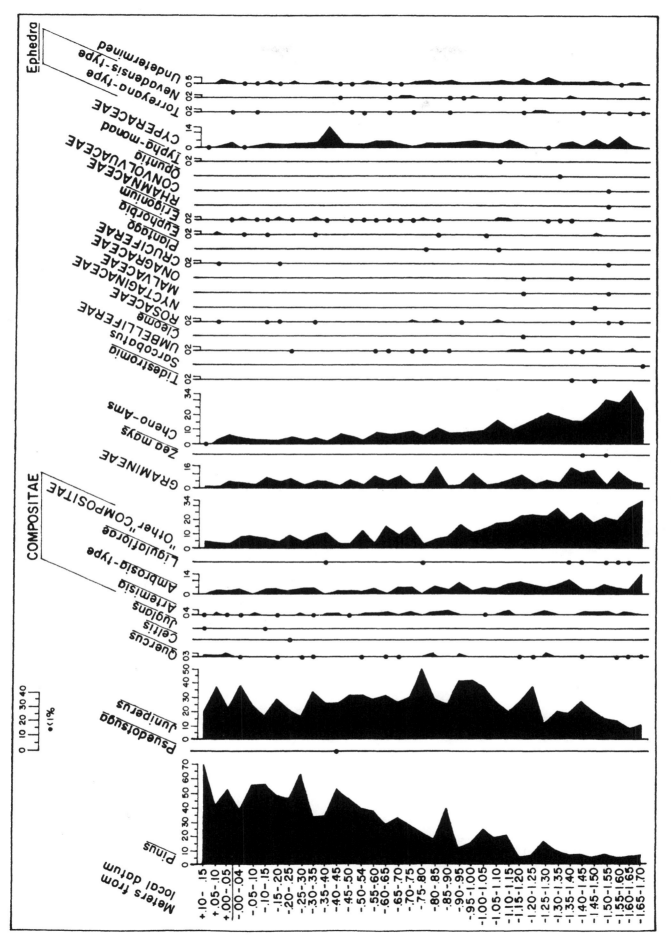

Figure 14.1. Pollen profile B at Grasshopper Pueblo. All counts are based on 200 grains.

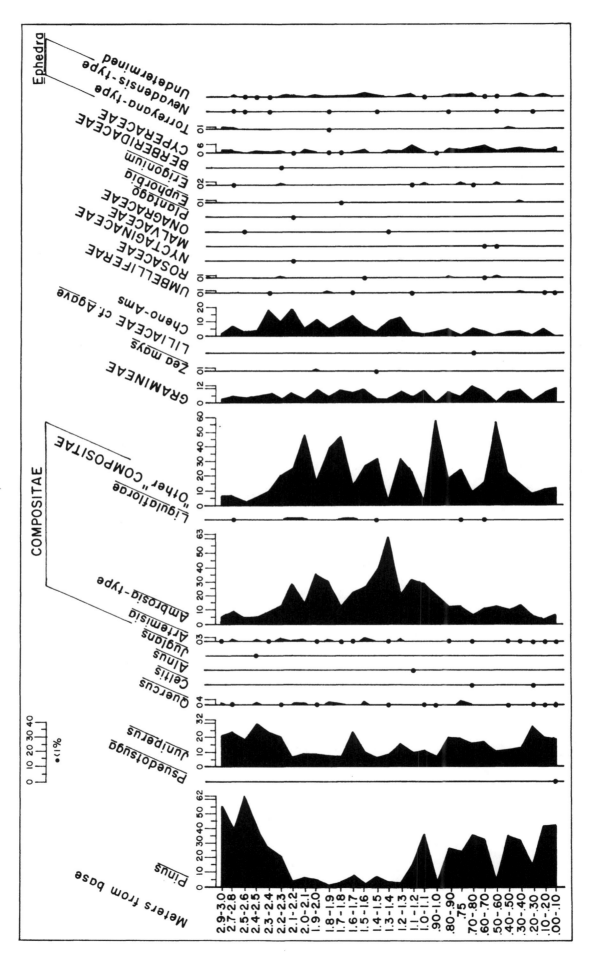

Figure 14.2. Pollen profile A at Grasshopper Pueblo. All counts based on 200 grains except for the interval 1.55 m to 1.60 m where n equals 100.

factor in the Grasshopper counts. Decrease in the pine pollen contribution to less than 10 percent during occupation of the Pueblo suggests that the trees were actually removed by cutting. A further indication that the trees were physically more distant during occupation of the village is suggested by a small rise in juniper representation after the village was abandoned and the subsequent tapering off of juniper as pine percentages recovered, a phenomenon perhaps reflecting the slightly faster migration rate of juniper during reforestation (Woodbury 1947).

The apparently abrupt nature of the drop in pine representation at 1.1 m to 1.2 m in Profile A and the fairly uniform pine contribution to the cultural segments of both pollen columns may indicate swift removal of trees from the vicinity, resulting from rapid growth of the village by aggregation as opposed to natural growth of the native population. Sharp change in the pine pollen configuration might also be a function of a fairly wide sampling interval (10 cm) and the relatively low sedimentation rate that might be expected on the higher ground above the arroyo, as implied by the relatively lengthy recovery period of pine pollen frequencies in Profile B (in contrast to Profile A). Absolute pollen frequencies, requiring knowledge of local sedimentation rates, are necessary for resolution of this question. In Profile A the rise of Ambrosia-type pollen, an indicator of disturbed soil, coincides with what may be the beginning of the juniper decline between 0.80 m and 1.0 m from the base. The juniper decline seems to precede the initial pine decline to a certain extent and suggests that the cutting of junipers began before the clearing of pines, perhaps reflecting prehistoric preference for vertical roof supports of juniper. Robinson (1967) has documented such a preference in the Colorado Plateau. Because construction presumably ceased some time prior to abandonment, local bias for juniper as an early construction material might partially explain the rise in juniper repre-

sentation below the point thought to mark abandonment in pollen Column B. Such interpretations are, of course, highly speculative.

When the pollen slides were scanned, three well-preserved pollen grains of *Zea mays* were noted at 2.3 m to 2.4 m from the bottom of Profile A, slightly above the point at which the arboreal types began to increase. The Cheno-ams did not drop off until later, and reforestation might have started while Grasshopper was still occupied. If true, then abandonment of the site was more or less gradual. Oak pollen is present in minor quantities in most samples of both profiles and shows no change in representation at abandonment. Oak trees grow in the immediate vicinity of the site today and may have constituted a protected resource during the life of the site.

Environmental chronologies based on pollen spectra from archaeological sites have been developed for various parts of the Southwest (Hevly 1964; Schoenwetter 1962, 1964, 1970). These chronologies may be biased by human activities that interfere with the natural pollen rain. Recent work indicates that such bias may be removed by application of principal component analysis (Fall, Kelso, and Markgraf 1981). In the absence of comparative environmental data from an independent source, however, it seems imprudent to attempt to elicit climatic information from the Grasshopper Pueblo pollen data at this time.

Some suggestions have been made concerning the nature of the local occupation and its effect on the local tree population, but these two profiles will best serve as a background for future pollen studies concerned with internal relations at the site. As at Broken K Pueblo (Hill and Hevly 1968), variation in the pine pollen frequencies might indicate relative room occupation dates when the longer, and perhaps more sensitive, Profile B is extended to cover the entire occupation period.

15. AGGREGATION AND ABANDONMENT AT GRASSHOPPER PUEBLO: EVOLUTIONARY TRENDS IN THE LATE PREHISTORY OF EAST-CENTRAL ARIZONA

Michael W. Graves, Sally J. Holbrook, and William A. Longacre

The preceding chapters report the results of research conducted at a fourteenth century Late Mogollon pueblo (see Fig. 1.1) by the University of Arizona Archaeological Field School and specialists from a variety of scientific disciplines. Although new and continuing studies may add knowledge to or modify our concept of cultural processes associated with this time period and locality, we can integrate the findings of studies now completed and discuss local and regional events that affected the outcome of aggregation and abandonment in the Grasshopper region. These processes are evaluated in terms of three broad areas of causality—population growth, environmental stress, and economic reorganization. The evolutionary implications of aggregation and abandonment in this area of the Southwest (following Cordell and Plog 1979) are also explored.

PREAGGREGATION OCCUPATION IN THE GRASSHOPPER REGION

During the period A.D. 1200 to 1300 small dispersed settlements dotted the Grasshopper region (Fig. 15.1). Small groups of sedentary or semisedentary agriculturalists occupied settlements that varied in size from one or two rooms to, rarely, as many as 20 rooms. Tuggle (1970: 103) grouped these settlements into spatial clusters by analyzing ceramic design similarity. These clusters, due in part to the small size of individual settlements, were maintained by economic, social, and historical relationships such as kinship alliances, exchange of marital partners, foodstuffs, and material goods, and cooperation in the performance of ritual activities. Tuggle's findings are in general agreement with other studies of dispersed settlements in similar areas of the Southwest prior to and during this interval (Bluhm 1960; Cordell and Plog 1979; Longacre 1966; Olson 1959; F. Plog 1974a, 1974b; S. Plog 1977; Wendorf 1956). Tree-ring dates from hearths beneath the earliest pueblo-associated surface of Plaza III at Grasshopper cluster in the early part of the 1200s. Excavations elsewhere, in the subfloor levels of rooms and beneath plaza surfaces, have revealed occupation surfaces and features (usually hearths or other forms of fire pits) that predate the founding of the Grasshopper pueblo community. In 1975 Frank Bayham reported a large pit structure, possibly representing a pit house, was partially excavated in the southeast corner of Plaza I. The structure was situated in a deposit of sterile clay and appeared to be associated with a low limestone wall. Both the wall and the pit structure occurred stratigraphically below

the east wall of Plaza I, which was composed of sandstone blocks and was clearly associated with the pueblo occupation.

The historical relationship of these earlier site components to the founding of the three major masonry room blocks of Grasshopper Pueblo is still unclear. Subsequent building and surface modification activities (for example, filling of low areas, dismantling walls and features) have apparently obscured many of these earlier remains. A period of time may have elapsed between construction of the earlier and later site components during which the vicinity was only sporadically occupied. The Grasshopper locale may have been used as a base camp for seasonal exploitation of resources associated with the riparian vegetation (walnuts, grapes, cottonwood) along Salt River Draw.

THE FOUNDING OF GRASSHOPPER PUEBLO

The founding of the pueblo settlement at Grasshopper between A.D. 1295 and 1305 was the result of a series of climatic and natural events set in motion nearly 25 years earlier. During the final quarter of the thirteenth century major portions of the Colorado Plateau and the mountainous Transition Zone in Arizona and New Mexico experienced a period of reduced effective moisture (Chapter 8; Douglass 1929: 751), often called the Great Drought. This drying trend was variable in its extent and in its effect on local environments and human populations. On the Colorado Plateau, this period of aridity corresponds temporally with relocation of several prehistoric groups to areas along major stream systems (Euler and others 1979; Mackey and Holbrook 1978; Jewett 1978; Jorde 1977; Lightfoot 1978). The climate was buffered during this interval, however, in the mountainous area south of the Mogollon Rim where a greater amount of precipitation fell during dry intervals than in areas to the north and south (Chapter 8; Euler and others 1979). Yet, climatic trends of the late 1200s did lead to environmental alterations in the Grasshopper Plateau (the drainage of the Salt River Draw) that we believe affected the establishment and aggregation of the community at Grasshopper. Whereas environmental or subsistence stress was implicated in aggregation on the Colorado Plateau (Hill 1970a; Jewett 1978; Lightfoot 1978; Longacre 1966; Schoenwetter and Dittert 1968), and was once hypothesized to have initiated aggregation at Grasshopper (Longacre 1974; Reid 1973), there is now sufficient evidence to substantiate a much different interpretation.

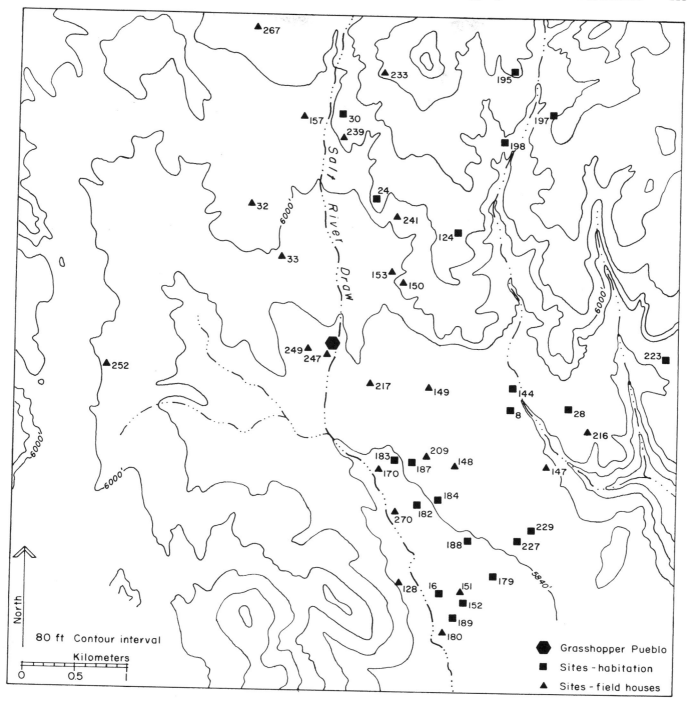

Figure 15.1. Location of preaggregation pueblos within a two-mile radius of Grasshopper Pueblo. Numbers refer to Arizona P:14 site designations of the Arizona State Museum.

Prior to the onset of drier conditions, beginning about A.D. 1275, the valley bottom of Salt River Draw was characterized by water-saturated soil conditions (at least on a seasonal basis) associated with well-developed riparian vegetation (Chapters 7, 8, 9, 11). These conditions probably extended from a point just north of Grasshopper to an area nearly 10 km south, and were probably similar to conditions along the upper portion of Cibecue

Creek today. The stream flow of Salt River Draw was greater than its current volume, and the water table may have been near the ground surface of the valley bottom.

During the interval from A.D. 1275 to 1300, when effective moisture in the region decreased significantly, the mean annual temperature may have risen slightly, thus increasing the length of the growing season. Water held near the soil surface of the valley would have evaporated at faster rates. It is also likely that Salt River Draw underwent a period of channel downcutting at this time (Chapters 8, 9), because intervals of drier conditions gradually lead to channel entrenchment (see Antevs 1955; Euler and others 1979). Excavations in the channel adjacent to Grasshopper revealed a gravel bar associated with prehistoric sherds contemporaneous with the pueblo occupation (Chapter 9), suggesting that after A.D. 1300 Salt River Draw flowed in a deeply cut channel. Such channel entrenchment would have lowered the water table and reduced the availability of moisture in the upper levels of the alluvium (Chapters 7, 8), perhaps affecting the riparian vegetation along the margins of the wash and vegetation on the valley floor. Vegetation would have been thinned by competition over the loss of ground water near the surface (Chapter 13) and the distribution of riparian species would have gradually clustered near the edge of the wash.

Toward the end of the period of diminished precipitation, during the five years before or after the beginning of the fourteenth century, the community at Grasshopper was established (Chapter 3), documented by tree-ring dates from early constructed rooms (Chapter 8). Three areas were selected for occupation, two on the west side of Salt River Draw and one on the east side. The size of each founding group, as indicated by the number of core rooms constructed in each area of the settlement, was not equivalent (Reid 1973). Between 5 and 10 rooms were built in the core sections of Room Blocks 1 and 3, whereas 21 rooms were constructed as a single unit in Room Block 2. This pattern of community settlement, the construction of small unit pueblos (Prudden 1914, 1918), is a direct outgrowth of trends established earlier in the area. However, the location of three contemporaneous room blocks within 100 m of one another and the variation in the number of rooms built within each room block suggest that a different set of occupation processes were operating in the Grasshopper vicinity by A.D. 1300, processes which were distinct from those of earlier settlements. A new trajectory of community development in the region was thus beginning (Fig. 15.2).

The two smaller construction units at the Grasshopper locality could have been built by groups "budding off" (Binford 1968; Birdsell 1957) from other settlements in the area. However, construction of 21 rooms in Room Block 2 suggests a different process—the movement of an entire village at one time. Excavations at the Chodistaas site (Crown 1981), a settlement of approximately 20 rooms located about one km northwest of Grasshopper, have disclosed that just prior to A.D. 1300 the entire pueblo was burned to the ground while it was being occupied. This conjunction, the end of occupation at Chodistaas and the establishment of a large core unit at Grasshopper by A.D. 1300 is remarkable and suggestive.

The major factor promoting the initial occupation of Grasshopper by three distinct social groups was the richness of the resources in the surrounding area. The settlement lies over an extensive limestone outcrop useful for construction (Scarborough and Shimada 1974), and

outcrops of other deposits of limestone and sandstone occur within a short distance of the site (Scarborough and Shimada 1974). A small seep or spring is located just north of the main ruin (Hough 1930). The settlement is a short distance from a variety of local environments, including the riparian habitats along Salt River Draw, which provided a number of hunted and gathered resources.

Perhaps the most important resource available to the inhabitants at Grasshopper was the expanse of alluvial bottomland suitable for cultivation, extending over four square km immediately south of the Pueblo. As a result of water saturation of the soil this area was previously uncultivated or, at best, minimally utilized for agriculture, but the drying trend that began 25 years earlier led to changes in the water table and in the vegetation of the valley. This interpretation is supported by analyses of pollen samples from Plaza I (McLaughlin and Trick 1974), from rooms (Chapter 13), and from test trenches outside the Pueblo (Chapter 14), and from analysis of the microfauna (Chapter 11). By A.D. 1300 dry farming could be practiced in the valley. At that time the expansion of agriculture in Salt River Draw did not require technological developments (new tools or water control devices) or extensive labor practices because the valley was apparently thinly forested, it had been only sporadically farmed previously, and it may have lacked a continuous or deep sod layer. Thus, the *initial* occupation at Grasshopper was conditioned by a brief and temporary climatic shift that in turn led to several crucial environmental changes, opening up a large area of fertile alluvium exploited for farming by the population at Grasshopper. The community was located at the northern terminus of this expanse of alluvium at a point where the flow of water down the Draw could be monitored and controlled. Above Grasshopper, Salt River Draw is characterized by a steep gradient and narrow valley, and below this point the grade decreases and the valley widens. A reservoir was built just north of the Pueblo to control water flow, and perhaps, to ensure an adequate supply of water for domestic use.

The founding of Grasshopper Pueblo thus represents a significant event in the prehistory of the region. The human population shifted their utilization of the Salt River Draw valley from seasonal or sporadic exploitation of wild resources and perhaps occasional farming along the drier fringes, to a fully agricultural commitment. This change in exploitative activity increased the productivity of the local subsistence system and fueled additional demographic and settlement changes in the community and region. Furthermore, none of these changes can be linked to environmental or subsistence stress, technological innovation, or population pressure (Cowgill 1974).

EXPANSION AND GROWTH AT GRASSHOPPER PUEBLO

The initial occupation at Grasshopper was based on agricultural exploitation of the previously unavailable

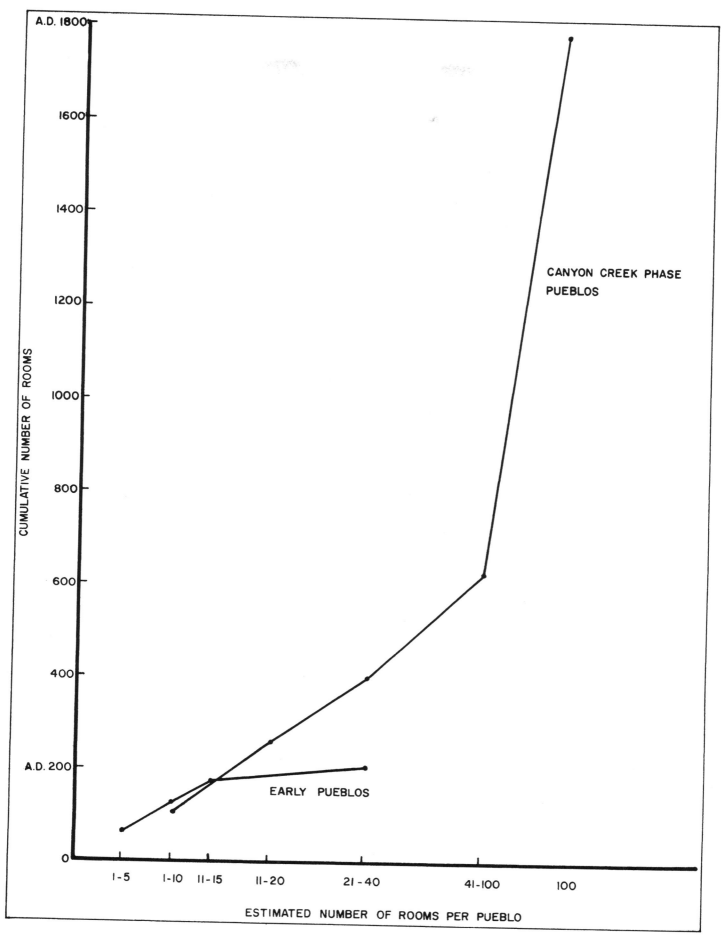

Figure 15.2. Cumulative number of rooms by estimated number of rooms per pueblo for two time periods, Grasshopper region.

valley bottom along Salt River Draw that had been favorably altered for cultivation by climatic and environmental change in the region. These events played an important role in the subsequent rapid population growth within the community (Chapter 3; Longacre 1974, 1975, 1976; Reid 1973) and the Grasshopper Plateau (Tuggle 1970). However, other factors also affected population increase and aggregation at Grasshopper and other contemporaneous pueblos in the region.

Much of the building activity at Grasshopper was completed by A.D. 1330. The corridor connecting the southern portion of Room Blocks 2 and 3 was roofed between 1320 to 1325. By 1325 these two room blocks had reached their maximum southward extension; the prehistoric pond and low-lying areas constrained expansion in other directions. Few tree-ring specimens recovered from the site date after A.D. 1330. The conversion of Plaza III to a Great Kiva sometime after 1330 represents the last major construction event (Chapter 8). Thus, within 30 to 40 years a small community initially composed of about 35 structures grew to encompass nearly 500 rooms, although not all 500 were contemporaneously occupied. By 1325 most of the three main room blocks, containing nearly 300 ground story rooms, had been built and were in use. After 1325 rooms were abandoned at an increasing rate so that through time the number of contemporaneously occupied rooms decreased.

The rapid rate of human population growth, as indicated by the rate of room construction, did not result from increases in the local population by births alone (Longacre 1975, 1976; Reid 1973). Given the initial size and reproductive capacity of the group inhabiting the core rooms, the size of the community could not have achieved a ten-fold increase within the period of one or two generations solely by reproduction. A substantial immigration of individuals into the community accounted for the rapid rate of construction that has been documented. At first these individuals may have been attracted by the availability of agricultural land, but at least two other factors operated to promote aggregation at Grasshopper.

First, once the process of aggregation was initiated at communities such as Grasshopper, it may have been difficult to stop. As stated above, prior to A.D. 1300 each village or hamlet depended for survival on the set of mutual arrangements between it and other settlements within its cluster. Under these conditions marriageable men and women were exchanged, foodstuffs may have been traded during temporary shortages, and villagers cooperated in ritual activities to ensure ideological maintenance. The initial loss of households and possibly sets of related households to the developing nucleated communities disrupted the set of exchange relations and alliances that had enabled the perpetuation of dispersed hamlets. Perhaps most importantly, it was no longer possible for small settlements to depend on reciprocal exchange of marital partners, and access to persons who could maintain a settlement's viability was limited. Individuals who moved to Grasshopper would have been incorporated into a nucleated community that provided suitable marital partners, supplemental foodstuffs, and cooperation in ritual activities both within and between large settlements. There was, therefore, little reason to sustain these links with individuals in dispersed settlements. As a result, those who attempted to remain in dispersed settlements would have come under increasing pressure to migrate to Grasshopper or to one of the other large pueblos in the region. This concept may help explain why small dispersed settlements on the Grasshopper Plateau were quickly abandoned and replaced by larger pueblos in the fourteenth century (Table 15.1).

TABLE 15.1

Distribution by Time Period of the Number of Rooms in Prehistoric Pueblos in the Grasshopper Region

Number of rooms per pueblo	All earlier pueblos	Canyon Creek phase pueblos	Total
1-20	33	22	55
Over 20	2	21	23
Total	35	43	78

Note: $X^2 = 18.25$, 1 d.f., $p < .001$

Grasshopper represents one of the earliest aggregated communities in the region, and it may have been instrumental in the process of aggregation of other communities in the drainage of Salt River Draw (Fig. 15.3). Once the process of aggregation had started at Grasshopper and dispersed settlements were abandoned, the effect may have rippled across the region. Because there were spatial (and we assume logistic) constraints on the occupation in the vicinity around Grasshopper, other communities were established to the south and toward the western escarpment of the Grasshopper Plateau. Although smaller in size than Grasshopper, there is no evidence that these communities were hierarchically ranked by access to traded goods (such as the White Mountain Red Wares) as has been reported for the Chavez Pass region during this interval (Cordell and Plog 1979).

Tree-ring data from Canyon Creek Pueblo (Haury 1934) indicate that portions of the regional population were aware of these settlement trends and anticipated aggregation. The ruin at Canyon Creek is located on the western escarpment of Grasshopper Plateau. According to Michael Graves, secondary beams of the dwelling were cut as early as A.D. 1305 and then stockpiled on a yearly basis until 1327 when the first room was built (Haury 1934). Nearly 70 percent of the sample of core and dated secondary beams that remain at the site were cut prior to 1327. Most have incompletely formed final rings, indicating that death (presumably due to cutting) occurred during the latter part of the summer growing season.

As early as A.D. 1305, then, a group exploiting the resources of the canyon area west of the Grasshopper Plateau recognized the potential of building at a location

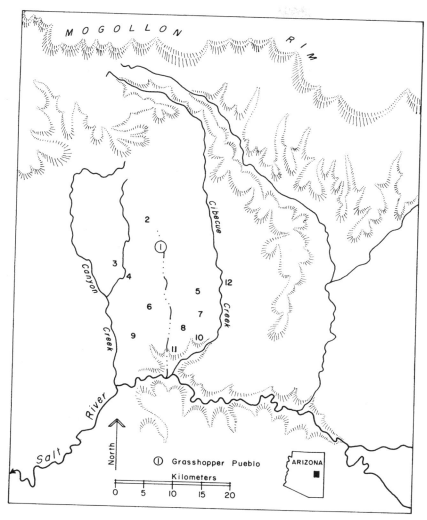

Figure 15.3.
Location of large contemporaneous
late prehistoric pueblos
in the Grasshopper region.
(Site numbers are in the
Arizona State Museum Site Survey.)

1. AZ P:14:1, Grasshopper Pueblo
2. AZ P:14:12
3. AZ P:14:15
4. AZ P:14:14
5. AZ P:14:25
6. AZ P:14:13
7. AZ V:2:13
8. AZ V:2:3
9. AZ V:2:1, Canyon Creek Pueblo
10. AZ V:2:7
11. AZ V:2:49
12. AZ P:15:15

along Canyon Creek and the possibility of aggregation there. Every summer or early fall for the next 25 years secondary beams were stockpiled, presumably in anticipation of a projected settlement shift. Although some of the individuals who settled at Canyon Creek may have been drawn from the larger pueblos, the timing of the stockpiling prior to and during the expansion phases of aggregation suggests that the founding population at Canyon Creek was composed of individuals from dispersed settlements.

The second factor that encouraged rapid population growth in the Grasshopper region was intercommunity exchange. Although the best documented evidence for exchange suggests interregional trade, exchange among contemporary late prehistoric pueblos within the region was probably widespread as well (Lightfoot 1979; Tuggle 1970). Three classes of material items seem to have been traded into the community in large quantities from outside the Grasshopper Plateau—White Mountain Red Ware (Carlson 1970; Whittlesey 1974), turquoise, and shell. Other introduced items included small quantities of certain kinds of pottery (such as Kinishba Polychrome and Kinishba Red, Jeddito wares, and Zuni glaze wares),

and mineral and lithic resources (quartz, obsidian, serpentine, gypsum). Although comparison with late Mogollon communities in other regions is difficult, it is clear that large quantities of pottery, shell, and turquoise found their way to Grasshopper Pueblo. Furthermore, a minimum of 20 macaws (*Ara* sp.) have been recovered from the site, one of the largest collections of macaws recorded from a prehistoric pueblo north of the Mexican border (Chapter 12; Olsen and Olsen 1974).

Traded products were derived from widely divergent sources. White Mountain Red Ware was produced in communities just north of the Mogollon Rim such as Showlow and Fourmile (Fewkes 1904; Gladwin and Gladwin 1931; Haury and Hargrave 1931). Most of the shell came from the Gulf of California or Pacific Coast (Brand 1938); it may have been procured and worked by Hohokam communities in the Salt River and Gila River areas (Hayden 1972; Weaver 1976) and then traded to communities north of the Salt River. The macaws were probably transported from Casas Grandes in the Mexican state of Chihuahua (Chapter 12; Hargrave 1970b). Also, according to John Olsen, two individuals of the White-fronted parrot, *Amazona albifrons* (Sparrman), whose most northern occurrence is in southern Sonora, Mexico, have been found at Grasshopper. Thus far this particular parrot has been recovered in the Southwest from only two other pueblos, Pecos and Gran Quivira, both of which engaged in extensive trading operations during the sixteenth and seventeenth centuries (Kidder 1958; Vivian 1964). Two prehistoric turquoise quarries have been identified near the confluence of Canyon Creek and the Salt River (Haury 1934; Moore 1968), but specific procurement locations remain unknown.

Interregional exchange occurred in the Southwest prior to A.D. 1300 (S. Plog 1977; Shepard in Judd 1954), although little is known about its extent or importance. Significantly, the Grasshopper region seems to have had only limited involvement in interregional trade during this period. Survey and excavation at earlier (pre-1300) sites suggest that the Grasshopper vicinity was remote (Tuggle 1970) from better established trade networks to the east (Point of Pines and Forestdale) and west (the Flagstaff area). With the founding of Grasshopper this situation changed and interregional trade increased dramatically.

In 1976 Gordon Bronitsky noted that during the early period of occupation at Grasshopper, greater amounts of exotic goods were included as mortuary offerings with deceased individuals than with individuals interred later in time (Whittlesey 1978). Agricultural surplus may have been the major item traded from Grasshopper during the early 1300s. Manufactured goods became more important for trade only in the latter portion of the occupation span. Through time, ground story rooms around extramural areas of the Pueblo (the plazas and the Great Kiva) shifted in function from domestic activities to specialized manufacturing areas for trade items such as chipped and ground stone, iron-based pigments, and bone tools and ornaments (Ciolek-Torrello 1978).

Clearly, production for exchange and transport of goods provided one way for individuals to perform tasks that were not agriculturally based on at least a part-time basis. This trend—diverting some of the work force to manufacturing activities—seems to have increased through the occupation span of Grasshopper, perhaps as a result of decreasing availability of new farm land coupled with the success of established trading enterprises within and between regions.

Other evidence supports the argument that the Grasshopper population increasingly engaged in trade as the local economy shifted away from agricultural self-sufficiency. There appears to have been a growing dependency on game animals, both imported and locally obtained, during certain seasons of the year or during unfavorable years. A wide variety of mammal and bird species were exploited (Chapters 10, 12), and wild turkeys were hunted during late winter. Subadult mule deer were heavily cropped on a year-round basis (Mathews and Greene 1972), and dogs were occasionally butchered. In addition, agricultural features occur only sporadically in the Grasshopper vicinity and the construction dates of only a few have been reliably shown to fall within this time period. Thus agricultural intensification by a more effi-

cient means of water retention was not implemented. Trade would have buffered the Grasshopper population from subsistence stress and at the same time sustained continued population growth by ensuring that resources matched or exceeded the needs of the community.

Our interpretation of the process of aggregation at Grasshopper has focused on the role of expanded availability of habitat suitable for agriculture (resulting from climatic fluctuation) and subsequent increases in agricultural productivity leading to immigration to Grasshopper of groups of households from both local and nonlocal areas. This process eventually terminated previously existing relations among small dispersed settlements while at the same time new relations were established in the large communities, including more far-reaching exchange networks. The new settlement system, however, was based on traditional, relatively unchanged, farming practices (Athens 1977; Binford 1972). Intercommunity exchange stabilized the flow of energy to those communities during the period of rapid immigration and population growth. The outcome of these events was a system of economically interdependent communities not unlike the settlement system it had replaced but involving considerably larger, localized populations and exchange as the dominant intercommunity relationship.

ABANDONMENT

The process of abandonment may involve a number of complexly related events, including movement by individuals, households, and larger social groups, and changes in birth and death rates (Martin and Plog 1973; Stanislawski 1973; Titiev 1944). Factors influencing these events may act differentially on groups within a community. We do not have much information as to why the Grasshopper region was depopulated, but data are accumulating that may shed some light on the events that played a role in this process.

Room construction at Grasshopper decreased rapidly after A.D. 1350. Similarly, between 1360 and 1370 room construction ended at Canyon Creek Pueblo. On the Grasshopper Plateau, expansion of communities had reached its peak before 1375 (see Fig. 15.3). Although population size may not have begun to decrease immediately thereafter, the rate of population growth probably fell rapidly. Archaeological evidence suggests that by A.D. 1400 Grasshopper and the other communities in the region were occupied by few, if any, inhabitants. This implies that after 1375 segments of the regional population (perhaps new or younger households) began to leave the area. Remaining households composed of older individuals would have been characterized by declining birth rates and increasing death rates. In combination, these events would have resulted in the rapid decline of the regional population.

Numerous rooms at Grasshopper are 'late abandoned' (Ciolek-Torrello 1978; Reid 1973, 1978). They are characterized by abundant and varied material remains abandoned in situ on the last occupied floor. Storage vesse and grinding bins, grinding stones, and a wide array of stone and bone tools and raw materials were clearly left in place when the rooms, and presumably the community, were abandoned. The lack of evidence of scavenging from these rooms is consistent with a trend toward regional depopulation—the distance that people were moving prevented transport of large, replaceable goods (Wasley 1952). Apparently return trips were not anticipated or made to Grasshopper to gather what had been left behind.

The nearly synchronous abandonment of Grasshopper and other pueblos in the region was not coincidental, and it shifts the focus from Grasshopper to the region in which Grasshopper was but one component. Furthermore, this process reflects the collapse of an entire system of interdependent communities within the region. We are unable to attribute this collapse directly to climatic fluctuations or environmental change. Climatic conditions throughout most of the fourteenth century in the Grasshopper region were within the range of normal variability except for a period of increased rainfall at the beginning of the century (Chapter 8). This region is part of the White Mountain Refugia (Euler and others 1979), one of the few areas of the puebloan Southwest occupied after A.D. 1300. Such refuge areas, including the Zuni Mountains, Rio Grande Valley, and Hopi mesas, were still occupied by historic pueblo groups when the Spanish entered the Southwest. Thus, depopulation of the Grasshopper region, while puebloan occupation continued elsewhere, does not reflect large scale climatic change.

Certain characteristics of the aggregation process at Grasshopper are implicated in the eventual abandonment of the town and region. Aggregation occurred over a fairly short period of time and involved a substantial number of people. Data from Grasshopper and Canyon Creek suggest that although temporal changes occurred in the production of agricultural and material goods and the organization of exchange relations, the political organization of these communities did not undergo significant development in the direction of increased complexity and differentiation (Ciolek-Torrello 1978; Whittlesey 1978; contrary opinion, see Molloy 1978). Essentially, the political organization of a low density dispersed settlement system was mapped onto a new high density nucleated settlement system (Jennings 1966). The changes in social organization that have been documented involved shifts in the spatial organization of households and in the activities conducted within these units (Ciolek-Torrello 1978), and a shift from a pattern of small kivas dispersed across the community to one large kiva presumably serving most, if not all, of the community. Study of mortuary treatment has indicated that no major structural changes occurred related to access to wealth or power in the community that might emerge in a vertical hierarchical system (Whittlesey 1978), contrasting with previously analyzed data from Grasshopper that suggested that status differentiation had occurred (Cassells 1972; Griffin 1967, 1969). This does not mean that the community was characterized by an egalitarian organi-

zation. Sex and age appear to be the primary attributes that influenced the quantity and quality of mortuary offerings. Residual variation in mortuary treatment may be explained by differences among ranked sodalities or clans that do not appear to have exercised considerable power, suggesting that individuals gained influence by force of their sodality association, personality, and pursuit of successful careers. It is unlikely that this power would have extended across major kinship divisions within the community.

On the basis of a cross-cultural survey, Naroll (1956: 640) proposed "...when settlements contain more than about 500 people they must have authoritative officials and if they contain over a thousand some kind of specialized organization or corps of officials to perform police functions...the larger the organization the greater the proportion of control officials needed." We suspect the population size of Grasshopper attained, if not exceeded, 500 persons, and certainly the region of interdependent communities contained many more than a thousand persons, yet there is no evidence of hierarchical regulatory control. The conversion of Plaza III to a Great Kiva late in the occupation of the Pueblo may reflect an attempt, albeit an unsuccessful one, to create a pan-community integrating mechanism. Because the Pueblo probably lacked strong institutional controls, disputes between groups may have divided the community into various factions, a process associated with historic Western Pueblo communities (Bradfield 1971; Parsons 1922; Titiev 1944).

Although factional disputes may arise independently, we believe two events triggered these irresolvable conflicts. First, in the latter portion of the fourteenth century agricultural productivity within the region may have been expanded to capacity, at least in the context of traditional means and concepts. Few technological innovations were used to increase agricultural production, except sporadic deployment of features designed to control erosion and increase absorption of water into the soil. In light of the rapid population increase and the amount and extent of human related environmental disturbance (Chapters 11, 13, 14) that perhaps led to increased soil erosion and loss of soil fertility, the regional population may have faced occasional food shortages.

These shortages would not have posed a danger to the region or the community within the context of extensive large scale interregional trade. As long as material goods were moving out of or through the region, other goods could be obtained that at some point could be exchanged for food. We argue that some event or set of events disrupted the trading relationships established between regions. John Molloy has linked abandonment of the region to state-level changes in Mesoamerica and their impact on the northern frontier, including the puebloan Southwest. Alternatively, goods produced within the Grasshopper region may have failed to find a market. Oversupply, lack of demand, and limited availability of agricultural products may have affected the ability of individuals in the region to gain access to critical goods, including food. Or, the failure of the interregional trading system may have occurred as populations to the north and south became reduced in size and withdrew to other areas along the major stream systems (Euler and others 1979).

Whatever the ultimate cause, it appears that by A.D. 1400 the large scale interregional trading system had vanished. There is some evidence that regional populations tried to substitute locally-made products (Wasley 1952; Wendorf 1950), perhaps to stimulate the flow of goods. Loss of trade, coupled with rapid population growth and agricultural productivity constraints among loosely-linked social groups lacking institutionalized controls, may have led to factional disputes. The process of abandonment may have been irreversibly triggered by the loss of personnel sometime after A.D. 1350. Just as the dispersed sedentary system present in the area prior to 1300 could not withstand the loss of personnel, the loss of groups to areas outside the region may have disrupted one of the primary means by which the system of interdependent communities came into being—exchange.

In addition, the population structure of the region had been irreversibly altered by the new settlement system. For a number of reasons, it was no longer possible to revert to a system of dispersed hamlets. First, that system no longer existed in the area; second, there was probably no unoccupied area in which to establish such a system within the region; and third, the set of mutually supporting relations had been organized among a larger number of individuals under a new settlement system, and to return to a successful dispersed system it would have been necessary to re-create those links simultaneously between newly-formed hamlets.

Given this perspective, it is understandable why the entire region was rapidly abandoned. Since the population could not re-create the dispersed settlement system, and since intra- and intercommunity relations had been disrupted, groups would have had two choices. First, they could move to areas in which there were successful nucleated systems still in operation, or second, they could try to re-create smaller (and perhaps unsuccessful) systems elsewhere in sparsely occupied areas such as the canyons to the west of the Grasshopper Plateau. It has been difficult to determine the destination of the dispersing groups, probably because they did not all go in the same direction or to any one region (S. Plog 1969). Some may have joined various communities in different regions known to them through former trading relationships.

REGIONAL COMPARISONS

The Grasshopper region was not the only area in which large pueblo towns developed after A.D. 1200; settlement trends in other portions of the Southwest were undergoing similar changes (Bluhm 1960; Danson 1957; Johnson 1965; Tuggle 1970). The area included in this discussion encompasses the mountainous region below the Mogollon Rim, from Canyon Creek in the northwest to Eagle Creek in the southeast. Several regional social systems were present in this area and we focus on two in addition to Grasshopper: Forestdale-Kinishba (Cummings 1940; Haury 1940a, 1950; Hough 1903) and Point of Pines (Haury 1958; Johnson 1965; Morris 1957; Wasley 1952; Wendorf 1950). Prior to A.D. 1000 cultural patterns in this area represented the Early Mogollon tradition (Wheat 1955), and during slightly different, yet overlapping intervals, communities were founded within these regions that conformed to a Late Mogollon (Rinaldo 1964b) or Western Pueblo (Johnson 1965; Reed 1948, 1950) configuration. This transition consisted of aggregation of groups of dispersed, regional populations into large pueblo communities (Fig. 15.4). The process began as early as A.D. 1240 at Turkey Creek Pueblo in the Point of Pines region, although the major agglomeration of individuals at Point of Pines Pueblo did not begin until about 1280 (Bannister and Robinson 1971: 38, 43; Parker 1967). The major period of aggregation at Kinishba began some time during the last quarter of the thirteenth century (Bannister and Robinson 1971: 31). No tree-ring materials have been recovered from Tundastusa, the largest pueblo in the Forestdale Valley (Hough 1903), but its ceramic assemblage indicates that aggregation probably started near the beginning of the fourteenth century. Grasshopper Pueblo was established between A.D. 1295 and 1305 and grew rapidly until 1325. Canyon Creek Pueblo was founded in A.D. 1327 and expanded until shortly after 1350. If the trend of these dates is correct the shift toward nucleated settlements below the Mogollon Rim began in the Point of Pines region and spread to the northwest. The Flagstaff region experienced a period of pueblo aggregation between A.D. 1100 and 1200, but that growth does not appear to have influenced events in the Grasshopper area.

Many of the large pueblos that were forming incorporated the same kinds of construction features, suggesting that similar processes were operating to promote aggregation. Each pueblo was composed of several room blocks arranged around enclosed or interior plazas and associated with a Great Kiva (Chapter 3; Baldwin 1938; Cummings 1940; Haury 1958; Hough 1903, 1930). The major period of construction probably lasted less than 35 to 50 years at each community. The pueblos at Kinishba and Grasshopper, which architecturally are mirror images of one another, were founded by groups occupying from three to six core construction units of varying sizes arranged across the settlement. Study of offsetting and abutting walls at Kinishba (Cummings 1940; Jones 1935) and analysis of the room construction sequence at Grasshopper (Chapter 3) indicate that the early constructed units consisted of multi-room sets; later additions usually consisted of one or two rooms. There was at least one large influx of immigrants, derived from the Kayenta area of northeastern Arizona (Haury 1958), to Point of Pines Pueblo. This particular group, however, was not successfully assimilated into the community—in fact, they were burned out of their homes (Haury 1958: 6). Both Kinishba and Grasshopper were built on the banks of a wash, a convenient location for obtaining, monitoring, or con-

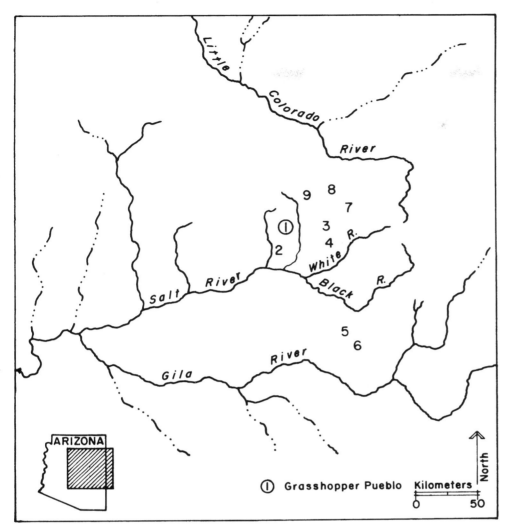

Figure 15.4.
Location of major
late prehistoric pueblos
in east-central
Arizona.

1. Grasshopper Pueblo
2. Canyon Creek Pueblo
3. Tundastusa
4. Kinishba
5. Turkey Creek Pueblo
6. Point of Pines Pueblo
7. Showlow Pueblo
8. Fourmile Pueblo
9. Pinedale Pueblo

trolling the flow of water down the channel (Reagan 1930). Late in the occupation of both Kinishba and Grasshopper one of the enclosed plazas was converted to a Great Kiva (Chapter 8; Haury 1950; Whittlesey 1978).

In each region, expansion of agricultural production disrupted the dispersed settlement system that was rapidly abandoned as groups aggregated into larger settlements. Despite the pressure to aggregate, some groups retained traditional house forms and construction practices, yet were in close association with the large pueblos. Examples include contemporaneous pit houses at Point of Pines (Bannister and Robinson 1971: 32), and outliers (small masonry structures) at Grasshopper (Chapter 3) and Kinishba (Cummings 1940).

Several features are common to the aggregation in these regions, including expansion of agricultural productivity (Woodbury 1966), disruption of the set of mutual relations among dispersed communities, and large scale exchange of goods within and between regions. At Point of Pines, construction of an extensive water control system across a variety of topographic and edaphic situations (Woodbury 1961) complemented dry farming in

alluvial areas surrounding Point of Pines, Turkey Creek, Clover Creek, and Willow Creek. Improving the water system may have been spurred by population growth after A.D. 1150. By constructing these features in areas marginal for agriculture (outside recent alluvium, within areas of conglomerate, sandstone, and moderately consolidated alluvial deposits), which differed in topographic and microclimatic conditions from the valley floor, the reliability and productivity of harvests may have been increased. Extensive alluvial areas are located near Kinishba and Tundastusa; they support dry farming by Apache groups today (Cummings 1940; Haury 1940a: 16).

Within each region communities participated extensively in the exchange of goods and services. White Mountain Red Wares from areas to the north were traded into the Point of Pines, Grasshopper, and Forestdale-Kinishba regions in large quantities until A.D. 1400 (Carlson 1970; Graves 1978; Wasley 1952; Wendorf 1950; Whittlesey 1974). Much of the Kinishba corrugated ware (Baldwin 1939), which has intricate patterns of indentations, may have been produced in the Point of Pines region (Breternitz, Gifford, and Olson 1957). Locally produced Kinishba Polychrome and Kinishba Red have been recovered at Canyon Creek Pueblo, Grasshopper, and Point of Pines. Black-on-white ceramics were imported into the Point of Pines region throughout its history. Cummings (1940: 58) describes a large cache of gypsum pendants recovered from a room at Kinishba. Gypsum occurs in exposures east of White River (Moore 1968: 63). Gypsum in both raw and worked forms has been recovered from Grasshopper. Similarly, hematite and diabase that occur predominately to the west of Grasshopper in upper Canyon Creek (Chapter 7; Moore 1968) have been found at Kinishba (Baldwin 1939; Cummings 1940) and Point of Pines (Smiley 1952; Wasley 1952; Wendorf 1950). More exotic goods such as macaws, turquoise, shell, obsidian, and quartz crystals have also been recovered. Exchange was probably promoted by naturally-occurring resource variability in the area (for example, the location of gypsum and hematite and other minerals) as well as by socially-imposed diversity (pottery making and possibly stone tool manufacture).

Despite rapid population growth, increased agricultural productivity, and an intricate system of exchange, there is no evidence to support the hypothesis that the prehistoric populations underwent significant social and political organizational changes, particularly in the direction of status differentiation. Whittlesey (1978) and Johnson (1965) found evidence of age-graded differences in the burial populations from Grasshopper and Turkey Creek Pueblo, respectively. Additional analyses have isolated sex and temporal differences in mortuary practices (Whittlesey 1978), but none have demonstrated a trend toward ascribed status differences. There are no architectural, residential, or ceremonial features associated with any of the settlements that indicate a developing political hierarchy.

By A.D. 1350 the population growth in this area of the Southwest had slowed. Between A.D. 1400 and 1450 the entire area was effectively abandoned. The timing and short duration of depopulation across the area suggest similarity in the underlying causes. Climatic events have not been implicated in the dispersion and depopulation of Grasshopper; it seems unlikely that they were of critical importance in nearby areas. Disruption of the extensive and important exchange network plus recurring subsistence stress may have led to disputes local authorities were unable to adjudicate. Lacking suitable habitat to re-create a dispersed settlement pattern or successful daughter communities, groups selected to journey to areas in which new settlements could be established or where individuals could be incorporated into existing communities. In the Point of Pines region a slightly different trend has been documented. After the abandonment of Point of Pines Pueblo (and the decline of regional population size), several smaller groups built isolated ten-to-twenty-room structures in the locality (Asch 1960; Morris 1957; Wasley 1952; Wendorf 1950). Their attempt to re-create a dispersed settlement system failed within a short period of time and the region was abandoned by A.D. 1450.

It has been suggested by Dean and Robinson in Chapter 8 that the aggregation of groups at Grasshopper, and by implication, in other regions below the Mogollon Rim, represents a "...fairly successful adaptation to the local environment, including normal year-to-year variation in that environment." Although at one time we may have been in general agreement with this position, we are beginning to suspect that aggregation in this area may have been successful in the short run, only to fail as a long-term solution (Tuggle 1970: 118).

The process of aggregation was evidently spurred by increased agricultural productivity in each region. Yet with the exception of Point of Pines there is no evidence that increased productivity was the result of intensification of labor or investment in new technology. Thus, aggregation that did lead to significant changes in settlement pattern did not lead to, nor was it the result of or accompanied by, major structural changes in the organization of political power. This seeming anomaly—the failure of the settlement changes to lead to increased sociocultural complexity—can best be explained by a lack of pressures that would have made such changes advantageous. Initially, agricultural productivity was sufficient to support each local population and surplus crops may have been used as an exchange commodity. Through time, as populations grew and agricultural productivity leveled off, exchange was used as a means to subsidize energy flow into the system in place of agricultural intensification, a situation that buffered the population of these communities (Athens 1977: 374). This development was successful in the short run; it maintained population growth and aggregation, and it enabled the population to retain traditional forms of sociocultural organization. There were no local elites who controlled and administered exchange relations between communities. Ethnographers have documented the operation of extensive direct reciprocal exchange of large quantities of goods and services within and between communities organized by individual households (Ford 1972a, 1972b; Takaki 1977; contrary opinion, see Cordell and Plog 1979). This kind of exchange system best fits our archaeological evidence.

In contrast, intercommunity relations among historic Western Pueblos exemplify a successful and temporally stable exchange system. Here, communities cooperate in various activities and ceremonies and cross-community marriages are arranged, yet these are transactions between individuals and households that are undertaken opportunistically or infrequently. Exchange between Western Puebloan communities has been documented (Winship 1896), but it never approached either the areal extent or quantity of goods of earlier exchange systems. The result of these practices ensured that individual communities remained independent. Occasionally, when the population of a pueblo grew sufficiently, a small daughter community was formed at some distance from the mother pueblo (Stanislawski 1973; Titiev 1944). Daughter villages were dependent on the mother pueblo for a number of years for ritual, defensive, and, periodically, for subsistence needs.

The type of social system represented by historic Western Pueblo groups in which the communities, although linked by historic and cultural traditions, act independently of each other appears to be a more stable alternative. Communities can fail for one reason or another, even randomly through time and space, but the remaining communities and the cultural tradition are relatively unaffected. Individuals from other communities may be aided in time of need or incorporated into a community, but there is no set of economic, marital, or social relations between communities that create reverberating effects when one pueblo disperses. As a result, through time, population may fluctuate; during intervals of decreasing population settlements may be abandoned, but during periods of increase daughter settlements will be founded to colonize abandoned or unused land, and the cultural system will be maintained.

In contrast, the prehistoric groups below the Mogollon Rim were inextricably linked to one another through a variety of social and economic arrangements (Chapter 6; Tuggle 1970). This degree of community interdependency, however, may not be a viable system among relatively egalitarian groups occupying uncertain or fluctuating environments. As a result, the loss of a community affects the remaining populations. The loss of energy is slowed through exchange, but the lack of a political structure that could have countered divisive trends within and between communities, intensified agricultural production, or controlled the exchange of goods, could then lead to regional depopulation in any case. Under these conditions movement to other regions in which successful nucleated communities were already located involved less risk and expenditure of energy than local dispersion to smaller settlements or increased cultural complexity in the form of a new political structure.

REFERENCES

Adams, William Y.
1968   Settlement pattern in microcosm: The changing aspect of a Nubian village during twelve centuries. In *Settlement Archaeology*, edited by Kwang-chih Chang, pp. 174-207. Palo Alto: National Press.

Anderson, Sydney
1961   Mammals of Mesa Verde National Park, Colorado. *University of Kansas Publications* 14(3): 29-67. Lawrence: Museum of Natural History, University of Kansas.

Antevs, Ernst
1955   Geologic-climate dating in the West. *American Antiquity* 20(4): 317-335.

Armstrong, David M.
1972   Distribution of mammals in Colorado. *Museum of Natural History, Monograph* 3. Lawrence: Museum of Natural History, University of Kansas.

Asch, C. M.
1960   Post-pueblo occupation at the Willow Creek Ruin, Point of Pines. *The Kiva* 26(2): 31-42.

Ascher, Robert
1968   Time's arrow and the archaeology of a contemporary community. In *Settlement Archaeology*, edited by Kwang-chih Chang, pp. 43-52. Palo Alto: National Press.

Athens, J. Stephen
1977   Theory building and the study of evolutionary process in complex societies. In *For Theory Building in Archaeology*, edited by Lewis R. Binford, pp. 353-384. New York: Academic Press.

Bailey, Vernon
1931   Mammals of New Mexico. *North American Fauna* 53. Washington: U.S. Department of Agriculture.

Baldwin, Gordon C.
1935   Ring record of the Great Drought (1276-1299) in eastern Arizona. *Tree-Ring Bulletin* 2(2): 11-12.
1938   Excavations at Kinishba Pueblo, Arizona. *American Antiquity* 4(1): 11-21.
1939   The material culture of Kinishba. *American Antiquity* 4(4): 314-327.

Bannister, Bryant
1962   The interpretation of tree-ring dates. *American Antiquity* 27(4): 508-514.

Bannister, Bryant, and William J. Robinson
1971   *Tree-Ring Dates from Arizona U-W: Gila-Salt Rivers Area*. Tucson: Laboratory of Tree-Ring Research, University of Arizona.

Bannister, Bryant, Elizabeth A. M. Gell, and John W. Hannah
1966   *Tree-Ring Dates from Arizona N-Q. Verde-Showlow-St. Johns Area*. Tucson: Laboratory of Tree-Ring Research, University of Arizona.

Barr, Anthony J., James H. Goodnight, John P. Sall, and Jane T. Helwig
1976   *A User's Guide to SAS 76*. Raleigh: Sparks Press.

Beals, Ralph L.
1932   Comparative ethnology of northern Mexico before 1750. *Ibero-Americana* 2.

Beck, Alan M., and Richard J. Vogl
1972   The effects of spring burning on rodent populations in a brush prairie savannah. *Journal of Mammalogy* 53: 336-346.

Benfer, Robert A.
1970   Associations among cranial traits. *American Journal of Physical Anthropology* 32(3): 463-464.

Bennett, Kenneth A.
1973   The Indians of Point of Pines, Arizona: A comparative study of their physical characteristics. *Anthropological Papers of the University of Arizona* 23. Tucson: University of Arizona Press.

Berry, A. Caroline, and R. J. Berry
1967   Epigenetic variation in the human cranium. *Journal of Anatomy* 101: 316-379.

Berry, R. J.
1968   The biology of non-metrical variation in mice and men. In *The Skeletal Biology of Earlier Human Populations*, edited by Don R. Brothwell, pp. 103-133. London: Pergamon Press.

Binford, Lewis R.
1964   A consideration of archaeological research design. *American Antiquity* 29(4): 425-441.
1968   Post-Pleistocene adaptations. In *New Perspectives in Archaeology*, edited by Sally R. Binford and Lewis R. Binford, pp. 313-341. Chicago: Aldine.
1972   Comments on evolution. In *An Archaeological Perspective*, by Lewis R. Binford, pp. 105-113. New York: Seminar Press.
1979   *Nunamiut Ethnoarchaeology*. New York: Academic Press.

Birdsell, Joseph B.
1957   Some Population Problems Involving Pleistocene Man. *Cold Spring Harbor Symposia on Quantitative Biology* 22: 47-69.

Birkby, Walter H.
1972   The Grasshopper Ruin skeletal remains. Paper presented at the 37th Annual Meeting of the Society for American Archaeology, Bal Harbour, Florida.
1973   *Discontinuous Morphological Traits of the Skull as Population Markers in the Prehistoric Southwest*. Doctoral dissertation, University of Arizona, Tucson. Ann Arbor: University Microfilms.

Blackith, R. E., and Richard A. Reyment
1971   *Multivariate Morphometrics*. London: Academic Press.

Blair, W. Frank
1940   A contribution to the ecology and faunal relationships of the mammals of the Davis Mountains region, southwestern Texas. *University of Michigan Museum of Zoology Miscellaneous Publications* 46. Ann Arbor: University of Michigan.

Blasing, Terence Jack
1975   Methods for Analyzing Climatic Variations in the North Pacific Sector and Western North America for the Last Few Centuries. MS, doctoral dissertation, University of Wisconsin, Madison.

Blasing, Terence J., and Harold C. Fritts
1975 Past climate of Alaska and northwestern Canada as reconstructed from tree rings. In "Climate of the Arctic," edited by Gunter Weller and Sue Ann Bowling, pp. 48-58. *Proceedings of the 24th Alaskan Science Conference, August 1973.* Fairbanks: Geophysical Institute, University of Alaska.
1976 Reconstructing past climatic anomalies in the north Pacific and western North America from tree-ring data. *Quaternary Research* 6: 563-579.

Bloom, Lansing B.
1933- Bourke in the Southwest. *New Mexico Historical Review*
1938 10: 271-322; 11: 188-207, 217-282; 12: 41-77, 337-379; 13: 192-238.

Bluhm, Elaine A.
1960 Mogollon settlement patterns in Pine Lawn Valley, New Mexico. *American Antiquity* 25(4): 538-546.

Bohrer, Vorsila L.
1962 Nature and interpretation of ethnobotanical materials from Tonto National Monument. In "Archaeological Studies at Tonto National Monument, Arizona," by Charlie R. Steen, Lloyd Peterson, Vorsila L. Bohrer, and Kate Peck Kent, pp. 79-114. *Southwestern Monuments Association Technical Series* 2.
1970 Ethnobotanical aspects of Snaketown, a Hohokam village in southern Arizona. *American Antiquity* 35(4): 413-430.
1972 Paleoecology of the Hay Hollow Site, Arizona. *Fieldiana: Anthropology* 63(1): 1-30.
1973 Ethnobotany of Point of Pines, Arizona. *Economic Botany* 27: 423-437.

Bradfield, Maitland
1971 The changing pattern of Hopi agriculture. *Occasional Paper* 30. London: Royal Anthropological Institute of Great Britain and Ireland.

Bradfield, Wesley
1931 Cameron Creek Village. *Monographs of the School of American Research* 1. Santa Fe: School of American Research.

Bradley, W. Glen, and Roger A. Mauer
1973 Rodents of a creosote bush community in southern Nevada. *Southwestern Naturalist* 17: 333-344.

Brand, Donald D.
1938 Aboriginal trade routes for sea shells in the Southwest. *Yearbook of the Association of Pacific Coast Geographers* 4: 3-10.

Breternitz, David A., James C. Gifford, and Alan P. Olson
1957 Point of Pines phase sequence and utility pottery type revisions. *American Antiquity* 22(4): 412-416.

Brew, John Otis
1946 Archaeology of Alkali Ridge, southeastern Utah. *Papers of the Peabody Museum, Harvard University,* 21. Cambridge: Harvard University.

Brothwell, Don R.
1965 Of mice and men. Epigenetic polymorphism in the skeleton. In *Homenaje a Juan Comas en su 65 Aniversario* II, pp. 9-21. Mexico.

Brown, James H., and Gerald A. Lieberman
1973 Resource utilization and coexistence of seed-eating desert rodents in sand dune habitats. *Ecology* 54: 788-797.

Brown, James M.
1968 *The Photosynthetic Regime of Some Southern Arizona Pine.* Doctoral dissertation, University of Arizona, Tucson. Ann Arbor: University Microfilms.

Buchler, Ira R., and Henry A. Selby
1968 *Kinship and Social Organization, An Introduction to Theory and Method.* New York: Macmillan.

Budelsky, Carl Albert
1969 *Variation in Transpiration and its Relationship with Growth for Pinus Ponderosa Lawson in Southern Arizona.* Doctoral dissertation, University of Arizona, Tucson. Ann Arbor: University Microfilms.

Buehrer, T. F.
1950 Appendix: Chemical study of the material from several horizons of the Ventana Cave profile. In *The Stratigraphy and Archaeology of Ventana Cave, Arizona,* by Emil W. Haury, pp. 549-563. Tucson: University of Arizona Press, and Albuquerque: University of New Mexico Press.

Buikstra, Jane E.
1972 Hopewell in the Lower Illinois River Valley: A Regional Approach to the Study of Biological Variability and Mortuary Activity. MS, doctoral dissertation, University of Chicago, Chicago.

Bukasov, Sergei M.
1930 The cultivated plants of Mexico, Guatemala, and Colombia. *Bulletin of Applied Botany of Genetics and Plant Breeding,* 47th Supplement. Leningrad.

Buol, Stanley W., Francis D. Hole, and Ralph J. McCraken
1973 *Soil Genesis and Classification.* Ames: The Iowa State University Press.

Burgh, Robert F.
1959 Ceramic profiles in the western mound at Awatovi, northeastern Arizona. *American Antiquity* 25(2): 184-202.

Burns, John
1975 CONTOUR Computer Program. MS, on file at the Laboratory of Tree-Ring Research, University of Arizona, Tucson.

Burt, William H.
1933 Additional notes on the mammals of southern Arizona. *Journal of Mammalogy* 14: 114-122.

Burt, William H., and Richard P. Grossenheider
1952 *A Field Guide to the Mammals.* Boston: Houghton Mifflin Company.

Butler, Barbara H.
1971 The People of Casas Grandes: Cranial and Dental Morphology through Time. MS, doctoral dissertation, Southern Methodist University, Dallas.

Butzer, Karl W.
1964 *Environment and Archaeology.* Chicago: Aldine Publishing Company.
1974 Geo-archaeological interpretation of Acheulian Calc-Pan sites at Doornlaagte and Rooidan (Kimberley, South Africa). *Journal of Archaeological Science* 1: 1-25.
1977 Geo-archaeology in practice. *Reviews in Anthropology* 4: 125-131.

Calahane, Victor H.
1939 Mammals of the Chiricahua Mountains, Cochise County, Arizona. *Journal of Mammalogy* 20: 418-440.

Carlson, Roy L.
1970 White Mountain Redware, A pottery tradition of east-central Arizona and western New Mexico. *Anthropological Papers of the University of Arizona* 19. Tucson: University of Arizona Press.

Carneiro, Robert L.
1967 On the relationship between size of population and complexity of social organization. *Southwestern Journal of Anthropology* 23(3): 234-243.

Cassells, E. Steve
1972 A test concerning artificial cranial deformation and status from the Grasshopper Site, east-central Arizona. *The Kiva* 37(2): 84-92.

Casteel, Richard W.
1976   *Fish Remains in Archaeology and Paleo-environmental Studies.* London and New York: Academic Press.

Chang, Kwang-chih
1958   A study of the Neolithic social grouping: Examples from the New World. *American Anthropologist* 60(2): 298-334.

Ciolek-Torrello, Richard S.
1978   *A Statistical Analysis of Activity Organization, Grasshopper Pueblo, Arizona.* Doctoral dissertation, University of Arizona, Tucson. Ann Arbor: University Microfilms.

Ciolek-Torrello, Richard, and J. Jefferson Reid
1974   Change in household size at Grasshopper. *The Kiva* 40(1-2): 39-47.

Clark, Geoffrey A.
1967   A Preliminary Analysis of Burial Clusters at the Grasshopper Site, East-Central Arizona. MS, master's thesis, Department of Anthropology, University of Arizona, Tucson.
1969   A preliminary analysis of burial clusters at the Grasshopper Site, east-central Arizona. *The Kiva* 35(2): 57-86.

Cockrum, E. Lendell
1960   *The Recent Mammals of Arizona: Their Taxonomy and Distribution.* Tucson: University of Arizona Press.
1964   Recent mammals of Arizona. In *The Vertebrates of Arizona,* edited by Charles H. Lowe, pp. 249-259. Tucson: University of Arizona Press.

Connell, Joseph H.
1978   Diversity in tropical rain forests and coral reefs. *Science* 199(4335): 1302-1310.

Connell, Joseph H., and Ralph O. Slatyer
1977   Mechanisms of succession in natural communities and their role in community stability and organization. *American Naturalist* III: 1119-1144.

Constandse-Westermann, T. S.
1972   Coefficients of biological distance. *Anthropological Publications.* The Netherlands: Oosterhout N.B.

Cook, Sherburne F., Jr.
1959   The effects of fire on a population of small rodents. *Ecology* 40: 102-108.
1972   Prehistoric demography. *Addison-Wesley Module* 16, pp. 1-42. Reading, Massachusetts: Addison-Wesley.

Cook, Sherburne F., Jr., and Robert F. Heizer
1962   Chemical analysis of the Hotchkiss Site (CCo-138). *University of California Archaeological Survey Report* 57. Berkeley: University of California.
1965   Studies on the chemical analysis of archaeological sites. *University of California Publications in Anthropology* 2. Berkeley: University of California.

Cooper, Charles F.
1960   Changes in vegetation, structure and growth of Southwestern pine forests since White settlement. *Ecological Monographs* 30(2): 129-164.

Cordell, Linda S., and Fred Plog
1979   Escaping the confines of normative thought: A reevaluation of Puebloan prehistory. *American Antiquity* 44(3): 405-429.

Cornwall, I. W.
1958   *Soils for the Archaeologist.* London: Phoenix House. New York: MacMillan.
1960   Soil investigations in the service of archaeology. In "The Application of Quantitative Methods in Archaeology," edited by Robert F. Heizer and Sherburne F. Cook, pp. 265-284. *Viking Fund Publications in Anthropology* 28.

Cotner, Melvin L.
1963   Controlling pinyon-juniper on Southwestern rangelands. U.S. Department of Agriculture Experiment Station, Tucson, Arizona, in cooperation with the Farm Economics Division. *Economic Research Service Report* 210.

Cowgill, George L.
1974   Comments on Professor Longacre's paper. In "Reconstructing Complex Societies," edited by Charlotte B. Moore, pp. 36-39. *Supplement to the Bulletin of the American Schools of Oriental Reserach* 20.

Cowgill, Pete
1978   Trout or squawfish in the Colorado River? *Arizona Daily Star,* February 5, Section B, p. 8. Tucson.

Cox, George W.
1967   *Laboratory Manual for General Ecology.* Dubuque, Iowa: William C. Brown.

Crown, (Robertson), Patricia
1981   *Variability in Ceramic Manufacture at the Chodistaas Site, East-central Arizona.* Doctoral dissertation, University of Arizona, Tucson. Ann Arbor: University Microfilms.

Cummings, Byron
1940   *Kinishba, A Prehistoric Pueblo of the Great Pueblo Period.* Tucson: Hohokam Museums Association and the University of Arizona.

Cushing, Frank H.
1896   Outline of Zuni creation myths. *Bureau of American Ethnology Thirteenth Annual Report, 1891-1892.* Washington.

Danson, Edward B.
1957   An archaeological survey of west central New Mexico and east central Arizona. *Papers of the Peabody Museum, Harvard University,* 44(1). Cambridge: Harvard University.

Daubenmeyer, Rexford
1959   *Plants and Environment.* New York: John Wiley and Sons.

David, Nicholas
1971   The Fulani compound and the archaeologist. *World Archaeology* 3(2): 111-131.

Davidson, Donald A.
1973   Particle size and phosphate analysis: Evidence for the evolution of a tell. *Archaeometry* 15: 143-152.

Davidson, Donald A., and Myra L. Shackley, editors
1976   *Geoarchaeology: Earth Science and the Past.* Boulder: Westview Press.

Deacon, James E., William G. Bradley, and Karl M. Larsen
1964   Ecological distribution of the mammals of Clark Canyon, Charleston Mountains, Nevada. *Journal of Mammalogy* 45: 397-509.

Dean, Jeffery S.
1969   Chronological analysis of Tsegi phase sites in northeastern Arizona. *Papers of the Laboratory of Tree-Ring Research* 3. Tucson: University of Arizona Press.
1970   Aspects of Tsegi phase social organization: A trial reconstruction. In *Reconstructing Prehistoric Pueblo Societies,* edited by William A. Longacre, pp. 140-174. Albuquerque: University of New Mexico Press.
1978   Independent dating in archaeological analysis. In *Advances in Archaeological Method and Theory* 1, edited by Michael B. Schiffer, pp. 223-255. New York: Academic Press.

Dean, Jeffrey S., and William J. Robinson
1977   *Dendroclimatic Variability in the American Southwest, A.D. 680 to 1970.* Tucson: Laboratory of Tree-Ring Research, University of Arizona.

Dean, Jeffrey S., and William J. Robinson *(continued)*
1979   Computer cartography and the reconstruction of dendroclimatic variability in the American Southwest, A.D. 680 to 1970. In "Computer Graphics in Archaeology: Statistical Cartographic Applications to Spatial Analysis in Archaeological Contexts," edited by Steadman Upham, pp. 79-94. *Arizona State University Anthropological Research Papers* 15. Tempe: Arizona State University.

Dice, Lee R.
1930   Mammal distribution in the Alamogordo region, New Mexico. *University of Michigan Museum of Zoology Occasional Papers* 213.

Dietz, Eugene F.
1957   Phosphorus accumulation in soil in an Indian habitation site. *American Antiquity* 22(4): 405-409.

Di Peso, Charles C.
1974   Casas Grandes, A fallen trading center of the Gran Chichimeca, Vols. 1-3. *Amerind Foundation Publications* 9. Dragoon: Amerind Foundation, Inc., and Flagstaff: Northland Press.

Di Peso, Charles C., John B. Rinaldo, and Gloria J. Fenner
1974   Casas Grandes, A fallen trading center of the Gran Chichimeca, Vols. 4-8. *Amerind Foundation Publications* 9. Dragoon: Amerind Foundation, Inc., and Flagstaff: Northland Press.

Doran, James E., and Frank R. Hodson
1975   *Mathematics and Computers in Archaeology.* Cambridge: Harvard University Press.

Douglass, Andrew E.
1914   A method of estimating rainfall by the growth of trees. In "The Climatic Factor as Illustrated in Arid America," by Ellsworth Huntington, pp. 101-121. *Carnegie Institution of Washington Publication* 192. Washington.
1929   The secret of the Southwest solved by talkative tree-rings. *National Geographic Magazine* 56(6): 737-770.
1941   Age of Forestdale Ruin excavated in 1939. *Tree-Ring Bulletin* 8(1): 7-8.
1942   Checking the date of the Bluff Ruin, Forestdale: A study in technique. *Tree-Ring Bulletin* 9(2): 2-7.
1944   Tabulation of dates of Bluff Ruin, Forestdale, Arizona. *Tree-Ring Bulletin* 11(2): 10-16.

Dozier, Edward P.
1965   Southwestern social units and archaeology. *American Antiquity* 31(1): 38-47.
1966   *Hano, A Tewa Indian Community in Arizona.* New York: Holt, Rinehart and Winston.
1970   *The Pueblo Indians of North America.* New York: Holt, Rinehart and Winston.

Eddy, Frank W., and Harold E. Dregne
1964   Soil tests on alluvial and archaeological deposits, Navajo Reservoir District. *El Palacio* 71(4): 5-21.

Eggan, Fred
1950   *Social Organization of the Western Pueblos.* Chicago: University of Chicago Press.
1964   *The American Indian, Perspectives for the Study of Social Change.* Chicago: Aldine.

Einarsen, Arthur D.
1948   *The Pronghorn Antelope and its Management.* Washington: The Wildlife Management Institute.
1956   Life of the mule deer. In *The Deer of North America*, edited by W. P. Taylor, pp. 363-520. Harrisburg: The Stackpole Company, and Washington: Wildlife Management Institute.

Emery, Dara
1964   Seed propagation of native California plants. *Leaflets of the Santa Barbara Botanic Garden* 1(10): 81-96.

Euler, Robert C., George J. Gumerman, Thor N. V. Karlstrom, Jeffrey S. Dean, and Richard H. Hevly
1979   The Colorado Plateau: cultural dynamics and paleoenvironment. *Science* 205(4411): 1089-1101.

Fall, Patricia, Gerald K. Kelso, and Vera Markgraf
1981   Paleoenvironmental reconstruction at Canyon del Muerto, Arizona, based on principal-component analysis. *Journal of Archaeological Science* 8: 297-307.

Farrand, William R.
1975   Sediment analysis of a prehistoric rock shelter: The Abri Pataud. *Quaternary Research* 5: 1-26.

Fewkes, J. W.
1904   Two summers' work in pueblo ruins. *Twenty-second Annual Report of the Bureau of American Ethnology*, Part 1, pp. 3-195. Washington.

Findley, James S., and Clyde J. Jones
1962   Distribution and variation of voles of the genus *Microtus* in New Mexico and adjacent areas. *Journal of Mammalogy* 43: 154-166.

Findley, James S., Arthur H. Harris, Donald E. Wilson, and Clyde Jones
1975   *Mammals of New Mexico.* Albuquerque: University of New Mexico Press.

Finnegan, Michael J.
1972   Population Definition on the Northwest Coast by Analysis of Discrete Character Variation. MS, doctoral dissertation, University of Colorado, Boulder.

Ford, Richard I.
1968   An Ecological Analysis Involving the Population of San Juan Pueblo, New Mexico. MS, doctoral dissertation, University of Michigan, Ann Arbor.
1972a   Barter, gift, or violence: An analysis of Tewa intertribal exchange. In "Social Exchange and Interaction," edited by Edwin N. Wilmsen, pp. 21-45. *Anthropological Papers, Museum of Anthropology*, 46. Ann Arbor: University of Michigan.
1972b   An ecological perspective on the eastern pueblos. In *New Perspectives on the Pueblos*, edited by Alfonso Ortiz, pp. 1-17. Albuquerque: University of New Mexico Press.

Fortes, Meyer
1971   Introduction. In "The Developmental Cycle in Domestic Groups," edited by Jack Goody, pp. 1-14. *Cambridge Papers in Social Anthropology* 1. Cambridge: Cambridge University Press.

Foth, H. D., H. S. Jacobs, and L. V. Withee
1971   *Laboratory Manual for Introductory Soil Science.* Third edition. Dubuque: William C. Brown.

Freeman, Leslie
1968   A theoretical framework for interpreting archaeological materials. In *Man the Hunter*, edited by Richard B. Lee and Irven DeVore, pp. 262-267. Chicago: Aldine.

Fritts, Harold C.
1965   Tree-ring evidence for climatic changes in western North America. *Monthly Weather Review* 93(7): 421-443. Washington.
1966   Growth-rings of trees: Their correlation with climate. *Science* 154(3752): 973-979.
1969   Bristlecone Pine in the White Mountains of California: Growth and ring-width characteristics. *Papers of the Laboratory of Tree-Ring Research* 4. Tucson: University of Arizona Press.
1971   Dendroclimatology and dendroecology. *Quaternary Research* 1(4): 419-449. New York.
1974   Relationships of ring widths in arid-site conifers to variations in monthly temperature and precipitation. *Ecological Monographs* 44(4): 411-440.
1976   *Tree Rings and Climate.* London: Academic Press.

Fritts, Harold C., James E. Mosimann, and Christine P. Bottorff
1969   A revised computer program for standardizing tree-ring series. *Tree-Ring Bulletin* 29(1-2): 15-20.

Fritts, Harold C., David G. Smith, and Marvin A. Stokes
1965 The biological model for paleoclimatic interpretation of Mesa Verde tree-ring series. In "Contributions of the Wetherill Mesa Archeological Project," assembled by Douglas Osborne, pp. 101-121. *Memoirs of the Society for American Archaeology* 19.

Fritts, Harold C., Terence J. Blasing, Bruce P. Hayden, and John E. Kutzbach
1971 Multivariate techniques for specifying tree-growth and climatic relations and for reconstructing anomalies in paleoclimate. *Journal of Applied Meteorology* 10(5): 845-864.

Fritts, Harold C., David G. Smith, John W. Cardis, and Carl A. Budelsky
1965 Tree-ring characteristics along a vegetation gradient in northern Arizona. *Ecology* 46(4): 393-401.

Fryer, Holly C.
1966 *Concepts and Methods of Experimental Statistics.* Boston: Allyn and Bacon.

Gennaro, Antonio L.
1968 Northern geographic limits of four desert rodents of the genera *Peromyscus, Perognathus, Dipodomys*, and *Onychomys* in the Rio Grande Valley. *American Midland Naturalist* 80: 477-493.

Gifford, Diane P.
1977 *Observations of Contemporary Human Settlements as an Aid to Archaeological Interpretation.* Doctoral dissertation, University of California, Berkeley. Ann Arbor: University Microfilms.
1978 Ethnoarchaeological observations on natural processes affecting cultural materials. In *Explorations in Ethnoarchaeology*, edited by Richard A. Gould, p. 77-101. Albuquerque: University of New Mexico Press.
1980 Ethnoarchaeological contributions to the taphonomy of human sites. In *Fossils in the Making*, edited by Anna K. Behrensmeyer and Andrew P. Hill, pp. 93-106. Chicago: University of Chicago Press.
1981 Taphonomy and paleoecology: A critical review of archaeology's sister disciplines. In *Advances in Archaeological Method and Theory* 4, edited by Michael B. Schiffer, pp. 365-438. New York: Academic Press.

Gilpin, Laura
1968 *The Enduring Navajo.* Austin: University of Texas Press.

Gladfelter, Bruce G.
1977 Geoarchaeology: The geomorphologist and archaeology. *American Antiquity* 42(4): 519-538.
1981 Developments and directions in geoarchaeology. In *Advances in Archaeological Method and Theory* 4, edited by Michael B. Schiffer, pp. 344-364. New York: Academic Press.

Gladwin, Winifred, and Harold S. Gladwin
1931 Some southwestern pottery types: Series II. *Medallion Papers* 10. Globe, Arizona: Gila Pueblo.

Goody, Jack, editor
1971 The developmental cycle in domestic groups. *Cambridge Papers in Social Anthropology* 1. Cambridge: Cambridge University Press.

Graves, Michael W.
1978 White Mountain Redware Design Variability. Paper presented at the 77th Annual Meeting of the American Anthropological Association, Los Angeles, California.

Gould, Stephen J., and Robert F. Johnston
1972 Geographic variation. *Annual Review of Ecology and Systematics* 3: 457-498.

Greene, Christine R., and William D. Sellers, editors
1964 *Arizona Climate.* Tucson: University of Arizona Press.

Griffin, P. Bion
1967 A high status burial from Grasshopper Ruin, Arizona. *The Kiva* 33(2): 37-53.

1969 *Late Mogollon Readaptation in East-Central Arizona.* Doctoral dissertation, University of Arizona, Tucson. Ann Arbor: University Microfilms.

Griffin, P. Bion, Mark P. Leone, and Keith H. Basso
1971 Western Apache ecology: From horticulture to agriculture. In "Apachean Culture History and Ethnology," edited by Keith H. Basso and Morris E. Opler, pp. 69-73. *Anthropological Papers of the University of Arizona* 21. Tucson: University of Arizona Press.

Hanson, C. Bruce
1980 Pluvial taphonomic Processes: Models and experiment. In *Fossils in the Making*, edited by Anna K. Behrensmeyer and Andrew P. Hill, pp. 156-181. Chicago: University of Chicago Press.

Hargrave, Lyndon L.
1970a Feathers from Sand Dune Cave. *Technical Series* 9. Flagstaff: Museum of Northern Arizona.
1970b Mexican macaws: Comparative osteology and survey of remains from the Southwest. *Anthropological Papers of the University of Arizona* 20. Tucson: University of Arizona Press.

Harradine, Frank
1953 Report on pedologic observations made at the "Capay Man" Site in western Yolo County. *University of California Archaeological Survey Reports* 22, *Papers on California Archaeology* 25. Berkeley: University of California.

Harrington, Harold D.
1967 *Edible Native Plants of the Rocky Mountains.* Albuquerque: University of New Mexico Press.

Harris, Arthur
1963 Ecological distribution of some vertebrates in the San Juan Basin, New Mexico. *Museum of New Mexico Papers in Anthropology* 8. Santa Fe: Museum of New Mexico Press.

Harris, Arthur, James Schoenwetter, and A. H. Warren
1967 An archaeological survey of the Chuska Valley and the Chaco Plateau, New Mexico, Part. 1. *Museum of New Mexico Research Records* 4. Santa Fe: Museum of New Mexico Press.

Hassan, Fekri A.
1978 Sediments in archaeology: Methods and implications for paleoenvironmental and cultural analysis. *Journal of Field Archaeology* 5: 197-213.
1979 Geoarchaeology: The geologist and archaeology. *American Antiquity* 44(2): 267-270.

Haury, Emil W.
1934 The Canyon Creek Ruin and cliff dwellings of the Sierra Ancha. *Medallion Papers* 14. Globe, Arizona: Gila Pueblo.
1940a Excavations in the Forestdale Valley, East-central Arizona. *Social Science Bulletin* 12. Tucson: University of Arizona.
1940b New tree-ring dates from the Forestdale Valley, East-central Arizona. *Tree-Ring Bulletin* 7(2): 14-16.
1950 A sequence of great kivas in the Forestdale Valley, Arizona. In *For the Dean, Essays in Anthropology in Honor of Byron Cummings*, edited by Erik K. Reed and Dale S. King, pp. 29-39. Tucson: Hohokam Museums Association, and Santa Fe: Southwestern Monument Association.
1958 Evidence at Point of Pines for a prehistoric migration from northern Arizona. In "Migrations in New World Culture History," edited by Raymond H. Thompson, pp. 1-8. *Social Science Bulletin* 27. Tucson: University of Arizona.

Haury, Emil W., and Carl M. Conrad
1938 The comparison of fiber properties of Arizona cliff-dweller and Hopi cotton. *American Antiquity* 3(3): 224-227.

Haury, Emil W., and Lyndon L. Hargrave
1931   Recently dated pueblo ruins in Arizona. *Smithsonian Miscellaneous Collections* 82(11): 4-79. Washington.

Havard, Valéry
1895   Food plants of the North American Indian. *Bulletin of the Torrey Botanical Club* 22(3): 98-103.
1896   Drink plants of the North American Indians. *Bulletin of the Torrey Botanical Club* 23(2): 34-46.

Hay, Richard L.
1976   *Geology of Olduvai Gorge: A Study of Sedimentation in a Semi-arid Basin.* Berkeley: University of California Press.

Hayden, Julian D.
1972   Hohokam petroglyphs of the Sierra Pinaate, Sonora, and the Hohokam shell expeditions. *The Kiva* 37(2): 74-83.

Haynes, C. Vance
1975   Pleistocene and Recent Stratigraphy. In "Late Pleistocene Environments of the Southern High Plains," edited by Fred Wendorf and James J. Hester, pp. 57-96. *Fort Burgwin Research Center Publication* 9.

Heiser, Charles B.
1945   The Hopi sunflower. *Missouri Botanical Garden Bulletin* 33(8): 163-166.

Hertzog, Keith P.
1968   Associations between discontinuous cranial traits. *American Journal of Physical Anthropology* 29(3): 397-403.

Hevly, Richard H.
1964   Pollen Analysis of Quaternary Archaeological and Lacustrine Sediments from the Colorado Plateau. MS, doctoral dissertation, University of Arizona, Tucson.
1968   Studies of the modern pollen rain in northern Arizona. *Journal of the Arizona Academy of Science* 5(2): 116-126.

Hevly, Richard H., Peter J. Mehringer, and Harrison G. Yokum
1965   Modern pollen rain in the Sonoran desert. *Journal of the Arizona Academy of Science* 3(3): 123-135.

Hewitt, Oliver H., editor
1967   *The Wild Turkey and its Management.* Washington: The Wildlife Society.

Hill, Andrew P.
1979   Butchery and natural disarticulation: An investigatory technique. *American Antiquity* 44(4): 739-744.

Hill, James N.
1967   The problem of sampling. In "Chapters in the Prehistory of Eastern Arizona III," by Paul S. Martin, William A. Longacre, and James N. Hill, pp. 145-157. *Fieldiana: Anthropology* 57.
1970a   Broken K Pueblo: Prehistoric social organization in the American Southwest. *Anthropological Papers of the University of Arizona* 18. Tucson: University of Arizona Press.
1970b   Prehistoric social organization in the American Southwest: Theory and method. In *Reconstructing Prehistoric Pueblo Societies*, edited by William A. Longacre, pp. 11-58. Albuquerque: University of New Mexico Press.
1971   Research propositions for consideration: Southwestern Anthropological Research Group. In "The Distribution of Prehistoric Population Aggregates," edited by George J. Gumerman, pp. 55-62. *Prescott College Anthropological Reports* 1. Prescott.

Hill, James N., and Richard H. Hevly
1968   Pollen at Broken K Pueblo: Some new interpretations. *American Antiquity* 33(2): 200-210.

Hill, John E.
1942   Notes on mammals of northeastern New Mexico. *Journal of Mammalogy* 23: 75-82.

Hoffmeister, Donald F.
1956   Mammals of the Graham (Piñaleno) Mountains, Arizona. *American Midland Naturalist* 55: 257-288.
1971   *Mammals of the Grand Canyon.* Urbana: University of Illinois Press.

Hoffmeister, Donald F., and Woodrow W. Goodpaster
1954   The mammals of the Huachuca Mountains, southeastern Arizona. *Illinois Biological Monographs* 24(1).

Holbrook, Sally J.
1975   Prehistoric Paleoecology of Northwestern New Mexico. MS, doctoral dissertation, University of California, Berkeley.
1977   Rodent faunal turnover and prehistoric community stability in northwestern New Mexico. *American Naturalist* 111: 1195-1208.
1978   Habitat relationships and coexistence of four sympatric species of *Peromyscus* in northwestern New Mexico. *Journal of Mammalogy* 59: 18-26.
1979a   Habitat utilization, competitive interactions, and coexistence of three species of Cricetine rodents of east-central Arizona. *Ecology* 60(4): 758-769.
1979b   Vegetation affinities, arboreal activity and coexistence of three species of rodents. *Journal of Mammalogy* 60: 528-542.
In   Paleoecology of Grasshopper Pueblo, Arizona. *National Geographic Society Research Reports.*
press

Hooper, Emmet T.
1957   Dental patterns in mice of the genus *Peromyscus*. *Miscellaneous Publications of the Museum of Zoology* 99. Ann Arbor: University of Michigan.

Hooven, Edward F., and Hugh C. Black
1976   Effects of some clearcutting practices on small mammal populations in western Oregon. *Northwest Science* 50:189-208.

Hough, Walter
1903   Archaeological field work in northeastern Arizona. The Museum-Gates expedition of 1901. *Annual Report of the U.S. National Museum for 1901*, pp. 278-358. Washington.
1919   Archaeological exploration in Arizona. *Smithsonian Miscellaneous Collections* 70(2): 3-90. Washington.
1920   Archaeological excavations in Arizona. *Smithsonian Miscellaneous Collections* 72(1): 6-64. Washington.
1930   Exploration of ruins in the White Mountain Apache Indian Reservation, Arizona. *Proceedings, U.S. National Museum*, 78(2856): 1-21. Washington.

Hughes, P. J., and R. J. Lampert
1977   Occupational disturbance and types of archaeological deposits. *Journal of Archaeological Science* 4: 135-140.

Ingles, Lloyd G.
1941   Natural history observations on the Audubon Cottontail. *Journal of Mammalogy* 22(3): 227-250.

Isaac, Glynn L.
1968   Towards the interpretation of occupation debris: Some experiments and observations. *Kroeber Anthropological Society Papers* 37: 31-57.

Ivey, R. DeWitt
1957   Ecological notes on the mammals of Bernalillo County, New Mexico. *Journal of Mammalogy* 38: 490-502.

Jaehnig, Manfred E. W.
1971   A buried soil profile at the site of Aztalan, 47, J E 1, Wisconsin. *Wisconsin Archaeologist* 52: 71-77.

Jantz, Richard L.
1970   Change and Variation in Skeletal Populations of Arikara Indians. MS, doctoral dissertation, University of Kansas, Lawrence.

Jennings, Jesse D.
1966 Glen Canyon: A summary. *Univerity of Utah Anthropological Papers* 81. Salt Lake City: University of Utah Press.

Jewell, Peter A., and Geoffrey W. Dimbleby, editors
1966 The experimental earthwork on Overton Down, Wiltshire, England: The first four years. *Proceedings of the Prehistoric Society* 32: 313-342.

Jewett, Roberta
1978 Locational analysis of the settlement pattern and colonization of the Pinedale region, east-central Arizona. In "An Analytical Approach to Cultural Resource Management: The Little Colorado Planning Unit," edited by Fred Plog, pp. 221-263. *Arizona State University Anthropological Research Papers* 13, and *USDA Forest Service Cultural Resources Report* 19. Tempe: Arizona State University.

Johnson, Alfred E.
1965 *The Development of Western Pueblo Culture.* Doctoral dissertation, University of Arizona, Tucson. Ann Arbor: University Microfilms.

Jones, David
1935 Progress of the excavations at Kinishba. *he Kiva* 1(3): 1-4.

Jorde, L. B.
1977 Precipitation cycles and cultural buffering in the prehistoric Southwest. In *For Theory Building in Archaeology: Essays on Faunal Remains, Aquatic Resources, Spatial Analysis, and Systemic Modeling,* edited by Lewis R. Binford, pp. 385-396. New York: Academic Press.

Judd, Neil M.
1954 The material culture of Pueblo Bonito. *Smithsonian Miscellaneous Collections* 124. Washington.
1964 The architecture of Pueblo Bonito. *Smithsonian Miscellaneous Collections* 147(1). Washington.

Julian, Paul R., and Harold C. Fritts
1968 On the possibility of quantitatively extending climatic records by means of dendroclimatological analysis. *Proceedings of the First Statistical Meteorological Conference.* Hartford: American Meteorological Society.

Kaplan, Lawrence
1963 Archeoethnobotany at Cordova Cave, New Mexico. *Economic Botany* 17(4): 350-359.

Kapp, Ronald O.
1969 *How to Know Pollen and Spores.* Dubuque, Iowa: William C. Brown.

Karcz, I., and U. Kafri
1978 Evaluation of supposed archaeoseismic damage in Israel. *Journal of Archaeological Science* 5: 237-253.

Kelley, James E.
1974 Bighorn Sheep at Grasshopper Ruin: Precautions in analysis. *The Kiva* 40(1-2): 71-79.

Kellock, W. L., and P. A. Parsons
1970a Variation of minor non-metrical cranial variants in Australian aborigines. *American Journal of Physical Anthropology* 32(3): 409-421.
1970b A comparison of the incidence of minor non-metrical cranial variants in Australian aborigines with those of Melanesia and Polynesia. *American Journal of Physical Anthropology* 33: 235-239.

Kelso, Gerald K.
1974 Pollen analysis of Reservoir No. 2 and macaw nesting boxes. In "Casas Grandes: A Fallen Trading Center of the Gran Chichimeca," Vol. 4, by Charles C. Di Peso, John B. Rinaldo, and Gloria J. Fenner, pp. 33-36. *Amerind Foundation Publication* 9. Dragoon: Amerind Foundation, Inc., and Flagstaff: Northland Press

Kemrer, Meade F.
1973 The Developmental Cycle of Domestic Groups in a Prehistoric Pueblo Community. Paper presented at the 38th Annual Meeting of the Society for American Archaeology, San Francisco.

Kemrer, Meade F., William J. Robinson, and Jeffrey S. Dean
1971 *Tree-rings as Indicators of Intra-Annual Climate.* Tucson: Laboratory of Tree-Ring Research, University of Arizona.

Kennerly, Thomas E., Jr.
1956 Comparisons between fossil and recent species of the genus *Perognathus. Texas Journal of Science* 8:74-86.

Kidder, Alfred Vincent
1958 Pecos, New Mexico: Archaeological notes. *Papers of the R. S. Peabody Foundation for Archaeology* 5. Andover.

Krause, Richard A.
1971 Review of analytical archaeology by David C. Clarke. *Plains Anthropologist* 16(53): 239-241.

Krause, Richard A., and Robert M. Thorne
1971 Toward a theory of archaeological things. *Plains Anthropologist* 16(54): 245-257.

Krefting, Laurits W., and Clifford E. Ahlgren
1974 Small mammals and vegetation changes after fire in a mixed conifer-hardwood forest. *Ecology* 55: 1391-1398.

Krieger, Alex D.
1940 Chemical alteration of archaeological remains. *Society for American Archaeology Notebook,* June, pp. 126-136.

Kroeber, Alfred L.
1917 Zuni kin and clan. *Anthropological Papers of the American Museum of Natural History* 28, Part 2. New York.

Lane, Rebecca A., and Audrey J. Sublett
1972 Osteology of social organization: Residence pattern. *American Antiquity* 37(2): 186-201.

Lewton, Frederick L.
1912 The cotton of the Hopi Indians: A new species of Gossypium. *Smithsonian Miscellaneous Collections* 60(6). Washington.

Lightfoot, Kent
1978 Population movements and social interactions in the prehistoric Southwest: An example from Springerville, Arizona. In "An Analytical Approach to Cultural Resource Management: The Little Colorado Planning Unit," edited by Fred Plog, pp. 188-199. *Arizona State University Anthropological Research Papers* 13, and *USDA Forest Service Cultural Resources Report* 19. Tempe: Arizona State University.
1979 Food redistribution among prehistoric pueblo groups. *The Kiva* 44(4): 319-339.

Ligon, J. Stokley
1964 *History and Management of Merriam's Wild Turkey.* Albuquerque: University of New Mexico Press.

Lillywhite, Harvey B.
1977 Effects of chaparral conversion on small vertebrates in southern California. *Biological Conservation* 11: 171-184.

Little, Elbert L., Jr.
1950 Southwestern trees. *U.S. Department of Agriculture Handbook* 9. Washington.

LoBue, Joseph and Rezneat M. Darnell
1959 Effect of habitat disturbance on a small mammal population. *Journal of Mammalogy* 40: 425-437.

Longacre, William A.
1966 Changing patterns of social integration: A prehistoric example from the American Southwest. *American Anthropologist* 68(1): 94-102.

Longacre, William A. *(continued)*
1970a Archaeology as anthropology: A case study. *Anthropological Papers of the University of Arizona* 17. Tucson: University of Arizona Press.
1970b (editor) *Reconstructing Prehistoric Pueblo Societies.* Albuquerque: University of New Mexico Press.
1974   Models of cultural process; testing hypothesis: Suggestions from southwestern archaeology. In "Reconstructing Complex Societies," edited by Charlotte B. Moore, pp. 29-36. *Supplement to the Bulletin of the American Schools of Oriental Research* 20.
1975   Population dynamics at the Grasshopper Pueblo, Arizona. In "Population Studies in Archaeology and Biological Anthropology: A Symposium," edited by Alan C. Swedlund, pp. 71-74. *Memoirs of the Society for American Archaeology* 30.
1976   Population dynamics at the Grasshopper Pueblo, Arizona. In *Demographic Anthropology: Quantitative Approaches,* edited by Ezra B.W. Zubrow, pp. 169-183. Albuquerque: University of New Mexico Press.

Longacre, William A., and James E. Ayres
1968   Archaeological lessons from an Apache wickiup. In *New Perspectives in Archaeology,* edited by Sally R. Binford and Lewis R. Binford, pp. 151-159. Chicago: Aldine.

Longacre, William A., and J. Jefferson Reid
1971   Research strategy for locational analysis: An outline. In "The Distribution of Prehistoric Population Aggregates," edited by George J. Gumerman, pp. 103-110. *Prescott College Anthropological Reports* 1. Prescott.
1974   The University of Arizona Archaeological Field School at Grasshopper: Eleven years of multidisciplinary research and teaching. *The Kiva* 40(1-2): 3-38.

Lowe, Charles H., editor
1964   *The Vertebrates of Arizona.* Tucson: University of Arizona Press.

Lubbell, David, Fekri A. Hassan, Achilles Gautier, and Jean-Louis Ballais
1976   The Caspian escargotieres. *Science* 191(4230): 910-920.

Mackey, James C., and Sally J. Holbrook
1978   Environmental reconstruction and the abandonment of the Largo-Gallina area. *New Mexico Journal of Field Archaeology* 5: 29-49.

Malde, Harold E.
1972   Geology of the Olsen-Chubbuck Site. Appendix I in "The Olsen-Chubbuck Site: A Paleo-Indian Bison Kill," by Joe Ben Wheat, pp. 171-177. *Society for American Archaeology Memoir* 26.

Martin, Paul Schultz
1963   *The Last 10,000 Years: A Fossil Pollen Record of the American Southwest.* Tucson: University of Arizona Press.

Martin, Paul Schultz, and William Byers
1965   Pollen and archaeology at Wetherill Mesa. In "Contributions of the Wetherill Mesa Archeological Project," assembled by Douglas Osborne, pp. 132-135. *Memoirs of the Society of American Archaeology* 19.

Martin, Paul Sidney
1936   Lowry Ruin in southwestern Colorado. *Fieldiana: Anthropology* 23(1).
1971   The revolution in archaeology. *American Antiquity* 36(1): 1-8.

Martin, Paul Sidney, and Fred Plog
1973   *The Archaeology of Arizona, A Study of the Southwest Region.* New York: Doubleday Natural History Press.

Martin, Paul Sidney, William A. Longacre, and James N. Hill
1967   Chapters in the prehistory of eastern Arizona, III. *Fieldiana: Anthropology* 57.

Martin, Robert A.
1968   Further study of the Friesenhahn *Peromyscus. Southwestern Naturalist* 13: 253-266.

Mathews, Thomas W., and Jerry L. Greene
1972   The Mammalian Fauna of Grasshopper Ruin, Navajo County, Arizona. Paper presented at the 37th Annual Meeting of the Society for American Archaeology, Bal Harbour, Florida.

Mauer, Michael D.
1970   Cibecue Polychrome: A Fourteenth Century Ceramic Type from East-Central Arizona. MS, master's thesis, University of Arizona, Tucson.

Mayro, Linda L., Stephanie M. Whittlesey, and J. Jefferson Reid
1976   Observations on the Salado presence at Grasshopper Pueblo. *The Kiva* 42(1): 85-94.

McCarthy, Phillip J.
1957   *Introduction to Statistical Reasoning.* New York: McGraw-Hill.

McKusick, Charmion R.
1972   Avian studies in archaeological investigation and interpretation. Paper presented at the 37th Annual Meeting of the Society for American Archaeology, Bal Harbour, Florida.
1974   The Casas Grandes avian report. In "Casas Grandes: A Fallen Trading Center of the Gran Chichimeca," Vol. 8, by Charles C. Di Peso, John B. Rinaldo, and Gloria J. Fenner, pp. 273-308. *Amerind Foundation Publications* 9. Dragoon: Amerind Foundation, Inc., and Flagstaff: Northland Press.

McLaughlin, Diane
1975   Results of Analyses of Pollen Samples from TT-75-1, Plaza I, AZ P:14:1. MS, on file in the Archives of the Arizona State Museum, Tucson.

McLaughlin, Diane, and Roger Trick
1974   Analyses of Pollen from Metates from Grasshopper Ruin. MS, on file in the Archives of the Arizona State Museum Library, Tucson.

Mehringer, Peter J., Jr.
1967   Pollen analysis of the Tule Springs area, Nevada. In "Pleistocene Studies in Southern Nevada," edited by Marie Wormington and Dorothy Ellis, pp. 130-200. *Nevada State Museum Anthropological Papers* 13. Carson City: Nevada State Museum.

Miller, Robert R.
1961   Man and the changing fish fauna of the American Southwest. *Papers of the Michigan Academy of Science, Arts, and Letters* 46: 365-404.

Minckley, William L.
1973   *Fishes of Arizona.* Phoenix: Arizona Game and Fish Department.

Minckley, William L., and Norman T. Alger
1968   Fish remains from an archaeological site along the Verde River, Yavapai County, Arizona. *Plateau* 40(3): 91-97.

Monson, Gale, and Allan R. Phillips
1964   Species of birds in Arizona. In *The Vertebrates of Arizona,* edited by Charles H. Lowe, pp. 175-248. Tucson: University of Arizona Press.

Moore, Richard T.
1968   The mineral deposits of the Fort Apache Indian Reservation, Arizona. *Arizona Bureau of Mines Bulletin* 177. Tucson: University of Arizona Press.

Morenon, E. Pierre
1972   Intra-site spatial change in the American Southwest: An alternative view. Paper presented at the 71st Annual Meeting of the American Anthropological Association, Toronto.

Morley, Sylvanus G.
1908 The excavation of the Cannonball Ruins in Southwestern, Colorado. *American Anthropologist* 10(4): 596-610.

Morris, Don P.
1975 Architectural development and masonry style at Antelope House. *The Kiva* 41(1): 33-37.

Morris, Elizabeth A.
1957 Stratigraphic Evidence for a Cultural Continuum at the Point of Pines Ruin. MS, master's thesis, Department of Anthropology, University of Arizona, Tucson.

Mueller, James W.
1974 The use of sampling in archaeological survey. *Memoirs of the Society for American Archaeology* 28.

Mueller, James W., editor
1975 *Sampling in Archaeology*. Tucson: University of Arizona Press.

Naroll, Raoul
1956 A preliminary index of social development. *American Anthropologist* 58(4): 687-715.

Nelson, Edward W.
1909 The rabbits of North America. *North American Fauna* 29: 9-314. Washington: U.S. Department of Agriculture.

Nequatewa, Edward
1943 Some Hopi recipes for the preparation of wild food plants. *Plateau* 16(1): 18-20.

Odum, Eugene P.
1971 *Fundamentals of Ecology*. 2nd edition. Philadelphia and London: W. B. Saunders.

Olsen, John W.
1980 *A Zooarchaeological Analysis of Vertebrate Faunal Remains from the Grasshopper Pueblo, Arizona*. Doctoral dissertation, University of California, Berkeley. Ann Arbor: University Microfilms.

Olsen, Sandra L.
1979 A study of bone artifacts from Grasshopper Pueblo, AZ P:14:1. *The Kiva* 44(4): 341-373.

Olsen, Stanley J.
1967 Osteology of the macaw and Thick-billed Parrot. *The Kiva* 33(3): 57-72.
1968 Canid remains from Grasshopper Ruin. *The Kiva* 34(1): 33-40.

Olsen, Stanley J., and John W. Olsen
1970 A preliminary report on the fish and herpetofauna of Grasshopper Ruin. *The Kiva* 36(2): 40-43.
1974 The macaws of Grasshopper Ruin. *The Kiva* 40(1-2): 67-70.

Olson, Alan P.
1959 An Evaluation of the Phase Concept in Southwestern Archaeology: As Applied to the Eleventh and Twelfth Century Occupations at Point of Pines, East Central Arizona. MS, doctoral dissertation, University of Arizona, Tucson.

Ossenberg, Nancy S.
1970 The influence of artificial cranial deformation on discontinuous morphological traits. *American Journal of Physical Anthropology* 33(3): 357-371.

Palmer, Edward
1878 Plants used by the Indians of the United States. *American Naturalist* 12: 593-606, 646-655.

Parker, Marion L.
1967 Dendrochronology of Point of Pines. MS, master's thesis, Department of Anthropology, University of Arizona, Tucson.

Parsons, Elsie C.
1922 Oraibi in 1920. Contributions to Hopi history. *American Anthropologist* 24(3): 283-294.
1939 *Pueblo Indian Religion*. Two volumes. Chicago: University of Chicago Press.

Parsons, Roger B.
1962 Indian mounds of northeast Iowa as soil genesis benchmarks. *Journal of the Iowa Archeological Society* 12: 1-30.

Parzen, Emmanuel
1960 *Modern Probability Theory and Its Applications*. New York: John Wiley and Sons.

Phillips, Allan R.
1968 The instability of the distribution of land birds in the Southwest. In "Collected Papers in Honor of Lyndon L. Hargrave," edited by Albert H. Schroeder, pp. 129-162. *Papers of the Archaeological Society of New Mexico* 1. Santa Fe: Museum of New Mexico Press.

Phillips, Allan R., Joe Marshall, and Gale Monson
1964 *The Birds of Arizona*. Tucson: University of Arizona Press.

Phillips, Edwin Allen
1959 *Methods of Vegetation Study*. New York: Henry Holt.

Pietrusewsky, Michael
1970 An osteological view of indigenous populations in Oceania. In "Studies in Oceanic Culture History I," edited by R. C. Green and M. Kelly, pp. 1-12. *Pacific Anthropological Records* 11. Honolulu: Bernice P. Bishop Museum.
1971a Application of distance statistics to anthroposcopic data and a comparison of results with those obtained by using discrete traits of the skull. *Archaeology and Physical Anthropology in Oceania* 6: 21-33.
1971b Human skeletal material from Anaehoomalu. *Department of Anthropology Report* 71-7. Honolulu: Bernice P. Bishop Museum.

Plog, Fred
1974a Settlement patterns and social history. In *Frontiers of Anthropology*, edited by Murray J. Leaf, pp. 68-91. New York: D. Van Nostrand.
1974b *The Study of Prehistoric Change*. New York: Academic Press.
1978 The Keresan bridge: An ecological and archaeological account. In *Social Archaeology: Beyond Subsistence and Dating*, edited by Charles L. Redman, Mary Jane Berman, Edward V. Curtin, William T. Langhorne, Jr., Nina M. Versaggi, and Jeffrey C. Wanser, pp. 349-372. New York: Academic Press.

Plog, Stephen E.
1969 Prehistoric Population Movements: Measurement and Explanation. MS, on file at the Field Museum of Natural History, Chicago.
1976 Relative efficiencies of sampling techniques for archaeological surveys. In *The Early Mesoamerican Village*, edited by Kent V. Flannery, pp. 136-158. New York: Academic Press.
1977 *A Multivariate Approach to the Explanation of Ceramic Design Variation*. Doctoral dissertation, University of Michigan, Ann Arbor. Ann Arbor: University Microfilms.

Prudden, T. Mitchell
1903 The prehistoric ruins of the San Juan watershed in Utah, Arizona, Colorado, and New Mexico. *American Anthropologist* 5(1): 224-288.
1914 The circular kivas of small ruins in the San Juan watershed. *American Anthropologist* 16(1): 33-58.
1918 A further study of prehistoric small house ruins in the San Juan watershed. *Memoirs of the American Anthropological Association* 5: 3-50.

Pyddocke, Edward
1961 *Stratification for the Archaeologist*. London: Phoenix House.

Reagan, Albert B.
1930 Archaeological notes on the Fort Apache region, Arizona. *Transactions of the Kansas Academy of Science* 33: 111-132.

Reed, Erik K.
1948   The Western Pueblo archaeological complex. *El Palacio* 55(1): 9-15.
1950   Eastern-central Arizona archaeology in relation to the Western Pueblos. *Southwestern Journal of Anthropology* 6(2): 120-138.
1968   Ponderosa pine, climatic history, and conifers as pioneers. In "Collected Papers in Honor of Lyndon L. Hargrave," edited by Albert H. Schroeder, pp. 165-170. *Papers of the Archaeological Society of New Mexico* 1. Santa Fe: Museum of New Mexico Press.

Reid, J. Jefferson
1971   Grasshopper Cornering Project, 1971. MS, on file in the Archives of the Arizona State Museum Library, Tucson.
1973   *Growth and Response to Stress at Grasshopper Pueblo, Arizona.* Doctoral dissertation, University of Arizona, Tucson. Ann Arbor: University Microfilms.
1975   Comments on environment and behavior at Antelope House. *The Kiva* 41(1): 127-132.
1978   Response to stress at Grasshopper Pueblo, Arizona. In *Discovering Past Behavior, Experiments in the Archaeology of the American Southwest*, edited by Paul Grebinger, pp. 195-213. New York: Gordon and Breach.

Reid, J. Jefferson, Michael B Schiffer, and Jeffrey M. Neff
1975   Archaeological considerations of intrasite sampling. In *Sampling in Archaeology*, edited by James W. Mueller, pp. 209-224. Tucson: University of Arizona Press.

Rick, John W.
1976   Downslope movement and archaeological intrasite spatial analysis. *American Antiquity* 41(2): 133-144.

Rinaldo, John B.
1964a Architectural details, Carter Ranch Pueblo. In "Chapters in the Prehistory of Eastern Arizona II," by Paul S. Martin, John B. Rinaldo, William A. Longacre, Leslie G. Freeman, Jr., James A. Brown, Richard H. Hevly, and M. E. Cooley, pp. 15-58. *Fieldiana: Anthropology* 55.
1964b Notes on the origins of historic Zuni culture. *The Kiva* 29(4): 86-98.

Roberts, Frank H. H.
1931   The ruins at Kiatuthlanna, eastern Arizona. *Bureau of American Ethnology Bulletin* 100. Washington.
1939   Archaeological remains in the Whitewater district, eastern Arizona. *Bureau of American Ethnology Bulletin* 121. Washington.

Robinson, William J.
1967   *Tree-Ring Materials as a Basis for Cultural Interpretations.* Doctoral dissertation, University of Arizona, Tucson. Ann Arbor: University Microfilms.

Robinson, William J., and Jeffrey S. Dean
1969   *Tree-Ring Evidence for Climatic Changes in the Prehistoric Southwest from A.D. 1000 to 1200.* Tucson: Laboratory of Tree-Ring Research, University of Arizona.

Robinson, William J., and Roderick Sprague
1965   Disposal of the dead at Point of Pines, Arizona. *American Antiquity* 30(4): 442-453.

Robinson, William J., Bruce G. Harrill, and Richard L. Warren
1975   *Tree-Ring Dates from Arizona H-I: Flagstaff Area.* Tucson: Laboratory of Tree-Ring Research, University of Arizona.

Rock, James T.
1974   The use of social models in archaeological interpretation. *The Kiva* 40(1-2): 81-91.

Rodeck, Hugh G.
1956   *Sorex merriami* and *Microtus mexicanus* in Colorado. *Journal of Mammalogy* 37: 436.

Rohn, Arthur
1965   Postulation of socio-economic groups from archaeological evidence. In "Contributions of the Wetherill Mesa Archeological Project," compiled by Douglas Osborne, pp. 65-69. *Society for American Archaeology Memoir* 19.
1971   *Mug House.* Washington: National Park Service.

Rosenzweig, Michael L., and Jerald Winakur
1969   Population ecology of desert rodent communities: Habitats and environmental complexity. *Ecology* 50: 558-572.

Roys, Lawrence
1936   Masonry of Lowry Ruin and of the Southwest. In "Lowry Ruin in Southwestern Colorado," by Paul S. Martin, pp. 115-142. *Fieldiana: Anthropology* 23(1).

Russell, Frank
1908   The Pima Indians. *Bureau of American Ethnology 26th Annual Report,* pp. 3-390. Washington

Scarborough, Robert, and Izumi Shimada
1974   Geological analysis of wall composition at Grasshopper with behavioral implications. *The Kiva* 40(1-2): 49-66.

Schellback, Louis, III
1930   An unusual burial in Mesa House Ruin. *Southwest Museum Papers* 4: 93-105.

Schiffer, Michael B.
1972   Archaeological context and systemic context. *American Antiquity* 37(2): 156-165.
1973a *Cultural Formation Processes of the Archaeological Record: Applications at the Joint Site, East-Central Arizona.* Doctoral dissertation, University of Arizona, Tucson. Ann Arbor: University Microfilms.
1973b The relationship between access volume and content diversity of storage facilities. *American Antiquity* 38(1): 114-116.
1975   Behavioral chain analysis: Activities, organization, and the use of space. In "Chapters in the Prehistory of Eastern Arizona IV," by Paul S. Martin, Ezra B. W. Zubrow, Daniel C. Bowman, David A. Gregory, John A. Hanson, Michael B. Schiffer, and David R. Wilcox, pp. 103-119. *Fieldiana: Anthropology* 65.
1976   *Behavioral Archaeology.* New York: Academic Press.

Schiffer, Michael B., and William L. Rathje
1973   Efficient exploitation of the archaeological record: Penetrating problems. In *Research and Theory in Current Archeology*, edited by Charles L. Redman, pp. 169-179. New York: Wiley (Interscience).

Schoenwetter, James
1962   The pollen analysis of eighteen archaeological sites in Arizona and New Mexico. In "Chapters in the Prehistory of Eastern Arizona, I," by Paul S. Martin, John B. Rinaldo, William A. Longacre, Constance Cronin, Leslie G. Freeman, Jr., and James Schoenwetter, pp. 168-209. *Fieldiana: Anthropology* 53.
1964   The palynological research. In "Alluvial and Palynological Reconstruction of Environments, Navajo Reservoir District," edited by James Schoenwetter and Frank W. Eddy. *Anthropological Papers* 13. Santa Fe: Museum of New Mexico Press.
1970   Archaeological pollen studies of the Colorado Plateau. *American Antiquity* 35(1): 35-47.

Schoenwetter, James, and Alfred E. Dittert, Jr.
1968   An ecological interpretation of Anasazi settlement patterns. In *Anthropological Archeology in the Americas*, edited by Betty J. Meggers, pp. 41-66. Washington: The Anthropological Society of Washington.

Schorger, A. W.
1966   *The Wild Turkey.* Norman: University of Oklahoma Press.

Schroeder, Albert H.
1968 Birds and feathers in documents relating to Indians of the Southwest. In "Collected Papers in Honor of Lyndon L. Hargrave," edited by Albert H. Schroeder, pp. 95-114. *Papers of the Archaeological Society of New Mexico* 1. Santa Fe: Museum of New Mexico Press.

Schulman, Edmund
1956 *Dendroclimatic Changes in Semiarid America*. Tucson: University of Arizona Press.

Schwartz, Douglas W.
1970 The postmigration culture: A base for archaeological inference. In *Reconstructing Prehistoric Pueblo Societies*, edited by William A. Longacre, pp. 175-193. Albuquerque: University of New Mexico Press.

Sellers, William D., and Richard H. Hill, editors
1974 *Arizona Climate, 1931-1972*. Tucson: University of Arizona Press.

Senter, Florence H.
1938 Southwestern dated ruins: IV. *Tree-Ring Bulletin* 5(1): 6-7.

Seton, Ernest T.
1929 *Lives of Game Animals*. 4 volumes. Garden City: Doubleday, Doran.

Shackley, Myra L.
1975 *Archaeological Sediments: A Survey of Analytical Methods*. London: Butterworths.
1976 Paleoenvironmental evidence from a late third millennium B.C. peat bed at New Shide Bridge, Isle of Wight. *Journal of Archaeological Science* 3: 385-389.

Sharp, Ward M.
1958 Evaluating mast yields in oaks. *Agricultural Experiment Station Bulletin* 635. Pennsylvania State University College of Agriculture.

Shimada, Izumi
1973 Field Report: The 1973 Cornering-Growth Project at Grasshopper. Paper presented at the Pecos Conference, Tucson, Arizona.
1978 Behavioral variability and organization in ancient constructions: An experimental approach. In "Papers on the Economy and Architecture of the Ancient Maya," edited by Raymond Sidrys, pp. 209-235. *Institute of Archaeology Monograph* 8. Los Angeles: University of California.

Sims, H. Percy, and Charles H. Buckner
1973 The effect of clearcutting and burning of *Pinus banksiana* forests on the populations of small animals in southeastern Manitoba. *American Midland Naturalist* 90: 228-231.

Sjöberg, Alf
1976 Phosphate analysis of anthropic soils. *Journal of Field Archaeology* 3: 447-454.

Smiley, Terah L.
1949 Tree-ring dates from Point of Pines. *Tree-Ring Bulletin* 15(3): 20-21.
1952 Four late prehistoric kivas at Point of Pines, Arizona. *Social Science Bulletin* 21. Tucson: University of Arizona.

Smith, Watson, Richard B. Woodbury, and Nathalie Woodbury
1966 The excavation of Hawaikuh by F. W. Hodge. *Contributions from the Museum of the American Indian* 20. New York: Heye Foundation.

Spier, Leslie
1919 Ruins in the White Mountains, Arizona. *Anthropological Papers of the American Museum of Natural History* 18(5): 363-387.

Stacy, Linda, and Candace Johnston
1969 Cornering Project—Grasshopper, 1969. MS, on file in the Archives of the Arizona State Museum Library, Tucson.

Standley, Paul C.
1912 Some useful native plants of New Mexico. *Smithsonian Institution Annual Report of 1911*, pp. 447-462. Washington.

Stanislawski, Michael B.
1973 Ethnoarchaeology and settlement archaeology. *Ethnohistory* 20(4): 375-392.

Stebbens, Robert C.
1954 *Amphibians and Reptiles of Western North America*. New York: McGraw-Hill.

Stein, Julie
1980 *Geoarchaeology of the Green River Shell Mounds, Kentucky*. Doctoral dissertation, Center for Ancient Studies, University of Minnesota, Minneapolis. Ann Arbor: University Microfilms.

Stein, Walter T.
1963 Mammal remains from archaeological sites in the Point of Pines region, Arizona. *American Antiquity* 29(2): 213-220.

Stevenson, Matilda C.
1915 Ethnobotany of the Zuni Indians. *Bureau of American Ethnology Thirtieth Annual Report, 1908-1909*, pp. 31-102. Washington.

Stockton, Charles W.
1975 Long-term streamflow records reconstructed from tree rings. *Papers of the Laboratory of Tree-Ring Research* 5. Tucson: University of Arizona Press.

Stockton, Charles W., and Harold C. Fritts
1971a Augmenting annual runoff records using tree-ring data. In "Hydrology and Water Resources in Arizona and the Southwest," pp. 1-12. *Proceedings of the 1971 Meetings of the Arizona Section—American Water Resources Association and the Hydrology Section—Arizona Academy of Science, Tempe* 1. Tempe.
1971b *An Empirical Reconstruction of Water Levels for Lake Athabasca (1810-1967) by Analysis of Tree Rings*. Tucson: Laboratory of Tree-Ring Research, University of Arizona.

Storie, R. Earl, and Frank Harradine
1950 An age estimate of the burials unearthed near Concord, California, based on pedologic observations. Appendix I in "Archaeology of CCo-137, the 'Concord Man' Site." *The University of California Archaeological Survey Papers on California Archaeology* 7: 16-19.

Sullivan, Alan P., III
1974 Problems in the estimation of original room function: A tentative solution from the Grasshopper Ruin. *The Kiva* 40(1-2): 93-100.

Swank, George
1932 Ethnobotany of the Acuma and Laguna Indians. MS, master's thesis, University of New Mexico, Albuquerque.

Swank, Wendell
1958 The mule deer in Arizona chaparral; and an analysis of other important deer herds. *Wildlife Bulletin* 3. Phoenix: State of Arizona Game and Fish Department.

Takaki, Michiko
1977 *Aspects of Exchange in a Kalinga Society, Northern Luzon*. Doctoral dissertation, Yale University, New Haven. Ann Arbor: University Microfilms.

Tamplin, Morgan
1969 The application of pedology to archaeological research. In *Pedology and Quaternary Research: Proceedings of the Symposium Held at Edmonton, Alberta, Canada, May 13-14*, edited by S. Pawluk, pp. 153-161.

Tamsitt, J. R.
1957 *Peromyscus* from the Late Pleistocene of Texas. *Texas Journal of Science* 9: 355-362.

Tevis, Lloyd, Jr.
1956a Responses of small mammal populations to logging of Douglas fir. *Journal of Mammalogy* 37: 189-196.
1956b Effect of a slash burn on forest mice. *Journal of Wildlife Management* 20: 405-409.

Thompson, Raymond H., editor
1958 Migration in New World culture history. *Social Science Bulletin* 27. Tucson: University of Arizona Press.

Thompson, Raymond H., and William A. Longacre
1966 The University of Arizona Archaeological Field School at Grasshopper, east-central Arizona. *The Kiva* 31(4): 255-275.

Thompson, Richard A.
1971 Structural statistics and structural mechanics: The analysis of *compdrazgo*. *Southwestern Journal of Anthropology* 27(4): 381-403.

Titiev, Mischa
1944 Old Oraibi, a study of the Hopi Indians of Third Mesa. *Papers of the Peabody Museum, Harvard University*, 22(1). Cambridge: Harvard University.

Train, Percy, James R. Henricks, and W. Andrew
1941 Medicinal plants used by the Indian tribes of Nevada. *Contributions Toward a Flora of Nevada* 33. Washington: U.S. Department of Agriculture.

Treganza, A., and S. F. Cook
1948 The quantitative investigation of aboriginal sites: Complete excavation with physical and archaeological analysis of a single mound. *American Antiquity* 13(4): 207-297.

Truslove, G. M.
1961 Genetical studies on the skeleton of the mouse. XXX: A search for correlations between some minor variants. *Genetic Research* 2: 431-438.

Tuggle, H. David
1970 *Prehistoric community relationships in East-Central Arizona*. Doctoral dissertation, University of Arizona, Tucson. Ann Arbor: University Microfilms.

Turkowski, Frank J., and Hudson G. Reynolds
1970 Response of some rodent populations to pinyon-juniper reduction on the Kaibab Plateau, Arizona. *Southwestern Naturalist* 15: 23-27.

Turkowski, Frank J., and Ross K. Watkins
1976 White-throated Woodrat (*Neotoma albigula*) habitat relations in modified pinyon-juniper woodland of southwestern New Mexico. *Journal of Mammalogy* 57: 586-591.

United States Department of Agriculture
1941 Climate and man. *Yearbook of Agriculture*. Washington.
1948 Woody plant seed manual. *Miscellaneous Publication* 654. Washington.

Vanzolini, Paulo E.
1952 Fossil snakes and lizards from the Lower Miocene of Florida. *Journal of Paleontology* 26(3): 452-457.

Vescelius, G. S.
1960 Archaeological sampling: A problem of statistical inference. In *Essays in Honor of Leslie A. White*, edited by Gertrude E. Dole and Robert L. Carneiro, pp. 457-470. New York: Thomas Y. Crowell.

Vestal, Paul A.
1952 Ethnobotany of the Ramah Navaho. *Papers of the Peabody Museum, Harvard University*, 40(4): 1-94. Cambridge: Harvard University.

Vivian, R. Gordon
1964 Excavations in a 17-century Jumano Pueblo, Gran Quivira, New Mexico. *Archeological Research Series* 8. Washington: National Park Service.

Vivian, R. Gordon, and Tom W. Mathews
1966 Kin Kletso, a Pueblo III community in Chaco Canyon, New Mexico. *Southwestern Monuments Association Technical Series* 6(1).Globe, Arizona: Southwest Monuments Association.

Vivian, R. Gwinn
1970 An inquiry into prehistoric social organization in Chaco Canyon, New Mexico. In *Reconstructing Prehistoric Pueblo Societies*, edited by William A. Longacre, pp. 59-83. Albuquerque: University of New Mexico Press.

Volkman, Toby
1972 Canyon Creek Project: The Kiva. MS, on file in the Archives of the Arizona State Museum Library, Tucson.

Wade, William D.
1970 Skeletal Remains of a Prehistoric Population from the Puerco Valley, Eastern Arizona. MS, doctoral dissertation, University of Colorado, Boulder.

Walker, Phillip L., and Jeffrey C. Long
1977 An experimental study of the morphological characteristics of tool marks. *American Antiquity* 42(4): 605-616.

Wasley, William W.
1952 The Late Pueblo Occupation at Point of Pines, East-central Arizona. MS, master's thesis, Department of Anthropology, University of Arizona, Tucson.

Watson, Patty Jo, and Richard Yarnell
1966 Archaeological and paleoethnobotanical investigations in Salts Cave, Mammoth Cave National Park, Kentucky. *American Antiquity* 31(6): 842-849.

Weaver, Donald E., Jr.
1976 Salado influences in the lower Salt River Valley. *The Kiva* 42(1): 17-26.

Wendorf, Fred
1950 A report on the excavation of a small ruin near Point of Pines, east central Arizona. *Social Science Bulletin* 19. Tucson: University of Arizona.
1956 Some distributions of settlement patterns in the Pueblo Southwest. In "Prehistoric Settlement Patterns in the New World," edited by Gordon R. Willey, pp. 18-25. *Viking Fund Publications in Anthropology* 23. New York: Wenner-Gren Foundation for Anthropological Research.

Wheat, Joe Ben
1952 Prehistoric water sources of the Point of Pines Area. *American Antiquity* 17(3): 185-196.
1955 Mogollon culture prior to A.D. 1000. *Memoirs of the Society for American Archaeology* 10.

Whiting, Alfred
1939 Ethnobotany of the Hopi. *Museum of Northern Arizona Bulletin* 15. Flagstaff: Museum of Northern Arizona.

Whittlesey, Stephanie M.
1974 Identification of imported ceramics through functional analysis of attributes. *The Kiva* 40(1-2): 101-112.
1978 *Status and Death at Grasshopper Pueblo: Experiments Toward an Archaeological Theory of Correlates*. Doctoral dissertation, University of Arizona, Tucson. Ann Arbor: University Microfilms.

Whittlesey, Stephanie M., Eric J. Arnould, and William E. Reynolds
1976 Stronger than Dirt: The Concept of an Archaeological Soil and Its Application. Paper presented at the 41st Annual Meeting of the Society for American Archaeology, St. Louis, Missouri.

Wilcox, David R.
1970 Cornering Project, 1969. MS, on file in the Archives of the Arizona State Museum Library, Tucson.

1975   A strategy for perceiving social groups in Puebloan sites. In "Chapters in the Prehistory of Eastern Arizona IV," by Paul S. Martin, Ezra B. W. Zubrow, Daniel C. Bowman, David A. Gregory, John A. Hanson, Michael B. Schiffer, and David R. Wilcox, pp. 120-159. *Fieldiana: Anthropology* 65.

1976   How the Pueblos Came To Be As They Are: The Problem Today. MS, on file in the Arizona State Museum Library, Tucson.

Wilcox, David R., and Michael B. Collins
1971   Toward the Analytical Perception of Social Groups at Ariz. P:14:1. MS, on file in the Grasshopper Collection, Department of Anthropology, University of Arizona, Tucson.

Wilcox, David R., and Lynette O. Shenk
1977   The architecture of the Casa Grande and its interpretation. *Arizona State Museum Archaeological Series* 115. Tucson: Arizona State Museum, University of Arizona.

Wilcox, David R., Thomas R. McGuire, and Charles Sternberg
1981   Snaketown revisited: A partial cultural resource survey, analysis of site structure, and an ethnohistoric study of the proposed Hohokam-Pima National Monument. *Arizona State Museum Archaeological Series* 155. Tucson: Arizona State Museum, University of Arizona.

Wilson, Donald E.
1968   Ecological distribution of the genus *Peromyscus* in the Sandia Mountains, New Mexico. *Southwestern Naturalist* 13: 267-274.

Wilson, Eldred D., and R. T. Moore
1959   Structure of the Basin and Range Province in Arizona. *Southern Arizona Guidebook II*, edited by Leo A. Heindl, pp. 89-107. Tucson: Arizona Geological Society.

Winship, George Parker
1896   The Coronado expedition, 1540-1542. *Fourteenth Annual Report of the Bureau of Ethnology, 1892-1893*, pp. 339-637. Washington.

Wood, Raymond W., and Donald Lee Johnson
1978   A study of disturbance processes in archaeological site formation. In *Advances in Archaeological Method and Theory* 1, edited by Michael B. Schiffer, pp. 315-381. New York: Academic Press.

Woodbury, Angus M.
1947   Distribution of pigmy conifers in Utah and northern Arizona. *Ecology* 28: 113-126.

Woodbury, Richard B.
1961   Prehistoric agriculture at Point of Pines, Arizona. *Memoirs of the Society for American Archaeology* 17.

1966   Village agriculture toward the peripheries — the North American Southwest. *36th International Congress of Americanists, 1964*, pp. 219-228. Seville.

Yaalon, Dan H.
1971   *Palaeopedology: Origin, Nature and Dating of Palaeosols.* Jerusalem: International Society of Soil Science and Israel University.

INDEX